MICROSOFT®
.NET REMOTING

Scott McLean
James Naftel
Kim Williams

Microsoft®
.net

PUBLISHED BY
Microsoft Press
A Division of Microsoft Corporation
One Microsoft Way
Redmond, Washington 98052-6399

Library of Congress Cataloging-in-Publication Data pending.

Printed and bound in the United States of America.

1 2 3 4 5 6 7 8 9   QWE   7 6 5 4 3 2

Distributed in Canada by H.B. Fenn and Company Ltd.

A CIP catalogue record for this book is available from the British Library.

Microsoft Press books are available through booksellers and distributors worldwide. For further information about international editions, contact your local Microsoft Corporation office or contact Microsoft Press International directly at fax (425) 936-7329. Visit our Web site at www.microsoft.com/mspress. Send comments to *mspinput@microsoft.com*.

Microsoft, Microsoft Press, Visual Basic, Visual Studio, Windows, and Windows NT are either registered trademarks or trademarks of Microsoft Corporation in the United States and/or other countries. Other product and company names mentioned herein may be the trademarks of their respective owners.

The example companies, organizations, products, domain names, e-mail addresses, logos, people, places, and events depicted herein are fictitious. No association with any real company, organization, product, domain name, e-mail address, logo, person, place, or event is intended or should be inferred.

Acquisitions Editor: Danielle Bird
Project Editor: Kathleen Atkins
Technical Editor: Dail Magee, Jr.

Body Part No. X08-81840

To my parents, for never doubting me, and to my wife, Nancy, the love of my life.

Scott

I dedicate this book to my two daughters, Meagan and Emma, my wife, April, and my family. All have played major roles in shaping my life.

James

To my wife, Patty, and son, Sean. I love you both and appreciate your support more than you'll ever know.

Kim

Table of Contents

4   SOAP and Message Flows   105

Acknowledgments

We couldn't have written this book without the help of many people. We'd like to thank the following people in particular.

First, we'd like to thank members of the Microsoft Press book team for making this book possible: Danielle Bird, acquisition editor; Kathleen Atkins, project editor; Michelle Goodman, copy editor; Dail Magee Jr., technical editor; Rob Nance, electronic artist; Kerri DeVault, compositor; and Marc Young, a technical editor who read our chapters early in the project. We'd like to thank our peer reviewers: Allen Jones and Adam Freeman. We'd also like to thank the folks at Moore Literary Agency for helping to make this book possible: Mike Meehan, Claudette Moore, and Debbie McKenna.

Finally, a very significant amount of time goes into writing a book, which is time that we stole from our loved ones. Each of us would like to extend our gratitude to our loved ones, for without their full support, we wouldn't have been able to complete this monumental task.

Introduction

Distributed computing has become an integral part of almost all software development. Before the advent of .NET Remoting, DCOM was the preferred method of developing distributed applications on Microsoft platforms. Unfortunately, DCOM is difficult for the average developer to understand and use. Enter .NET Remoting—an object-oriented architecture that facilitates distributed application development using Microsoft .NET. Just as the .NET Framework replaces COM as the preferred way to build components, .NET Remoting replaces DCOM as the preferred way to build distributed applications using the .NET Framework. Furthermore, .NET Remoting provides the basic underpinnings of .NET Web services. Hence, a fundamental understanding of .NET Remoting is crucial as developers shift to more Internet-based distributed application development using the .NET Framework.

This book discusses the .NET Remoting architecture in depth and provides concrete examples in C# that demonstrate how to extend and customize .NET Remoting. We'll explore the capabilities provided by .NET Remoting and develop examples that clearly demonstrate how to customize key aspects of .NET Remoting. This is where .NET Remoting really shines. Furthermore, the .NET Remoting architecture provides many extensibility hooks that let you use a variety of protocols and configuration options.

When we started working with the .NET Framework, we were pleasantly surprised to learn how easy it is to build distributed applications using .NET Remoting. This is quite a contrast to our experiences with DCOM! Furthermore, we quickly realized the true power of .NET Remoting when we started extending the .NET Remoting infrastructure. In general, we found that .NET Remoting has a logical and cohesive object model that facilitates both simple configuration changes and advanced extensions to the .NET Remoting infrastructure. In addition, .NET Remoting supports open and Internet-based standards such as Web Services and Simple Object Access Protocol (SOAP). It's not a perfect world though; any new technology usually has its warts. However, we almost always could find reasonable workarounds to the problems we encountered. (We'll point out these workarounds throughout the book.) We've seen our share of new technologies, and we believe .NET Remoting is a strong replacement for its predecessor (DCOM) as well as a powerful tool to support distributed application development in today's open, Internet-connected environment.

Our Audience

This book is written for anyone who has some experience writing programs using the .NET Framework and wants to learn how to build distributed applications using .NET Remoting. We cover .NET Remoting in detail; no prior knowledge of the subject is required. All examples are in C#, and a working knowledge of C# is recommended; however, we don't use many advanced features of the language. Although you should have a working familiarity with the .NET Framework and C#, this book will be easily understood by someone with a background in C++, Microsoft Visual Basic .NET, or Java. If you've written remote applications using any of these languages, you should have enough knowledge to get the most out of this book.

Organization

We've organized this book into the following eight chapters. The first two chapters are conceptual in nature. The remaining chapters of the book focus on advanced concepts and demonstrate how to exploit the extreme extensibility provided by .NET Remoting.

■   **Chapter 1: Understanding Distributed Application Development**   This chapter sets the stage by discussing the history of distributed application architecture and technology. The chapter discusses remote procedure calls (RPC), DCOM, Remote Method Invocation (RMI), and SOAP/XML technologies. The goal of the chapter is to address the successes and shortcomings of these past technologies. We then take an in-depth look at how .NET Remoting meets the challenges of both historical and modern distributed application development.

■   **Chapter 2: Understanding the .NET Remoting Architecture**   Here we introduce the major architectural components of the .NET Remoting infrastructure. We'll explore these components in depth in subsequent chapters. This chapter serves as both an introduction and a reference for these .NET Remoting concepts. It provides introductory explanations of each of the major components comprising the .NET Remoting architecture: activation (server activated and client activated), marshal-by-reference, marshal-by-value, leases, channels, messages, and formatters.

- **Chapter 3: Building Distributed Applications with .NET Remoting**   This chapter offers a detailed look at constructing a distributed application using the various stock features provided by .NET Remoting. Here we create a hypothetical job assignment application and use it to demonstrate fundamental .NET Remoting concepts, such as client-activated and server-activated objects. In addition, this application demonstrates how to use .NET Remoting to implement Web Services. This chapter also shows you how to add security to .NET Remoting applications by using the powerful security features of Microsoft Internet Information Services (IIS) and demonstrates how to expose a remote object as a Web Service.

- **Chapter 4: SOAP and Message Flows**   This chapter is a primer on SOAP and examines the messages exchanged between the client applications and server applications developed in Chapter 3. We give you with an extra learning experience by showing you the external artifacts produced and consumed by .NET Remoting.

- **Chapter 5: Messages and Proxies**   In this chapter, we begin by examining messages, which are fundamental to extending and customizing the .NET Remoting infrastructure. The chapter also examines proxies, which act as bridges between local objects and remote objects. Client code makes calls on the proxy object, which in turn invokes methods on the remote object. We show three methods of developing custom proxies and examine how to plug them into the .NET Remoting infrastructure. We use custom proxies to develop two sample applications: one that can dynamically switch from using TCP to HTTP if a connection via TCP isn't possible (for example, because of a firewall), and another that provides load balancing.

- **Chapter 6: Message Sinks and Contexts**   This chapter shows you how to use a .NET Remoting context to enforce rules and behavior for objects executing within the context. This chapter explains what message sink chains are and why they're a major extensibility point in the .NET Remoting framework, providing the foundation upon which the powerful interception capabilities of contexts rest. We also explain each of the different context-related message sinks and show you how to use them.

■ **Chapter 7: Channels and Channel Sinks** Channels are fundamental components of .NET Remoting. This chapter first explains the architecture of the .NET Remoting *HttpChannel* and its supporting classes so that you gain a better understanding of how to create a custom channel. The chapter then covers extending .NET Remoting with a custom channel type example that uses the file system as a transport mechanism for .NET Remoting messages. Finally, this chapter creates a custom sink that blocks method calls during a user-defined time period.

■ **Chapter 8: Serialization Formatters** The final chapter continues to build on the concepts discussed in the previous chapters and describes serialization formatters in detail. After introducing general serialization concepts, we show you how to extend .NET Remoting by creating a custom serialization formatter and formatter sink.

System Requirements

To build and execute the sample code, you'll need Microsoft Visual Studio .NET. You'll also need IIS to run the Web Service and to demonstrate the security techniques discussed in Chapter 3. Although many .NET Remoting features are best demonstrated by using a network with two or more machines, all the sample code in this book will run on a single machine.

Sample Files

The sample files for this book can be found on the Web at *http://www.microsoft.com/mspress/books/6172.asp*. To get to the companion content for this book once you reach the Web site, click on the Companion Content link in the More Information menu on the right of the Web page. That action loads the companion content page, which includes links for downloading the sample files.

1

Understanding Distributed Application Development

Distributed application technologies such as DCOM, Java RMI, and CORBA have evolved over many years to keep up with the constantly increasing requirements of the enterprise. In today's environment, a distributed application technology should be efficient, be extensible, support transactions, interoperate with different technologies, be highly configurable, work over the Internet, and more. But not all applications are large enough in scope to require all this support. To support smaller systems, a distributed application technology needs to provide common default behavior and be simple to configure so that distributing these systems is as easy as possible. It might seem impossible for a single remoting technology to meet this entire list of requirements. In fact, most of today's distributed application technologies began with a more modest list of requirements and then acquired support for other requirements over many years.

Every so often, it's better to wipe the slate clean and start over. This was the approach taken with the design of .NET Remoting. .NET Remoting provides a cohesive object model with extensibility hooks to support the kinds of systems developers have built until now by using DCOM. The designers of .NET Remoting had the advantage of taking into account the recent technology requirements that were initially unknown to DCOM's designers.

Although this chapter is not intended to help you decide which distributed application technology to use, .NET Remoting offers clear advantages. .NET Remoting is probably the best choice if you're doing all new development in .NET and you implement both client and server by using the .NET Framework. On the other hand, if your existing distributed application is implemented with a non-.NET remoting technology, the .NET Framework provides an unprecedented level of interoperability with legacy technologies:

- If your existing system is COM/DCOM, the .NET Framework's .NET-to-COM interoperability layer is full-featured and easy to use. This layer allows flexible, incremental migration to .NET Remoting over time.

- If your existing system is based on a non-Microsoft distributed technology such as Java Remote Method Invocation (RMI) or Common Object Request Broker Architecture (CORBA), there's still good news. .NET Remoting's support for open standards such as XML and Simple Object Access Protocol (SOAP) makes it possible to communicate with multivendor, multiplatform environments as these open standards are adopted by other vendors At present, a number of Java-based SOAP toolkits are available. Although CORBA's SOAP support is lagging, the Object Management Group (OMG) is currently working on an official CORBA/SOAP standard.

A Brief History

In the broadest sense, a *distributed application* is one in which the application processing is divided among two or more machines. This division of processing implies that the data involved is also distributed.

Distributed Architectures

A number of distributed application solutions predate .NET Remoting. These early systems technologies are the foundation from which many lessons about distributed computing have been learned and of which .NET Remoting is the latest incarnation.

Modular Programming

Properly managing complexity is an essential part of developing all but the most trivial software applications. One of the most fundamental techniques for managing this complexity is organizing code into related units of functionality. You can apply this technique at many levels by organizing code into procedures; procedures into classes; classes into components; and components into larger, related subsystems. Distributed applications greatly benefit from—and in many cases help enforce—this concept because modularity is required to distribute code to various machines. In fact, the broad categories of distributed architectures mainly differ in the responsibilities assigned to different modules and their interactions.

Client/Server

Client/server is the earliest and most fundamental of distributed architectures. In broad terms, client/server is simply a client process that requests services from a server process. The client process typically is responsible for the presentation layer (or user interface). This layer includes validating user input, dispatching calls to the server, and possibly executing some business rules. The server then acts as an engine—fulfilling client requests by executing business logic and interoperating with resources such as databases and file systems. Often many clients communicate with a single server. Although this book is about distributed application development, we should point out that client and server responsibilities generally don't have to be divided among multiple machines. The separation of application functionality is a good design approach for processes running on a single machine.

N-Tier

Client/server applications are also referred to as *two-tier applications* because the client talks directly to the server. Two-tier architectures are usually fairly easy to implement but tend to have limited scalability. In the past, developers frequently discovered the need for *n*-tier designs this way: An application ran on a single machine. Someone decided the application needed to be distributed for some reason. These reasons might have included intentions to service more than one client, gate access to a resource, or utilize the advanced processing power of a single powerful machine. The first attempt was usually based on a two-tier design—the prototype worked fine, and all was considered well. As more clients were added, things started to slow down a bit. Adding even more clients brought the system to its knees. Next, the server's hardware was upgraded in an attempt to fix the problem, but this was an expensive option and only delayed confronting the real problem.

A possible solution to this problem is to change the architecture to use a three-tier or *n*-tier design. Figure 1-1 shows how three-tier architectures involve adding a middle tier to the system to perform a variety of tasks. One option is to put business logic in the middle tier. In this case, the middle tier checks the client-supplied data for consistency and works with the data based on the needs of the business. This work could involve collaborating with a data tier or performing in-memory calculations. If all goes well, the middle tier commonly submits its results to a data tier for storage or returns results to the client. The key strength of this design is a granular distribution of processing responsibilities.

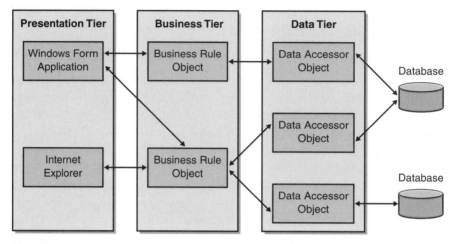

Figure 1-1   Three-tier architecture

Even if more than one tier of an *n*-tier system is located on the same machine, a logical separation of system functions can be beneficial. Developers or administrators can maintain the tiers separately, swap them out altogether, or migrate them to separate machines to accommodate future scalability needs. This is why three-tier (or really *n*-tier) architectures are optimal for scalability as well as flexibility of software maintenance and deployment.

Peer-to-Peer

The preceding distributed architectures have clear roles for each of the tiers. Client/server tiers can easily be labeled as either master/slave or producer/consumer. Tiers in an *n*-tier model tend to fall into roles such as presentation layer, business layer, or data layer. This needn't always be the case, however. Some designs benefit from a more collaborative model in which the lines between client and server are blurred. Workgroup scenarios are constructed this way because the main function of these distributed applications is to share information and processing.

A pure peer-to-peer design is comprised of many individual nodes with no centralized server, as shown in Figure 1-2. Without a well-known main server, there must be a mechanism that enables peers to find each other. This usually is achieved through broadcast techniques or some predefined configuration settings.

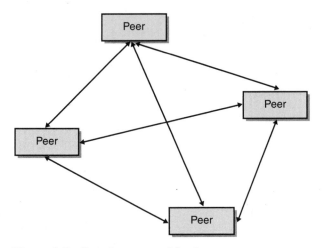

Figure 1-2   Peer-to-peer architecture

The Internet is usually considered a classic client/server architecture with a monolithic Web server servicing many thin clients. But the Internet has also given rise to some quasi-peer-to-peer applications, such as Napster and Gnutella. These systems allow collaborative sharing of data between peer machines. These peers use a centralized server for peer discovery and lookup, as shown in Figure 1-3. Although they're not a pure peer-to-peer architecture, these hybrid models usually scale much better than a completely decentralized peer model and deliver the same collaborative benefits.

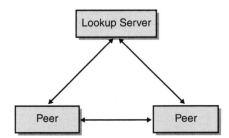

Figure 1-3   Peer-to-peer architecture with centralized lookup server

Even multitier designs can benefit from loosening the client-server role distinction. It's common for a client module to also be a server and for a server to be a client. We'll discuss this blurring of client-server roles when we look at client callbacks and events in Chapter 3, "Building Distributed Applications with .NET Remoting."

Distributed Technologies

The various distributed architectures we discussed have been implemented over the years by using a variety of technologies. Although these architectures are tried and true, the big improvements in distributed application development have been in the technology. Compared to the tools and abstractions used to develop distributed applications 10 years ago, today's developers have it made! Today we can spend a lot more time on solving business problems than on constructing an infrastructure just to move data from machine to machine. Let's look at how far we've come.

Sockets

Sockets are one of the fundamental abstractions of modern network applications. Sockets shield programmers from the low-level details of a network by making the communication look like stream-based I/O. Although sockets provide full control over communications, they require too much work for building complex, full-featured distributed applications. Using stream-based I/O for data communications means that developers have to construct message-passing systems and build and interpret streams of data. This kind of work is too tedious for most general-purpose distributed applications. What developers need is a higher-level abstraction—one that gives you the illusion of making a local function or procedure call.

Remote Procedure Calls

The Distributed Computing Environment (DCE) of the Open Group (formerly the Open Software Foundation) defined, among other technologies, a specification for making remote procedure calls (RPC). With RPC and proper configuration and data type constraints, developers could enable remote communications by using many of the same semantics required by making a local procedure call. RPC introduced several fundamental concepts that are the basis for all modern distributed technologies, including DCOM, CORBA, Java RMI, and now .NET Remoting. Here are some of these basic concepts:

- **Stubs** These pieces of code run on the client and the server that make the remote procedure calls appear as though they're local. For example, client code calls procedures in the stub that look exactly like the ones implemented on the server. The stub then forwards the call to the remote procedure.

- **Marshaling** This is the process of passing parameters from one context to another. In RPC, function parameters are serialized into packets for transmission across the wire.

■   **Interface Definition Language (IDL)**   This language provides a standard means of describing the calling syntax and data types of remotely callable procedures independent of any specific programming language. IDL isn't needed for some Java RMI because this distributed application technology supports only one language: Java.

RPC represented a huge leap forward in making remote communications friendlier than socket programming. Over time, however, the industry moved away from procedural programming and toward object-oriented development. It was inevitable that distributed object technologies wouldn't be far behind.

Distributed Objects—A Welcome Abstraction

Today most developers accept object-oriented design and programming as the tenets of modern software development. Whenever humans have to deal with anything as complex as creating large software systems, using effective abstractions is critical. Objects are the fundamental abstractions used today. Therefore, if developers acknowledge the benefits of objects, it makes sense to apply them to distributed scenarios.

Distributed object technologies allow objects running on a certain machine to be accessed from applications or objects running on other machines. Just as RPC makes remote procedures seem like local ones, distributed object technologies make remote objects appear local. DCOM, CORBA, Java RMI, and .NET Remoting are examples of distributed object technologies. Although these technologies are implemented quite differently and are based on different business philosophies, they are remarkably similar in many ways:

■   They're based on objects that have identity and that either have or can have state. Developers can use remote objects with virtually the same semantics as local objects. This simplifies distributed programming by providing a single, unified programming model. Where possible, developers can factor out language artifacts specific to distributed programming and place them in a configuration layer.

■   They're associated with a component model. The term *component* can be defined in a number of ways, but for this discussion we'll say that a component is a separate, binary-deployable unit of functionality. Components represent the evolution of object-oriented practice from white-box reuse to black-box reuse. Because of their strict public contracts, components usually have fewer dependencies and can be assembled and relocated as functional units. Using components increases deployment flexibility as well as the factoring-out of common services.

■   They're associated with enterprise services. Enterprise services typically provide support for such tasks as transactions, object pooling, concurrency management, and object location. These services address common requirements for high-volume systems and are difficult to implement. When the client load on a distributed system reaches a certain point, these services become critical to scalability and data integrity. Because these services are difficult to implement and commonly needed, they're generally factored out of the developer's programming domain and supplied by the distributed object technology, an application server, or the operating system.

Benefits of Distributed Application Development

Because you've chosen to read a book on .NET Remoting, you probably have some specific scenarios in mind for distributing an application. For completeness, we should mention a few of the general reasons for choosing to distribute applications.

Fault Tolerance

One benefit of distributed applications—which arguably is also one challenge of using them—is the notion of fault tolerance. Although the concept is simple, a wide body of research is centered on fault-tolerant algorithms and architectures. Fault tolerance means that a system should be resilient when failures within the system occur. One cornerstone of building a fault-tolerant system is redundancy. For example, an automobile has two headlights. If one headlight burns out, it's likely that the second headlight will continue to operate for some time, allowing the driver to reach his or her destination. We can hope that the driver replaces the malfunctioning headlight before the remaining one burns out!

By its very nature, distributed application development affords the opportunity to build fault-tolerant software systems by applying the concept of redundancy to distributed objects. Distributing duplicate code functionality—or, in the case of object-oriented application development, copies of objects—to various nodes increases the probability that a fault occurring on one node won't affect the redundant objects running at the other nodes. Once the failure occurs, one of the redundant objects can begin performing the work for the failed node, allowing the system as a whole to continue to operate.

Scalability

Scalability is the ability of a system to handle increased load with only an incremental change in performance. Just as distributed applications enable fault-tolerant systems, they allow for scalability by distributing various functional areas of the application to separate nodes. This reduces the amount of processing performed on a single node and, depending on the design of the application, can allow more work to be done in parallel.

The most powerful cutting-edge hardware is always disproportionately expensive compared to slightly less powerful machines. As mentioned earlier in the three-tier design discussion, partitioning a monolithic application into separate modules running on different machines usually gives far better performance relative to hardware costs. This way, a few expensive and powerful server machines can service many cheaper, less powerful client machines. The expensive server CPUs can stay busy servicing multiple simultaneous client requests while the cheaper client CPUs idle, waiting for user input.

Administration

Few IT jobs are as challenging as managing the hardware and software configurations of a large network of PCs. Maintaining duplicate code across many geographically separated machines is labor intensive and failure prone. It's much easier to migrate most of the frequently changing code to a centralized repository and provide remote access to it.

With this model, changes to business rules can be made on the server with little or no interruption of client service. The prime example of this model is the thin-client revolution. Thin-client architectures (usually browser-based clients) have most, if not all, of the business rules centrally located on the server. With browser-based systems, deployment costs are virtually negligible because Web servers house even presentation-layer code that the clients download on every access.

The principle of reduced administration for server-based business rules holds true even with traditional thick-client architectures too. If thick clients are primarily responsible for presenting data and validating input, the application can be partitioned so that the server houses the logic most likely to change.

Challenges of Distributed Application Development

Developing distributed applications is challenging—there's no doubt about it. Although this section focuses on the challenges that a distributed application technology must meet, it also presents some of the challenges that a distributed application developer must overcome.

Performance

A number of factors can affect the performance of a distributed application. Some examples are factors outside the software system, such as network speed, network traffic, and other hardware issues local to specific machines, such as CPUs, I/O subsystems, and memory size and speed.

Given the current state of distributed application technologies, performance and interoperability are mutually exclusive goals. If your distributed application absolutely needs to perform as fast as possible, you usually have to constrain the application to run inside the firewall, and you have to use the same platform for both client and server. This way, the distributed application can use an efficient network protocol such as TCP and send data by using a proprietary binary format. These formats are far more efficient that the text-based formats usually required for open-standard support.

Assuming a distributed system's hardware (including the network) is optimally configured, proper coding techniques are essential to a scalable high-performance application. The best optimization is to avoid making distributed calls wherever possible. This optimization is usually referred to as the *chatty vs. chunky trade-off*. Most traditional object-oriented programming techniques and texts focus on designing elegant solutions to common programming problems. These solutions are usually most appropriate when collaborating objects are very close to each other (probably in the same process, or with .NET, in the same application domain).

For example, if you're working with a partner who sits beside you in the office, you two can chat as often as you want to solve problems. You can bounce ideas off each other, change your minds, and generally talk throughout the workday. On the other hand, if you're working with a buddy who lives on another continent, your work style needs to change dramatically. In this scenario, you do as much work as possible on your own, check it carefully, and try to make the most of your infrequent communication with your partner. Working this way isn't as elegant as working with a partner who sits beside you, and it requires you to learn a new approach to stay productive. For efficiency, you wind up sending back and forth bigger chunks of work more infrequently when distance becomes a factor.

Thus, if you're using local objects, you can perform tasks such as the following:

- **Use properties at will**   You can set the state of an object by setting many properties on it, each of which requires a round-trip to that object. This way, the client has the flexibility to change as few or as many properties as a scenario requires.

- **Use callbacks at will**   Because the communication time of local objects is negligible, an object can walk a list of client objects and call them even to update a trivial piece of status information. These client objects can call each other to update and retrieve any information they want, without too much worry about a performance hit.

If you're using remote objects, you need to adhere to these stipulations:

- **Avoid heavy use of properties**   Instead of using many properties, you should set remote object state by combining a number of these properties as parameters to one or a few methods. In fact, some very scalable distributed applications have methods with large parameter lists that seem ridiculous for local calls.

- **Think carefully about callbacks**   In the interest of avoiding expensive remote calls, many callbacks could be aggregated into a single or a few method calls with many parameters.

The bottom line is that good remote application design can frequently seem like poor object-oriented design. You simply can't apply every local object metaphor to distributed object scenarios without considering performance.

Note   Of course, you should always avoid writing sloppy, wasteful code. Thus, it's good object-oriented practice for objects to limit their communications where appropriate. Because of the chunky vs. chatty trade-off, scalable remote object design frequently means avoiding many patterns you might have grown accustomed to when dealing with local objects.

Security

No aspect of distributed systems has gotten more attention lately than security. With the increasing exposure of company networks and data to the Internet, the focus of security will only grow. To be considered secure, a distributed application needs to address three main security areas:

- **Authentication**   Servers need a way to make sure the client is who it says it is.

- **Cryptography**   After the server authenticates the client, it must be able to secure the communications.

- **Access control**   After the server authenticates the client, it must be able to determine what the client can do. For example, what operations can the client perform, and what files can it read or write?

DCOM provides strong support for authentication, cryptography, and access control by integrating closely with the Microsoft Windows NT security system. Although DCOM offers a robust and comprehensive security model, in practice, implementing DCOM security effectively is far from straightforward. When the complexity and scope of DCOM solutions encompass solving real-world problems, configuring security can become quite difficult. Because security is so critical to distributed applications, implementing it needs to be foolproof and as simple as possible.

Interoperability and Wire Formats

Most distributed application technologies including DCOM, CORBA, and Java RMI have their own proprietary wire format that's usually designed with performance in mind. A few years ago, interoperability wasn't nearly as important as staking out territory and possibly achieving vendor or technology lock-in. Some third-party "bridge" implementations have attempted to help the locked-in organizations talk to the other side. But none of these solutions are as seamless and easy to use as having the interoperability support baked into the various distributed application technologies.

The Internet and Firewalls

Most of the popular distributed application technologies were originally designed to operate over private networks. Even though the public Internet has been around for years, until recently, its use was mainly confined to file transfer, e-mail, and Web servers delivering HTML pages for viewing. Most people didn't use the Internet as a network for running distributed applications. Over time, companies started protecting their internal networks from all traffic other than HTTP, usually only over port 80. It's probably safe to say that, at this point in history, the majority of all client connections are over HTTP. It's not that HTTP is an efficient protocol. It's simply a convention that evolved because of the popularity of the Internet.

Legacy wire formats and protocols usually require exposing unsafe ports through firewalls. In addition, these formats and protocols tend not to restrict their communications to a single port but to several ports or to ranges of ports. The general feeling in the security community is that configuring firewalls to allow this kind of traffic essentially defeats the purpose of the firewall.

Thus, the next step for companies was to bridge private networks with HTTP. This task was and still is accomplished by tunneling a proprietary wire format over HTTP, writing a custom client and server to pass traffic, or relying on traditional Web servers to handle that hop. None of these alternatives is too attractive. They are labor-intensive, error-prone patches for wire protocol limitations.

This situation has made the use of such proprietary formats unsuitable for the Internet. Like it or not, the industry standard for getting through a firewall is to write distributed applications that communicate by using HTTP.

Configuration

Real-world distributed applications are usually quite complex. You have to control a number of factors just to enable remote communication, much less get any real work done. These variables include endpoint management, activation policies, security settings, and protocols. A number of configuration techniques have appeared in various distributed technologies, but it is now widely accepted that these systems should allow configuration both programmatically and administratively.

DCOM, for example, supports programmatic configuration access through the COM API. Unfortunately, DCOM configuration information is dependent on the registry for storage. Because editing the registry is error prone and dangerous, Microsoft supplies the Dcomcnfg tool to enable easier editing of DCOM configuration information. Even with this tool, using the registry to store distributed application configuration information makes deployment difficult because configuration requires human intervention or installation scripts.

Location Independence

All modern distributed object technologies have facilities to make a remote object appear as though the object is local. This is an important goal of distributed systems because it allows server objects to be moved or replicated without making expensive changes to the calling objects.

Object Lifetime Management

Networks are inherently unreliable. Client applications crash, users give up, and the network can have periods of unavailability. Precious server resources can't be held any longer than necessary, or scalability will suffer and the hardware requirements to support a given load will be unnecessarily large. Distributed application technologies need to provide ways to control object lifetimes and detect client failures so that server objects can be removed from memory as soon as possible.

DCOM's solution to object lifetime is based on a combination of pinging and client-managed reference counting. Unfortunately, placing responsibility for server lifetimes on the client usually forces programmers (at least C++ programmers) to pepper their code with calls to *AddRef* and *Release*. As with managing security, keeping track of *AddRef* and *Release* pairs gets increasingly difficult as interfaces are passed between objects and the number of objects and interfaces grows.

Dealing with multiple interfaces from different objects, passing their references to other objects both local and remote, vigilantly calling *Release* in error scenarios, and avoiding calling *Release* at the wrong time are common problems with complex COM applications

Although reference counting takes care of keeping the server alive, you need a way to detect clients that have failed before releasing the server references they were holding. DCOM's solution for detecting client failures is to use a pinging mechanism. Although pinging (or polling) the client periodically increases network traffic, DCOM's pinging mechanism is heavily optimized to piggyback these pings onto other requests destined for the machine.

Using .NET Remoting to Meet the Challenges

Ultimately, it's all about money. An organization can make more money if it can create better solutions faster and without having to fret over finding enough superstar developers who can juggle all the disparate complex technologies needed to develop large-scale, real-world solutions. Although DCOM is well-equipped to solve complex distributed application problems, it requires significant expertise. You can't always solve these sorts of problems with wizards and naïve development concepts, but you can do a lot to simplify and consolidate the configuration, programming model, and extensibility of DCOM. This is .NET Remoting's greatest strength. .NET Remoting greatly simplifies—or better yet, organizes—the approach to creating and extending distributed applications. This level of organization makes developers more productive, systems more maintainable, and possibly, organizations a bit richer.

Performance

If you configure a .NET Remoting application for optimal performance, the speed will be comparable to that of DCOM, which is very fast. Of course, when configured this way, .NET Remoting applications have the same interoperability constraints as the DCOM applications they're comparable with. Fortunately, configuring .NET Remoting applications for maximum performance versus interoperability is as easy as specifying a couple of entries in a configuration file.

> **Note**   .NET Remoting performance differs from DCOM performance when the client and server are on the same machine. The DCOM/ COM infrastructure detects that the processes are local and falls back to a pure COM (more optimized communication) method. .NET Remoting will still use the network protocol that it was configured to use (such as TCP) when communicating among application domains on the same machine.

Extending and Customizing Remoting

Making a system easy to use for simple, common scenarios yet logically extensible and customizable for more advanced ones is a universal software design problem. How well .NET Remoting solves this problem is probably the technology's strongest feature. For the common cases, .NET Remoting supports many distributed scenarios with little work or configuration through its pluggable architecture. Therefore, it's easy to get a distributed application running. You might say that pluggability is the next layer above component development. Component development provides greater encapsulation of objects into building blocks that can be assembled into working applications. In a similar vein, pluggable architectures support swapping entire subsystems of functionality as long as they support the same "plug." For example, the .NET Remoting architecture supports plugging in the type of channel you want (such as HTTP or TCP) and the type of formatter you want (such as binary or SOAP). This way, you can make common yet powerful configuration choices based on performance and interoperability, simply by plugging in a new module.

Configuration

.NET currently supports configuring remoting applications in three ways:

- **Using configuration files** Remoting can be easily configured by using XML-based files. Using an open standard such as XML for configuration data is a big improvement over using the Windows registry. For example, various instances of remoting applications can coexist on the same machine and be separately configured via configuration files located in their own private directories. Configuration files also facilitate what's known as *Xcopy deployment* for .NET Remoting applications. Xcopy deployment is a method of deploying applications by simply copying a directory tree to a target machine instead of writing setup programs and requiring the user to run them to configure applications. After the initial installation, maintenance is far easier because reconfiguring the application is as easy as copying a new configuration file into the same directory as the remote application's executable. This ease of configuration simply isn't possible when using the registry-based configuration of COM objects.

> **Note** Configuration files come in three flavors, based on their scope:
>
> - **Machine.config** Used for machinewide settings
> - **Web.config** Used to configure ASP.NET applications and .NET Remote objects hosted under Microsoft Internet Information Server (IIS)
> - **Application configuration file** Used to configure a specific application domain

- **Programmatically** Developers who don't want to allow changes to remoting configuration can retain full control over the settings within code.

■   **Using the .NET Framework Microsoft Management Console (MMC) snap-in**   Although programmatic and file-based configuration is considered the domain of the developer, MMC snap-in configuration is supplied to allow the administrator to configure remoting applications. Although this GUI-based configuration tool doesn't give you the control that code and configuration files provide, its scope is directed at the tasks an administrator would want to perform.

CLR and CTS Benefits

A distributed object technology derives a lot of its power and ease of use from its underlying type system and object model. DCOM is subject to the same limitations of COM's type system and object-oriented feature constraints. With COM, there's no implementation inheritance except through constructs such as aggregation and containment. Error handling is limited to return codes because COM doesn't support exceptions. COM's type system is also inconsistent and disparate. C++ COM systems use source code type descriptions (IDL), while Visual Basic and scripting languages rely on binary type representations (type libraries). Neither IDL nor type libraries are a definitive standard because both support constructs that aren't supported by the other. Finally, COM doesn't support a number of object-oriented features, such as static modifiers, virtual functions, and overloaded methods.

By contrast, .NET Remoting is easy to use and powerful, largely because it's based on the common type system (CTS) and the common language runtime (CLR). Type information, known as *metadata*, is consistent and accessible. The .NET Framework CTS defines the basic types that all .NET-compliant languages must support. These types are the atoms that all remoting clients and servers can count on for compatible communication with the same fidelity as classes communicating within a single project. Furthermore, this metadata is unified and stored within the defining assembly so that remote objects don't need separate type descriptions such as DCOM and CORBA.

Because .NET Remoting can use the full power of .NET's object-oriented features, it supports full implementation inheritance; properties; and static, virtual, and overloaded methods. The CLR and CTS allow developers to use a single object system for both local and remote objects and to avoid implementing designs in which the distribution of objects limits object-oriented programming choices. Finally, .NET fully supports exception propagation across remoting boundaries, meaning that handling errors in distributed objects is a big improvement over DCOM's return code error handling.

Interoperability

Customer demand for enterprise technologies such as distributed object technologies has changed during the past few years. For a technology to succeed today, it needs to balance power and ease of use in closed systems as well as possess an ability to interoperate with other potentially proprietary and legacy systems. This is one of .NET Remoting's key design goals. .NET Remoting meets the interoperability goal by supporting open standards such as HTTP, SOAP, Web Service Description Language (WSDL), and XML. To pass through firewalls, you can plug in an HTTP channel. (We'll discuss channels in Chapter 7, "Channels and Channel Sinks.") To communicate with non-.NET clients and servers, a developer can plug in a SOAP formatter. (We'll discuss formatters in Chapter 8, "Serialization Formatters.") Remoting objects can be exposed as Web Services, as we'll discuss in Chapter 3. The .NET Remoting Framework and IIS lets you generate Web Service descriptions that you can provide to developers of non-.NET clients so that they can interoperate over the Internet with the .NET remote objects.

In Figure 1-4, you'll see two common .NET Remoting scenarios: an HTTP channel/SOAP formatter configuration for maximum interoperability, and a higher-performing TCP channel/binary formatter configuration. Both configurations can be set by plugging in simple options.

Security

The security model for .NET Remoting systems has changed quite a bit from the complex and highly configurable model of DCOM. For the initial release of the .NET Framework, the best way to implement a secure remoting system is to host the remote server inside IIS. The best part of hosting inside IIS is that you can use its strong security features without changing the client's code or the server's code. This means you can secure a remoting system just by changing the hosting environment to IIS and passing credentials (user name, password, and optionally, the domain) by setting a client configuration option. We'll give an example of IIS hosting in Chapter 3, but for now we'll look at some of the security options IIS provides.

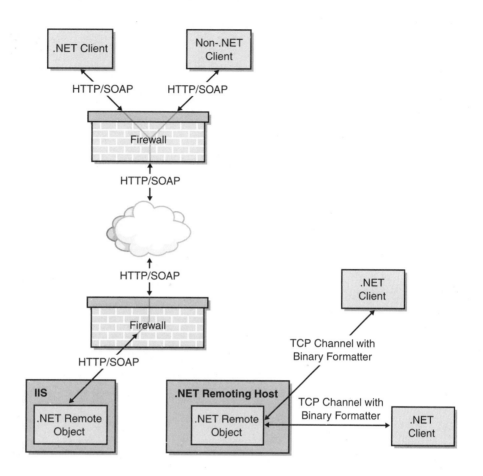

Figure 1-4   Interoperability vs. performance

Authentication

IIS has rich support for various authentication mechanisms, including Windows Integrated Security (NTLM), Basic authentication, Passport authentication, and certificate-based services. NTLM provides the same robust security system as Windows NT and its successors. This is an ideal choice for intranet applications because NTLM doesn't support authentication over firewalls and proxy servers. However, for Internet-based remoting and other authentication scenarios involving firewalls, you'll need a scheme such as Basic or Passport authentication.

Privacy

After the user is authenticated, your next concern might be to hide sensitive data that's being marshaled between remoting tiers. IIS also provides a strong solution for encryption: Secure Sockets Layer (SSL). SSL is an industry standard for encrypting data, and IIS fully supports SSL by using server-side certificates. .NET Remoting clients then need only specify *https* (instead of *http*) as the protocol in the server's URL.

Security with Other Hosts

The initial .NET Framework release doesn't support out-of-the-box remoting security by using hosts other than IIS. However, because the architecture is pluggable, you can write your own custom security solution and plug it in. Writing such a module is beyond the scope of this book. However, there will doubtlessly be many solutions available through the .NET community.

Lifetime Management

.NET Remoting's solution to object lifetime management is a prime example of the *easy to use in simple cases, logical to extend for complex ones* philosophy. First, reference counting and pinging are out. Lease-based lifetimes and sponsors are in. Although DCOM's reference-counting model is simple in concept, it can be complex, error prone, and poorly configurable in practice. .NET leases and sponsors are easy to use, and they customize both clients and servers and allow them to participate in server lifetime management if desired. As with other .NET Remoting parameters, you can configure object lifetimes both programmatically and via configuration files. (We'll look at lifetime management in detail in Chapter 2, "Understanding the .NET Remoting Architecture.")

Enterprise Services

Enterprise services are like medicine: If you don't need them, you should avoid them. But if you need them, you *really* need them. If you do need enterprise services such as distributed transactions, object pooling, and security services, the initial version of the .NET Framework can leverage the robust COM+ services.

When both client and server are running under the CLR, accessing COM+ services is as easy as deriving an object from *System.EnterpriseServices.ServicedComponent*. Because *ServicedComponent* ultimately derives from *MarshalByRefObject* (the type all .NET remote objects derive from), all .NET COM+ objects are automatically remotable. Any object derived from *ServicedComponent* can use COM+ services by adding attributes to its class or its methods. Attribute programming is a powerful paradigm that, among other things, allows a developer to describe code so that tools and other code can learn about his or her intentions and requirements. For example, a .NET remote object can participate in a transaction by simply applying an attribute to a remote object hosted by COM+.

> **Note**   .NET remote objects can participate in COM+ services and can service both .NET Remoting clients and traditional COM clients. However, to support legacy COM clients, the .NET objects hosted by COM+ use COM for the communication method rather than .NET Remoting. In addition, these .NET objects must be given strong names and registered as traditional COM objects by using the Regasm tool.

Summary

In this chapter, we discussed a number of challenges that a remoting technology must meet. These challenges include critical issues, such as performance, interoperability, and security, as well as "nice to haves," such as ease of configuration. .NET Remoting deals with these issues by offering the following features:

■ Strong, out-of-the-box support for common remoting scenarios such as high performance or strong interoperability

■ The ability to use the strong security features of IIS

■ Pluggable architecture for swapping in custom subsystems in the future

■ A logical object model for extending and customizing nearly every aspect of the remoting application.

Understanding the .NET Remoting Architecture

In Chapter 1, "Understanding Distributed Application Development," we took a tour of the distributed application development universe, noting various architectures, benefits, and challenges. This chapter will focus on the .NET Remoting architecture, introducing you to the various entities and concepts that you'll use when developing distributed applications with .NET Remoting. A thorough understanding of the concepts discussed in this chapter is critical to understanding the rest of this book. Throughout the chapter, we'll include some brief code snippets to give you a taste of the programmatic elements defined by the .NET Remoting infrastructure, but we'll defer discussing full-blown implementation details until Chapter 3, "Building Distributed Applications with .NET Remoting." If you're already familiar with the .NET Remoting architecture, feel free to skim through this chapter and skip ahead to Chapter 3.

Remoting Boundaries

In the unmanaged world, the Microsoft Windows operating system segregates applications into separate processes. In essence, the process forms a boundary around application code and data. All data and memory addresses are process relative, and code executing in one process can't access memory in another process without using some sort of interprocess communication (IPC) mechanism. One benefit of this address isolation is a more fault-tolerant environment because a fault occurring in one process doesn't affect other processes. Address isolation also prevents code in one process from directly manipulating data in another process.

Because the common language runtime verifies managed code as type-safe and verifies that the managed code does not access invalid memory locations, the runtime can run multiple applications within a single process and still provide the same isolation benefits as the unmanaged application-per-process model. The common language runtime defines two logical subdivisions for .NET applications: the *application domain* and the *context*.

Application Domains

You can think of the application domain as a logical process. We say this because it's possible for a single Win32 process to contain more than one application domain. Code and objects executing in one application domain can't directly access code and objects executing in another application domain. This provides a level of protection because a fault occurring in one application domain won't affect other application domains within the process. The division between application domains forms a .NET Remoting boundary.

Contexts

The common language runtime further subdivides an application domain into contexts. A context guarantees that a common set of constraints and usage semantics will govern all access to the objects within it. For example, a synchronization context might allow only one thread to execute within the context at a time. This means objects within the synchronization context don't have to provide extra synchronization code to handle concurrency issues. Every application domain contains at least one context, known as the *default context*. Unless an object explicitly requires a specialized context, the runtime will create that object in the default context. We'll discuss the mechanics of contexts in detail in Chapter 6, "Message Sinks and Contexts." For now, realize that, as with application domains, the division between contexts forms a .NET Remoting boundary.

Crossing the Boundaries

.NET Remoting enables objects executing within the logical subdivisions of application domains and contexts to interact with one another across .NET Remoting boundaries. A .NET Remoting boundary acts like a semipermeable membrane: in some cases, it allows an instance of a type to pass through unchanged; in other cases, the membrane allows an object instance outside the application domain or context to interact with the contained instance only through a well-defined protocol—or not at all.

The .NET Remoting infrastructure splits objects into two categories: *non-remotable* and *remotable*. A type is remotable if—and only if—at least one of the following conditions holds true:

■   Instances of the type can cross .NET Remoting boundaries.

■   Other objects can access instances of the type across .NET Remoting boundaries.

Conversely, if a type doesn't exhibit either of these qualities, that type is nonremotable.

Nonremotable Types

Not every type is remotable. Instances of a nonremotable type can't cross a .NET Remoting boundary, period. If you attempt to pass an instance of a nonremotable type to another application domain or context, the .NET Remoting infrastructure will throw an exception. Furthermore, object instances residing outside an application domain or a context containing an object instance of a nonremotable type can't directly access that instance.

Remotable Types

Depending on its category, a remotable type can pass through .NET Remoting boundaries or be accessed over .NET Remoting boundaries. .NET Remoting defines three categories of remotable types: marshal-by-value, marshal-by-reference, and context-bound.

Marshal-by-Value   Instances of marshal-by-value types can cross .NET Remoting boundaries through a process known as *serialization*. Serialization is the act of encoding the present state of an object into a sequence of bits. Once the object has been serialized, the .NET Remoting infrastructure transfers the sequence of bits across .NET Remoting boundaries into another application domain or context where the infrastructure then deserializes the sequence of bits into an instance of the type containing an exact copy of the state. In .NET, a type is serializable if it is declared by using the *Serializable* attribute. The following code snippet declares a class that's made serializable by using the *Serializable* attribute:

```
[Serializable]
class SomeSerializableClass
{
    ⋮
}
```

In addition, a *Serializable*-attributed type can implement the *ISerializable* interface to perform custom serialization. We'll discuss serialization in detail in

Chapter 8. Figure 2-1 shows the serialization and deserialization of an object instance from one application domain to another application domain.

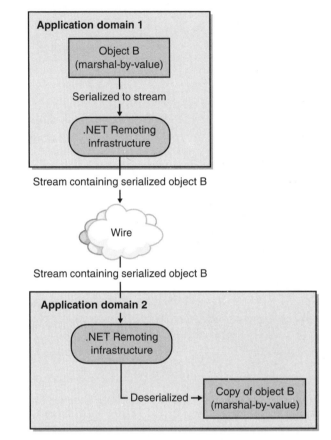

Figure 2-1   Marshal-by-value: object instance serialized from one application domain to another

Marshal-by-Reference   Marshal-by-value is fine for some circumstances, but sometimes you want to create an instance of a type in an application domain and know that all access to such an object will occur on the object instance in that application domain rather than on a copy of it in another application domain. For example, an object instance might require resources that are available only to object instances executing on a specific machine. In this case, we refer to such types as marshal-by-reference, because the .NET Remoting infrastructure marshals a reference to the object instance rather than serializing a copy of the object instance. To define a marshal-by-reference type, the .NET

Framework requires that you derive from *System.MarshalByRefObject*. Simply deriving from this class enables instances of the type to be remotely accessible. The following code snippet shows an example of a marshal-by-reference type:

```
class SomeMBRType : MarshalByRefObject
{
    ⋮
}
```

Figure 2-2 shows how a marshal-by-reference remote object instance remains in its "home" application domain and interacts with object instances outside the home application domain through the .NET Remoting infrastructure.

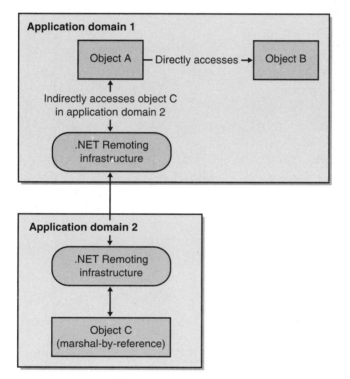

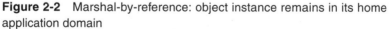

Figure 2-2   Marshal-by-reference: object instance remains in its home application domain

Context-Bound   A further refinement of marshal-by-reference is the context-bound type. Deriving a type from *System.ContextBoundObject* will restrict instances of such a type to remaining within a specific context. Objects external to the containing context can't directly access *ContextBoundObject* types, even if the other objects are within the same application domain. We'll discuss context-bound types in detail in Chapter 6, "Message Sinks and Contexts." The following code snippet declares a context-bound type:

```
class SomeContextBoundType : ContextBoundObject
{
    ⋮
}
```

Figure 2-3 shows the interactions between a Context-Bound object and other objects outside its context.

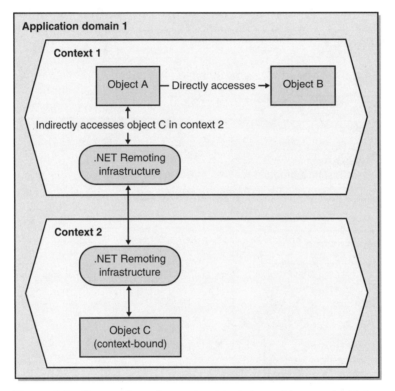

Figure 2-3   Context-bound: remote objects bound to a context interact with objects outside the context through the .NET Remoting infrastructure

Object Activation

Before an object instance of a remotable type can be accessed, it must be created and initialized by a process known as *activation*. In .NET Remoting, marshal-by-reference types support two categories of activation: *server activation* and *client activation*. Marshal-by-value types require no special activation mechanism because they're copied via the serialization process and, in effect, activated upon deserialization.

> **Note**   In .NET Remoting, a type's activation is determined by the configuration of the .NET Remoting infrastructure rather than by the type itself. For example, you could have the same type configured as server activated in one application and as client activated in another.

Server Activated

The .NET Remoting infrastructure refers to server-activated types as well-known object types because the server application publishes the type at a well-known Uniform Resource Identifier (URI) before activating object instances. The server process hosting the remotable type is responsible for configuring the type as a well-known object, publishing it at a specific well-known endpoint or address, and activating instances of the type only when necessary. .NET Remoting categorizes server activation into two modes that offer differing activation semantics: *Singleton mode* and *SingleCall mode*.

Singleton

No more than one instance of a Singleton-mode–configured type will be active at any time. An instance is activated when first accessed by a client if no other instance exists. While active, the Singleton instance will handle all subsequent client access requests by either the same client or other clients. The Singleton instance can maintain state between method calls.

The following code snippet shows the programmatic method of configuring a remotable object type as a Singleton in a server application hosting that remotable object type:

```
RemotingConfiguration.RegisterWellKnownServiceType(
                      typeof( SomeMBRType ),
                      "SomeURI",
                      WellKnownObjectMode.Singleton );
```

This code snippet uses the *System.Runtime.Remoting.RemotingConfiguration* class to register a type named *SomeMBRType* as a well-known object in Singleton mode. The client must also configure *SomeMBRType* as a well-known object in Singleton mode, as the following code snippet shows.

```
RemotingConfiguration.RegisterWellKnownClientType(
                            typeof( SomeMBRType ),
                            "http://SomeWellKnownURL/SomeURI" );
```

> **Note** .NET Remoting provides two mechanisms for configuring the .NET Remoting infrastructure: programmatic files and configuration files. We'll look at each of these configuration alternatives in more detail in Chapter 3.

Figure 2-4 shows how a Singleton-configured remotable object type handles multiple client requests.

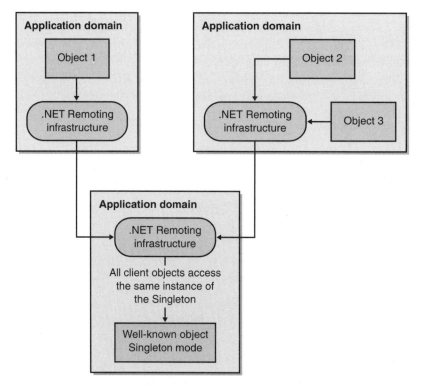

Figure 2-4 Server-activated remote object in Singleton mode

> **Caution**   The lifetime management system used by .NET Remoting imposes a default lifetime on server-activated Singleton-configured types. This implies that it's possible for subsequent client access to occur on various instances of a Singleton type. However, you can override the default lifetime to affect how long your Singleton-configured type can live. In Chapter 3, we'll look at overriding the default lifetime for a Singleton-configured type.

SingleCall

To better support a stateless programming model, server activation supports a second activation mode: SingleCall. When you configure a type as SingleCall, the .NET Remoting infrastructure will activate a new instance of that type for every method invocation a client makes. After the method invocation returns, the .NET Remoting infrastructure makes the remote object instance available for recycling on the next garbage collection. The following code snippet shows the programmatic method of configuring a remotable object type as a SingleCall in an application hosting that remotable object type:

```
RemotingConfiguration.RegisterWellKnownServiceType(
                        typeof( SomeMBRType ),
                        "SomeURI",
                        WellKnownObjectMode.SingleCall );
```

Except for the last parameter, this code snippet is identical to the code used for registering *SomeMBRType* as a Singleton. The client uses the same method to configure *SomeMBRType* as a well-known object in SingleCall mode as it used for the Singleton mode. Figure 2-5 shows a server-activated remote object in SingleCall mode. The .NET Remoting infrastructure ensures that a new remote object instance handles each method call request.

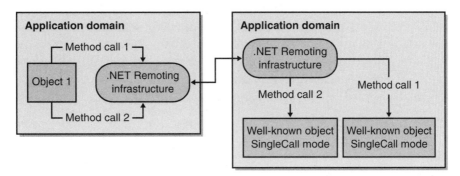

Figure 2-5   Server-activated remote object in SingleCall mode

Client Activated

Some scenarios require that each client reference to a remote object instance be distinct. .NET Remoting provides client activation for this purpose. In contrast to how it handles well-known server-activated types, the .NET Remoting infrastructure assigns a URI to each instance of a client-activated type when it activates each object instance.

Instances of client-activated types can remain active between method calls and participate in the same lifetime management scheme as the Singleton. However, instead of a single instance of the type servicing all client requests, each client reference maps to a separate instance of the remotable type.

The following code snippet shows the programmatic method of configuring a remotable object type as client activated in an application hosting that remotable object type:

```
RemotingConfiguration.RegisterActivatedServiceType(typeof( SomeMBRType ));
```

The corresponding configuration code on the client application would look like the following:

```
RemotingConfiguration.RegisterActivatedClientType(typeof( SomeMBRType ),
"http://SomeURL");
```

We'll look at more detailed examples of configuring and using client-activated objects in Chapter 3.

Note   The *RemotingConfiguration* class's methods for registering remote objects follow two naming patterns:

- *RegisterXXXXClientType* methods register remotable object types that a client application wants to consume.

- *RegisterXXXXServiceType* methods register remotable object types that a server application wants to publish.

XXXX can be either *WellKnown* or *Activated*. *WellKnown* indicates that the method registers a server-activated type; *Activated* indicates that the method registers a client-activated type. We'll look at the *RemotingConfiguration* class in more detail in Chapter 3.

Figure 2-6 shows how each client holds a reference to a different client-activated type instance.

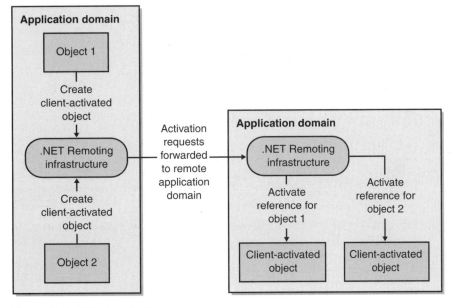

Figure 2-6   Client activation

An Object's Lease on Life

.NET Remoting uses a lease-based form of distributed garbage collection to manage the lifetime of remote objects. To understand the reasoning behind this choice of lifetime management systems, consider a situation in which many clients are communicating with a server-activated Singleton-mode remote object. Non-lease-based lifetime management schemes can use a combination of pinging and reference counting to determine when an object should be garbage collected. The reference count indicates the number of connected clients, while pinging ensures that the clients are still active. In this situation, the network traffic incurred by pinging might have adverse effects on the overall operation of the distributed application. In contrast, the lease-based lifetime management system uses a combination of leases, sponsors, and a lease manager. Because the lease-based lifetime management system doesn't use pinging, it offers an increase in overall performance. Figure 2-7 shows the distributed lifetime management architecture employed by .NET Remoting.

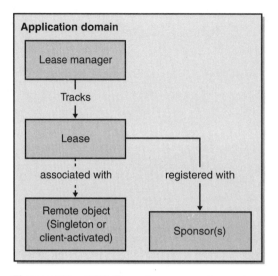

Figure 2-7   .NET Remoting uses a lease-based lifetime management system to achieve distributed garbage collection.

In Figure 2-7, each application domain contains a lease manager. The lease manager holds references to a lease object for each server-activated Singleton or each client-activated remote object activated within the lease manager's application domain. Each lease can have zero or more associated sponsors that are capable of renewing the lease when the lease manager determines that the lease has expired.

Leases

A *lease* is an object that encapsulates *TimeSpan* values that the .NET Remoting infrastructure uses to manage the lifetime of a remote object. The .NET Remoting infrastructure provides the *ILease* interface that defines this functionality. When the runtime activates an instance of either a well-known Singleton or a client-activated remote object, it asks the object for a lease by calling the object's *InitializeLifetimeServices* method, inherited from *System.MarshalByRefObject*. You can override this method to return a lease with values other than the default. The following code listing provides an override in the *SomeMBRType* class of the *InitializeLifetimeServices* method:

```
class SomeMBRType : MarshalByRefObject
{
    ⋮

    public override object InitializeLifetimeService()
    {
```

```
    // Returning null means the lease will never expire.
    return null;
}

    ⋮

}
```

We'll show another example of overriding the *InitializeLifetimeService* method in Chapter 3.

The *ILease* interface defines the following properties that the .NET Remoting infrastructure uses to manage an object's lifetime:

- *InitialLeaseTime*

- *RenewOnCallTime*

- *SponsorshipTimeout*

- *CurrentLeaseTime*

We'll look at an example of manipulating a lease's properties in Chapter 3. For now, it's important to understand the purpose of each of the properties that *ILease* defines. The *InitialLeaseTime* property is a *TimeSpan* value that determines how long the lease is initially valid. When the .NET Remoting infrastructure first obtains the lease for a remote object, the lease's *CurrentLeaseTime* will be equal to *InitialLeaseTime*. An *InitialLeaseTime* value of *0* indicates that the lease will never expire.

The .NET Remoting infrastructure uses the *RenewOnCallTime* property to renew a lease each time a client calls a method on the remote object associated with the lease. When the client calls a method on the remote object, the .NET Remoting infrastructure will determine how much time remains until the lease expires. If the time remaining is less than *RenewOnCallTime*, the .NET Remoting infrastructure renews the lease for the time span indicated by *RenewOnCallTime*.

The *SponsorshipTimeout* property is essentially a timeout value that indicates how long the .NET Remoting infrastructure will wait after notifying a sponsor that the lease has expired. We'll look at sponsors shortly.

The *CurrentLeaseTime* property indicates the amount of time remaining until the lease expires. This property is read-only.

Lease Manager

Each application domain contains a lease manager that manages leases for instances of remotable object types residing in the application domain. When the .NET Remoting infrastructure activates a remote object, the .NET Remoting infrastructure registers a lease for that object with the application domain's lease manager. The lease manager maintains a *System.Hashtable* member that maps leases to *System.DateTime* instances that represent when each lease is due to expire. The lease manager periodically enumerates all the leases it's currently managing to determine whether the current time is greater than the lease's expiration time. By default, the lease manager wakes up every 10 seconds and checks whether any leases have expired, but this polling interval is configurable. The following code snippet changes the lease manager's polling interval to 5 minutes:

```
LifetimeServices.LeaseManagerPollTime = System.TimeSpan.FromMinutes(5);
```

The lease manager notifies each expired lease that it has expired, at which point the lease will begin asking its sponsors to renew it. If the lease doesn't have any sponsors or if all sponsors fail to renew the lease, the lease will cancel itself by performing the following operations:

1. Sets its state to *System.Runtime.Remoting.Lifetime.LeaseState.Expired*

2. Notifies the lease manager that it should remove this lease from its lease table

3. Disconnects the remote object from the .NET Remoting infrastructure

4. Disconnects the lease object from the .NET Remoting infrastructure

At this point, the .NET Remoting infrastructure will no longer reference the remote object or its lease, and both objects will be available for garbage collection. Consider what will happen if a client attempts to make a method call on a remote object whose lease has expired. The remote object's activation mode will dictate the results. If the remote object is server activated in Singleton mode, the next method call will result in the activation of a new instance of the remote object. If the remote object is client activated, the .NET Remoting infrastructure will throw an exception because the client is attempting to reference an object that's no longer registered with the .NET Remoting infrastructure.

Sponsors

As mentioned earlier, sponsors are objects that can renew leases for remote objects. You can define a type that can act as a sponsor by implementing the *ISponsor* interface. Note that because the sponsor receives a callback from the remote object's application domain, the sponsor itself must be a type derived from *System.MarshalByRefObject*. Once you have a sponsor, you can register it with the lease by calling the *ILease.Register* method. A lease can have many sponsors.

For convenience, the .NET Framework defines the *ClientSponsor* class in the *System.Runtime.Remoting.Lifetime* namespace that you can use in your code. *ClientSponsor* derives from *System.MarshalByRefObject* and implements the *ISponsor* interface. The *ClientSponsor* class enables you to register remote object references for the class to sponsor. When you call the *ClientSponsor.Register* method and pass it a remote object reference, the method will register itself as a sponsor with the remote object's lease and map the remote object reference to the lease object in an internal hash table. You set the *ClientSponsor.RenewalTime* property to the time span by which you want the property to renew the lease. The following listing shows how to use the *ClientSponsor* class:

```
// Use the ClientSponsor class: assumes someMBR references an
// existing instance of a MarshalByRefObject derived type.
ClientSponsor cp = new ClientSponsor(TimeSpan.FromMinutes(5));
cp.Register(someMBR);
```

Crossing Application Boundaries

Earlier in this chapter, we mentioned that the divisions between application domains and contexts form .NET Remoting boundaries. The .NET Remoting infrastructure largely consists of facilities that handle the details of enabling objects to interact across these boundaries. Having defined some basic concepts in the previous sections, we can look at the overall sequence of events that occurs when a client of a remote object activates the object and then calls a method on that object.

Marshaling Remote Object References via an *ObjRef*

We mentioned earlier that objects in one .NET Remoting subdivision can't directly access instances of marshal-by-reference types in another .NET Remoting subdivision. So how does .NET Remoting enable objects to communicate across .NET Remoting boundaries? In simple terms, the client uses a proxy object to interact with the remote object by using some means of interprocess communication. We'll look at proxies in more detail shortly, but before we do, we'll discuss how the .NET Remoting infrastructure marshals a reference to a marshal-by-reference object from one .NET Remoting subdivision to another.

There are at least three cases in which a reference to a marshal-by-reference object might need to cross a .NET Remoting boundary:

■ Passing the marshal-by-reference object in a function argument

■ Returning the marshal-by-reference object from a function

■ Creating a client-activated marshal-by-reference object

In these cases, the .NET Remoting infrastructure employs the services of the *System.Runtime.Remoting.ObjRef* type. *Marshaling* is the process of transferring an object reference from one .NET Remoting subdivision to another. To marshal a reference to a marshal-by-reference type from one .NET Remoting subdivision to another, the .NET Remoting infrastructure performs the following tasks:

1. Creates an *ObjRef* instance that fully describes the type of the marshal-by-reference object

2. Serializes the *ObjRef* into a bit stream

3. Transfers the serialized *ObjRef* to the target .NET Remoting subdivision

After receiving the serialized *ObjRef*, the Remoting infrastructure operating in the target .NET Remoting subdivision performs the following tasks:

1. Deserializes the serialized *ObjRef* representation into an *ObjRef* instance

2. Unmarshals the *ObjRef* instance into a proxy object instance that the client can use to access the remote object

To achieve the functionality just described, the *ObjRef* type is serializable and encapsulates several vital pieces of information necessary for the .NET Remoting infrastructure to instantiate a proxy object in the client application domain.

URI

When the .NET Remoting infrastructure activates an instance of a marshal-by-reference object within an application, it assigns it a Uniform Resource Identifier that the client uses in all subsequent requests on that object reference. For server-activated types, the Uniform Resource Identifier corresponds to the published well-known endpoint configured by the host application. For client-activated types, the .NET Remoting infrastructure generates a Globally Unique Identifier (GUID) for the URI and maps it to the remote object instance.

Metadata

Metadata is the DNA of .NET. No, we're not talking about Distributed Network Applications; we're talking about the basic building blocks of the common language runtime. The *ObjRef* contains type information, or metadata, that describes the marshal-by-reference type. The type information consists of the marshal-by-reference object's fully qualified type name; the name of the assembly containing the type's implementation; and the assembly version, culture, and public key token information. The .NET Remoting infrastructure also serializes this type information for each type in the derivation hierarchy, along with any interfaces that the marshal-by-reference type implements, but the infrastructure doesn't serialize the type's implementation.

We can draw a subtle yet important conclusion from the type information conveyed in the *ObjRef* instance: because the *ObjRef* conveys information that describes a type's containing assembly and derivation hierarchy but fails to convey the type's implementation, the receiving application domain must have access to the assembly defining the type's implementation. This requirement has many implications for how you deploy your remote object, which we'll examine in Chapter 3.

Channel Information

Along with the URI and type information, the *ObjRef* carries information that informs the receiving .NET Remoting subdivision how it can access the remote object. .NET Remoting uses channels to convey the serialized *ObjRef* instance, as well as other information, across .NET Remoting boundaries. We'll examine channels shortly, but for now, it's enough to know that the *ObjRef* conveys two sets of channel information:

- Information identifying the context, application domain, and process containing the object being marshaled

- Information identifying the transport type (for example, HTTP), IP address, and port to which requests should be addressed

Clients Communicate with Remote Objects via Proxies

As we mentioned earlier, after the *ObjRef* arrives in the client .NET Remoting subdivision, the .NET Remoting infrastructure deserializes it into an *ObjRef* instance and unmarshals the *ObjRef* instance into a proxy object. The client uses the proxy object to interact with the remote object represented by the *ObjRef*. We'll discuss proxies in detail in Chapter 5, "Messages and Proxies." For now, we want to limit this discussion to the conceptual aspects of proxies to help you better understand their role in .NET Remoting.

Figure 2-8 shows the relationship between a client object and the two types of proxies: transparent and real. The .NET Remoting infrastructure utilizes these two proxy types to achieve seamless interaction between the client and the remote object.

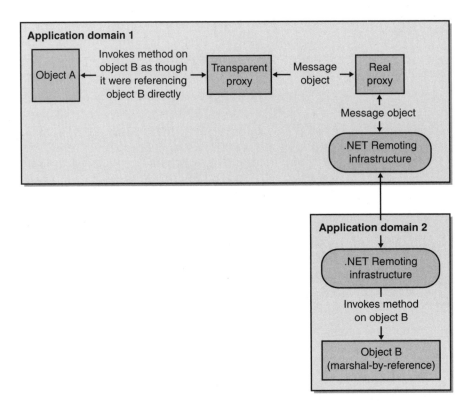

Figure 2-8 The .NET Remoting infrastructure utilizes two kinds of proxies to enable clients to interact with the remote object: transparent and real.

Transparent Proxy

The transparent proxy is the one that the client directly accesses. When the .NET Remoting infrastructure unmarshals an *ObjRef* into a proxy, it generates on the fly a *TransparentProxy* instance that has an interface identical to the interface of the remote object. The client has no idea it's interacting with anything other than the actual remote object's type. The .NET Remoting infrastructure defines and implements *TransparentProxy* internally as the *System.Runtime.Remoting.Proxies.__TransparentProxy* type.

When a client makes a method call on the transparent proxy, the proxy simply converts the method call into a message object, which we'll discuss shortly. The transparent proxy then forwards the message to the second proxy type, *RealProxy*.

Real Proxy

The real proxy is the workhorse that takes the message created by the transparent proxy and sends it to the .NET Remoting infrastructure for eventual delivery to the remote object.

The *System.Runtime.Remoting.Proxies.RealProxy* type is an abstract class; therefore, you can't create instances of it directly. This class is the base class for all proxy types that plug into the .NET Remoting infrastructure. In fact, the .NET Remoting infrastructure defines a *RemotingProxy* class that extends *RealProxy*. The infrastructure uses the *RemotingProxy* class to handle the role of *Real-Proxy*, but you can derive your own custom proxy type from *RealProxy* and use it in place of the one provided by the runtime. We'll demonstrate how to define and use a custom proxy in Chapter 5.

Messages Form the Basis of Remoting

Let's briefly digress from .NET Remoting to consider what happens when we make a method call in a nonremote object-oriented environment. Logically speaking, when you make a method call on an object, you're signaling the object to perform some function. In a way, you're sending the object a message composed of values passed as arguments to that method. The address of the method's entry point is the destination address for the message. At a very low level, the caller pushes the method arguments onto the stack, along with the address to which execution should return when the method completes. Then the caller calls the method by setting the application's instruction pointer to the method's entry point. Because the caller and the method agree on a calling convention, the method knows how to obtain its arguments from the stack in the correct order. In reality, the stack assumes the role of a communications transport layer between method calls, conveying function arguments and return results between the caller and the callee.

Encapsulating the information about the method call in a message object abstracts and models the method-call-as-message concept in an object-oriented way. The message object conveys the method name, arguments, and other information about the method call from the caller to the callee. .NET Remoting uses such a scheme to enable distributed objects to interact with one another. Message objects encapsulate all method calls, input arguments, constructor calls, method return values, output arguments, exceptions, and so on.

.NET Remoting message object types implement the *System.Runtime.Remoting.Messages.IMessage* interface and are serializable. *IMessage* defines a single property member of type *IDictionary* named *Properties*. The dictionary holds named properties and values that describe various aspects of the called method. The dictionary typically contains information such as the URI of the remote object, the name of the method to invoke, and any method parameters. The .NET Remoting infrastructure serializes the values in the dictionary when it transfers the message across a .NET Remoting boundary. The .NET Remoting infrastructure derives several kinds of message types from *IMessage*. We'll look at these types and messages in more detail in Chapter 5, "Messages and Proxies."

> **Note**   Remember that only instances of serializable types can cross .NET Remoting boundaries. Keep in mind that the .NET Remoting infrastructure will serialize the message object to transfer it across the .NET Remoting boundary. This means that any object placed in the message object's *Properties* dictionary must be serializable if you want it to flow across the .NET Remoting boundary with the message.

Channels Transport Messages Across Remoting Boundaries

.NET Remoting transports serialized message objects across .NET Remoting boundaries through channels. Channel objects on either side of the boundary provide a highly extensible communications transport mechanism that potentially can support a wide variety of protocols and wire formats. The .NET Remoting infrastructure provides two types of channels you can use to provide a transport mechanism for your distributed applications: TCP and HTTP. If these channels are inadequate for your transport requirements, you can create your own transport and plug it into the .NET Remoting infrastructure. We'll look at customizing and plugging into the channel architecture in Chapter 7, "Channels and Channel Sinks."

TCP

For maximum efficiency, the .NET Remoting infrastructure provides a socket-based transport that utilizes the TCP protocol for transporting the serialized message stream across .NET Remoting boundaries. The *TcpChannel* type defined in the *System.Runtime.Remoting.Channels.Tcp* namespace implements the *IChannel*, *IChannelReceiver*, and *IChannelSender* interfaces. This means that *TcpChannel* supports both sending and receiving data across .NET Remoting boundaries. The *TcpChannel* type serializes message objects by using a binary wire format by default. The following code snippet configures an application domain with an instance of the *TcpChannel* type that listens for incoming connections on port 2000:

```
using System.Runtime.Remoting.Channels;
using System.Runtime.Remoting.Channels.Tcp;
⋮
TcpChannel c = new TcpChannel( 2000 );
ChannelServices.Register(c);
```

HTTP

For maximum interoperability, the .NET Remoting infrastructure provides a transport that utilizes the HTTP protocol for transporting the serialized message stream across the Internet and through firewalls. The *HttpChannel* type defined in the *System.Runtime.Remoting.Channels.Http* namespace implements the HTTP transport functionality. Like the *TcpChannel* type, *HttpChannel* can send and receive data across .NET Remoting boundaries. The *HttpChannel* type serializes message objects by using a SOAP wire format by default. The following code snippet configures an application domain with an instance of the *HttpChannel* type that listens for incoming connections on port 80:

```
using System.Runtime.Remoting.Channels;
using System.Runtime.Remoting.Channels.Http;
⋮
HttpChannel c = new HttpChannel( 80 );
ChannelServices.Register(c);
```

Channel Sink Chains Can Act on Messages

The .NET Remoting architecture is highly flexible because it possesses a clear separation of object responsibilities. The channel architecture provides flexibility by employing a series of channel sink objects linked together into a sink chain. Each channel sink in the chain has a clearly defined role in the processing of the message. In general, each channel sink performs the following tasks:

1. Accepts the message and a stream from the previous sink in the chain

2. Performs some action based on the message or stream

3. Passes the message and stream to the next sink in the chain

At a minimum, channels transport the serialized messages across .NET Remoting boundaries by using two channel sink objects. Figure 2-9 shows the client-side channel architecture.

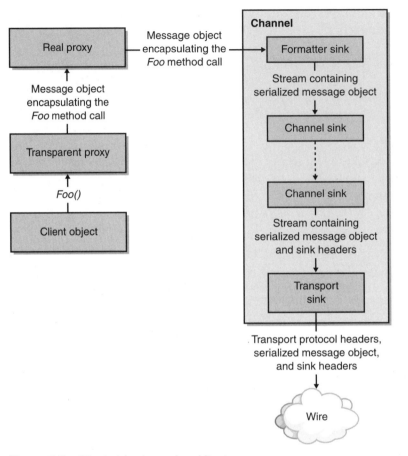

Figure 2-9 Client-side channel architecture

In Figure 2-9, the client object makes calls on a transparent proxy, which in turn converts the method call into a message object and passes that object to the *RealProxy*—actually a *RemotingProxy* derived from *RealProxy*. The *Remoting-Proxy* passes the message object to a set of specialized sink chains within the context (not shown in Figure 2-9), which we'll discuss in detail in Chapter 6, "Message Sinks and Contexts." The message object makes its way through the context sink chains until it reaches the first sink in the channel's sink chain: a formatter sink, which is responsible for serializing the message object to a byte stream by using a particular wire format. The formatter sink then passes the stream to the next sink in the chain for further processing. The last sink in the channel sink chain is responsible for transporting the stream over the wire by using a specific transport protocol.

Formatter Sinks Serialize Message Objects to a Stream

.NET Remoting provides two types of formatter sinks for serializing messages: *BinaryFormatter* and *SoapFormatter*. The type you choose largely depends on the type of network environment connecting your distributed objects. Because of the pluggable nature of the .NET Remoting architecture, you can create your own formatter sinks and plug them into the .NET Remoting infrastructure. This flexibility enables the infrastructure to support a potentially wide variety of wire formats. We'll look at creating a custom formatter in Chapter 8, "Formatters." For now, let's take a quick look at what .NET Remoting provides out of the box.

For network transports that allow you to send and receive binary data (such as TCP/IP), you can use the *BinaryFormatter* type defined in the *System.Runtime.Serialization.Formatters.Binary* namespace. As its name suggests, *BinaryFormatter* serializes message objects to a stream in a binary format. This can be the most efficient and compact way of representing a message object for transport over the wire.

Some network transports don't allow you to send and receive binary data. These transports force applications to convert all binary data into an ASCII text representation before sending it over the wire. In such situations or for maximum interoperability, .NET Remoting provides the *SoapFormatter* type in the *System.Runtime.Serialization.Formatters.Soap* namespace. *SoapFormatter* serializes messages to a stream by using a SOAP representation of the message. We'll discuss SOAP in more detail in Chapter 4, "SOAP and Message Flows."

Transport Sinks Interface with the Wire

The transport sink knows how to transfer data between itself and its counterpart across the .NET Remoting boundary by using a specific transport protocol. For example, *HttpChannel* uses a transport sink capable of sending and receiving HTTP requests and responses to transport the serialized message stream data from one .NET Remoting subdivision to another.

A transport sink terminates the client-side channel sink chain. When this sink receives the message stream, it first writes transport protocol header information to the wire and then copies the message stream to the wire, which transports the stream across the .NET Remoting boundary to the server-side .NET Remoting subdivision.

Figure 2-10 shows the server-side channel architecture. As you can see, it's largely the same as the client-side channel architecture.

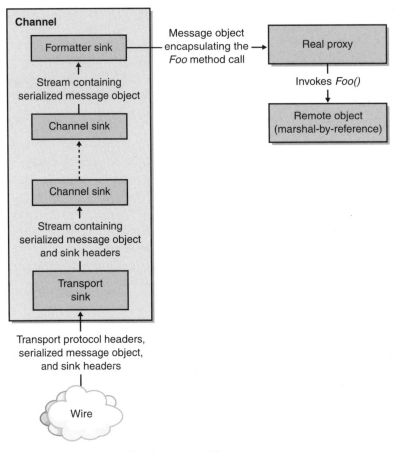

Figure 2-10 Server-side channel architecture

In Figure 2-10, the first sink on the server-side channel sink chain that the serialized message stream encounters is a transport sink that reads the transport protocol headers and the serialized message data from the stream. After pulling this data off the wire, the transport sink passes this information to the next sink in the server-side sink chain. Sinks in the chain perform their processing and pass the resulting message stream and headers up the channel sink chain until they reach the formatter sink. The formatter sink deserializes the message stream and headers into an *IMessage* object and passes the message object to the .NET Remoting infrastructure's *StackBuilderSink*, which actually makes the method call on the remote object. When the method call returns, the *Stack-BuilderSink* packages the return result and any output arguments into a message object of type *System.Runtime.Remoting.Messaging.ReturnMessage*, which the *StackBuilderSink* then passes back down the sink chain for eventual delivery to the proxy in the caller's .NET Remoting subdivision.

Summary

In this chapter, we took a high-level view of each of the major architectural components and concepts of the .NET Remoting infrastructure. Out of the box, .NET Remoting supports distributed object communications over the TCP and HTTP transports by using binary or SOAP representation of the data stream. Furthermore, .NET Remoting offers a highly extensible framework for building distributed applications. At almost every point in the processing of a remote method call, the architecture allows you to plug in customized components. Chapters 5 through 8 will show you how to exploit this extensibility in your .NET Remoting applications.

Now that we've discussed the .NET Remoting architecture, we can proceed to the subject of Chapter 3: using .NET Remoting to build distributed applications.

3

Building Distributed Applications with .NET Remoting

In Chapter 2, "Understanding the .NET Remoting Architecture," we discussed the overall architecture of .NET Remoting, explaining each of the major architectural components that make up the .NET Remoting infrastructure. In this chapter, we'll show you how to use .NET Remoting to build a distributed job assignment system.

The sample application in this chapter demonstrates how to apply the various aspects of the .NET Remoting technology discussed in Chapter 2 to the distributed application development concepts discussed in Chapter 1, "Understanding Distributed Application Development." In the second part of this book, we'll use this application to demonstrate the extensibility of .NET Remoting by developing a custom proxy, channel, and formatter.

In implementing the sample application, we'll discuss and demonstrate the following .NET Remoting tasks:

- Defining remote types

- Hosting remote objects

- Handling events over .NET Remoting boundaries

- Publishing and consuming remote objects

- Exposing a remote object as a Web Service

- Packaging metadata to minimize dependencies

Designing a Distributed Job Assignment Application

The job assignment application consists of two parts, a server and a client. The client will communicate with only a single server, whereas the server will communicate with any number of clients. The server application must maintain state for all clients as well as perform the following tasks:

■ Allow clients to choose job assignments

■ Allow clients to indicate a job is complete

■ Notify clients of new jobs in real time

■ Track all jobs assigned and completed by each client

The client's main purpose is data entry; therefore, a user interface is required. The main screen of the user interface should show a list of all jobs currently on the server and should contain controls that allow the user to create, assign, and update jobs. The client should meet the following additional requirements:

■ Allow the user to choose job assignments from available jobs

■ Allow the user to indicate a job is complete

■ Handle real-time notification of new jobs

■ Handle real-time notification of job assignments

Implementing the JobServer Application

The main purpose of the JobServer application is to host our remote object *JobServerImpl*. Notice in the code listings in this section that the interfaces, structs, and classes do not contain any .NET Remoting references. The unobtrusive nature of .NET Remoting is one of its major strengths.

Although it's not shown in this chapter, when developing this chapter's sample code listings we originally started with a simple client/server application that had both the client and server in the same application domain. One benefit of this approach is that you can ensure the proper functioning of your application before introducing more areas that might cause failures. In addition, debugging is easier in a single application domain.

Implementing the JobServer Application Logic

The JobServer application consists of the *JobInfo* struct, the *IJobServer* interface, the *JobEventArgs* class, and the *JobServerImpl* class. The server application, which we'll discuss shortly, publishes an instance of the *JobServerImpl* class as a remote object; the remaining types support the *JobServerImpl* class.

The *JobInfo* Struct

The following listing defines the *JobInfo* struct, which encapsulates a job's unique identifier, description, assigned user, and status:

```
public struct JobInfo
{
    public JobInfo(int nID, string sDescription,
                string sAssignedUser, string sStatus)
    {
        m_nID           = nID;
        m_sDescription  = sDescription;
        m_sAssignedUser = sAssignedUser;
        m_sStatus       = sStatus;
    }

    public int      m_nID;
    public string   m_sDescription;
    public string   m_sAssignedUser;
    public string   m_sStatus;
}
```

The *IJobServer* Interface

The following listing defines the *IJobServer* interface, which defines how clients interact with the *JobServerImpl* instance:

```
public interface IJobServer
{
    event       JobEventHandler JobEvent;
    void        CreateJob(string sDescription);
    void        UpdateJobState(int nJobID,
                            string sUser,
                            string sStatus);
    ArrayList   GetJobs();
}
```

As its name implies, the *IJobServer.CreateJob* method allows clients to create new jobs by specifying a job description. The *IJobServer.UpdateJobState* method allows a client to set the job status based on the job identifier and user. The status of a job can be either "Assigned" or "Completed." The *IJobServer.GetJobs* method returns a list of all *JobInfo* instances currently defined.

An *IJobServer* implementation should raise the *JobEvent* whenever a client creates a new job or updates the status of an existing job. We'll discuss implementing the *IJobServer* interface shortly, in the section "The *JobServerImpl* Class."

The *JobEventArgs* Class

The *JobEventArgs* class passes new and updated job information to any subscribed *JobEvent* handlers. We define *JobEventArgs* as follows:

```
public class JobEventArgs : System.EventArgs
{
    public enum ReasonCode { NEW, CHANGE };
    private ReasonCode      m_Reason;
    private JobInfo         m_JobInfo;

    public JobEventArgs( JobInfo NewJob, ReasonCode Reason )
    {
        m_JobInfo   = NewJob;
        m_Reason    = Reason;
    }

    public JobInfo Job
    {
        get
        { return m_JobInfo; }

        set
        { m_JobInfo = value; }
    }

    public ReasonCode Reason
    {
        get
        { return m_Reason; }
    }
}
```

Because our implementation of the *IJobServer* interface will raise the *JobEvent* whenever a client adds or updates a job, we'll use the *m_Reason* member to indicate whether the client has created or updated the *JobInfo* instance in *m_JobInfo*.

Notice in this listing that the *JobEventArgs* class derives from *System.EventArgs*. Deriving from *System.EventArgs* isn't a requirement, but it's recommended if the event sender needs to convey event-specific information to the event receiver. We'll discuss the *JobEventArgs* class in more detail in later sections of this chapter.

The *JobServerImpl* Class

The *JobServerImpl* class is the main class of the JobServer application, which hosts an instance of this class as a remote object. The following listing shows the *JobServerImpl* class definition:

```
public class JobServerImpl : IJobServer
{
    private int       m_nNextJobNumber;
    private ArrayList m_JobArray;
```

```
public JobServerImpl()
{
    m_nNextJobNumber = 0;
    m_JobArray      = new ArrayList();
}

// Helper function to raise IJobServer.JobEvent
private void NotifyClients(JobEventArgs args)
{
    // Defined later...
}

// Implement the IJobServer interface.
public event JobEventHandler    JobEvent;

public ArrayList GetJobs()
{
    // Defined later...
}

public void CreateJob( string sDescription )
{
    // Defined later...
}

public void UpdateJobState( int    nJobID,
                            string sUser,
                            string sStatus )
{
    // Defined later...
}
}
```

The *JobServerImpl.m_JobArray* member stores each *JobInfo* instance. The *JobServerImpl.m_nNextJobNumber* member uniquely identifies each newly created job.

The following listing shows the implementation of the *GetJobs* method:

```
public ArrayList GetJobs()
{
    return m_JobArray;
}
```

Both the *CreateJob* and *UpdateJobState* methods rely on a helper method named *NotifyClients* to raise the *JobEvent* when a client creates a new job or updates an existing job. The following listing shows the implementation of the *NotifyClients* method:

```
private void NotifyClients(JobEventArgs args)
{
    //
    // Manually invoke each event handler to
    // catch disconnected clients.
    System.Delegate[] invkList = JobEvent.GetInvocationList();

    IEnumerator ie = invkList.GetEnumerator();
    while(ie.MoveNext())
    {
        JobEventHandler handler = (JobEventHandler)ie.Current;
        try
        {
            IAsyncResult ar =
                    handler.BeginInvoke( this, args, null, null);
        }
        catch(System.Exception e)
        {
            JobEvent -= handler;
        }
    }
}
```

Note that instead of using the simple form of raising the event, the *Notify-Clients* method enumerates over the event's invocation list, manually invoking each handler. This guards against the possibility of a client becoming unreachable since subscribing to the event. If a client becomes unreachable, the *JobEvent* invocation list will contain a delegate that points to a disconnected remote object. When the code invokes the delegate, the runtime will throw an exception because it can't reach the remote object. This prevents the invocation of any remaining delegates in the invocation list and can lead to clients not receiving event notifications. To prevent this problem from occurring, we must manually invoke each delegate and remove any delegates that throw an exception. In production code, it's better to watch for specific errors so that you can handle them appropriately.

The following listing shows the *JobServerImpl* class implementation of the *CreateJob* method, which allows the user to create a new job:

```
public void CreateJob( string sDescription )
{
    // Create a new JobInfo instance.
    JobInfo oJobInfo = new JobInfo( m_nNextJobNumber,
                                    Description,
                                    "",
                                    "" );
    // Increment the next job number.
    m_nNextJobNumber++;
```

```
        // Add the JobInfo instance to our JobArray.
        m_JobArray.Add( oJobInfo );

        // Notify any attached clients of the new job.
        NotifyClients( new JobEventArgs( oJobInfo,
                                    JobEventArgs.ReasonCode.NEW ));
}
```

The following listing shows the implementation of the *UpdateJobState*
method, which allows clients to update the user and status for a job:

```
public void UpdateJobState( int nJobID,
                            string sUser,
                            string sStatus )
{
        // Get the specified job from the array.
        JobInfo oJobInfo = ( JobInfo ) m_JobArray[ nJobID ];

        // Update the user and status fields.
        oJobInfo.m_sAssignedUser = sUser;
        oJobInfo.m_sStatus = sStatus;

        // Update the array element because JobInfo is a value type.
        m_JobArray[ nJobID ] = oJobInfo;

        // Notify any attached clients of the new job.
        NotifyClients( new JobEventArgs( oJobInfo,
                                    JobEventArgs.ReasonCode.CHANGE));
}
```

Adding .NET Remoting

So far, we've implemented some types without regard to .NET Remoting. Now
let's walk through the steps required to add .NET Remoting to the JobServer
application:

1. Making a type remotable

2. Choosing a host application domain

3. Choosing an activation model

4. Choosing a channel and a port

5. Choosing how clients will obtain the server's metadata

6. Configuring the server for .NET Remoting

Making a Type Remotable

To prepare the *JobServerImpl* class and its supporting constructs for .NET Remoting, we need to enhance their functionality in several ways. Let's start with the *JobInfo* struct. The *JobServerImpl* class passes *JobInfo* structure instance information to the client; therefore, the structure must be *serializable*. With the .NET Framework, making an object serializable is as simple as applying the *[serializable]* pseudocustom attribute.

Next we must derive the *JobServerImpl* class, which is our remote object, from *System.MarshalByRefObject*. As you might recall from Chapter 2, an instance of a type derived from *System.MarshalByRefObject* interacts with objects in remote application domains via a proxy. Table 3-1 lists the public methods of *System.MarshalByRefObject*.

Table 3-1   Public Methods of *System.MarshalByRefObject*

Public Method	Description
CreateObjRef	Virtual method that returns a *System.Runtime.Remoting.ObjRef* instance used in marshaling a reference to the object instance across .NET Remoting boundaries. You can override this function in your derived types to return a custom version of the *ObjRef*.
GetLifetimeService	Use this method to obtain an *ILease* interface reference on the *MarshalByRefObject* instance's associated lease.
InitializeLifetimeService	The .NET Remoting infrastructure calls this virtual method during activation to obtain an object of type *ILease*. As explained in Chapter 2 and demonstrated later in this chapter in "Adding a Sponsor to the Lease," this method can be overridden in derived classes to control the object instance's initial lifetime policy.

The following listing shows how we override the *InitializeLifetimeService* method:

```
public override object InitializeLifetimeService()
{
    return null;
}
```

Returning *null* tells the .NET Remoting infrastructure that the object instance should live indefinitely. We'll see an alternative implementation of this method later in this chapter in the "Configuring the Client for Remoting Client-Activated Objects" section.

Choosing a Host Application Domain

The next step is to decide how to expose instances of *JobServerImpl* to the client application. The method you choose depends on your answers to the following questions:

- Will the application run all the time?

- Will the server and clients be on an intranet?

- Will the server application provide a user interface?

- Will you be exposing the remote type as a Web Service?

- How often will the application run?

- Will clients have access to the application only through a firewall?

    Fortunately, we have many options at our disposal, including the following:

- Console applications

- Windows Forms

- Windows Services

- Internet Information Services (IIS)/ASP.NET

- COM+

Because of their simplicity, you'll probably prefer to use console applications as the hosting environment for doing quick tests and developing prototypes. Console applications are full-featured .NET Remoting hosts, but they have one major drawback for real-world scenarios: they must be explicitly started. However, for testing and debugging, the ability to start and stop a host as well as monitor console output might be just what you want.

.NET Remoting hosts have the same benefits and limitations as console applications, only .NET Remoting hosts have a graphical display. Windows Forms applications are usually thought of as client applications rather than server applications. Using a GUI application for a .NET Remoting host underscores how you can blur lines between client and server. Of course, all the .NET Remoting hosts can simultaneously function as a client and a server or simply as a server.

Production-level hosting environments need to provide a way to register channels and listen for client connections automatically. You might be familiar with the DCOM server model in which the COM Service Control Manager (SCM) automatically launches DCOM servers in response to a client connection. In contrast, .NET Remoting hosts must be running prior to the first client connection. The remaining hosting environments in this discussion provide this capability.

Windows Services make an excellent choice for implementing a constantly available host because they can be configured to start automatically and don't require a user to be logged on to the machine. The downside of using Windows Services as .NET Remoting hosts is that they require more development effort and require that you run an installation utility to deploy the service.

The simplest .NET Remoting host to write is the one that's already written: IIS. Because IIS is a service, it's a constantly running remote object host. IIS also provides some unique features, such as allowing for easy security configuration for remote applications and enabling you to change the server's configuration file without restarting the host. The biggest drawback of using IIS as a .NET Remoting host is that IIS supports only the *HttpChannel* (discussed in Chapter 2), although you can increase performance by choosing the binary formatter.

Finally, if you need access to enterprise services, you can use COM+ services to host remote objects. In fact, .NET objects that use COM+ services are automatically remotable because the required base class for all COM+ objects (*System.EnterpriseServices.ServicedComponent*) ultimately derives from *System.MarshalByRefObject*. The litmus test for deciding whether to use COM+ as the hosting environment is whether you need access to COM+ services, such as distributed transactions and object pooling. If you don't need these services, you probably won't want to incur the performance penalties of running under COM+ services.

To help illustrate various .NET Remoting concepts, we've chosen the easiest host to create, run, and debug: a console application for the JobServer application. We'll use Windows Forms to develop the JobClient application in the next section of the chapter. We'll also use IIS as the hosting environment later in this chapter when we discuss Web Services.

The following code listing shows the entry point for the JobServer application:

```
namespace JobServer
{
    class JobServer
    {
        /// <summary>
        /// The main entry point for the application
        /// </summary>
        static void Main(string[] args)
        {
            // Insert .NET Remoting code.

            // Keep running until told to quit.
            System.Console.WriteLine( "Press Enter to exit" );
```

```
                    // Wait for user to press the Enter key.
                    System.Console.ReadLine();
                }
            }
        }
```

As we discuss .NET Remoting issues later in this section, we'll replace the "Insert .NET Remoting code" comment with code. Near the end of this section, you'll see a listing of the completed version of the *Main* method. You'll be surprised at how simple it remains.

Choosing an Activation Model

In Chapter 2, we discussed the two types of activation for marshal-by-reference objects: server activation and client activation. For our application, we want the client to create the remote object once, and we want the remote object to remain instantiated, regardless of which client created it. Recall from Chapter 2 that the client controls the lifetime of client-activated objects. We clearly don't want our object to be client activated. This leads us to selecting server activation. We have one more decision to make: selecting an activation mode, Singleton or SingleCall. In Chapter 2, we learned that in SingleCall mode, a separate instance handles each request. SingleCall mode won't work for our application because it persists data in memory for a particular instance. Singleton mode, however, is just what we want. In this mode, the application creates a single *JobServerImpl* instance when a client first accesses the remote object.

The .NET Remoting infrastructure provides a class named *RemotingConfiguration* that you use to configure a type for .NET Remoting. Table 3-2 lists the public members of the *RemotingConfiguration* class.

Table 3-2   Public Members of *System.Runtime.
Remoting.RemotingConfiguration*

Member	Member Type	Description
ApplicationId	Read-only property	A string containing a globally unique identifier (GUID) for the application.
ApplicationName	Read/write property	A string representing the application's name. This name forms a portion of the Uniform Resource Identifier (URI) for remote objects.
Configure	Method	Call this method to configure the .NET Remoting infrastructure by using a configuration file.

(continued)

**Table 3-2   Public Members of *System.Runtime.
Remoting.RemotingConfiguration***   *(continued)*

Member	Member Type	Description
GetRegisteredActivatedClientTypes	Method	Obtains an array of all currently registered client-activated types consumed by the application domain.
GetRegisteredActivatedServiceTypes	Method	Obtains an array of all currently registered server-activated types published by the application domain.
GetRegisteredWellKnownClientTypes	Method	Obtains an array of all currently registered server-activated types consumed by the application domain.
GetRegisteredWellKnownServiceTypes	Method	Obtains an array of all currently registered server-activated types published by the application domain.
IsActivationAllowed	Method	Determines whether the currently configured application domain supports client activation for a specific type.
IsRemotelyActivatedClientType	Method	Returns an *ActivatedClientTypeEntry* instance if the currently configured application domain has registered the specified type for client activation.
IsWellKnownClientType	Method	Returns a *WellKnownClientTypeEntry* instance if the currently configured application domain has registered the specified type for server activation.
ProcessId	Read-only property	A string in the form of a GUID that uniquely identifies the process that's currently executing.
RegisterActivatedClientType	Method	Registers a client-activated type consumed by the application domain.
RegisterActivatedServiceType	Method	Registers a client-activated type published by the application domain.
RegisterWellKnownClientType	Method	Registers a server-activated type consumed by the application domain.
RegisterWellKnownServiceType	Method	Registers a server-activated type published by the application domain.

The following code snippet demonstrates configuring the *JobServerImpl* type as a server-activated type, published with a URI of *JobURI* and published by using the Singleton activation mode:

```
RemotingConfiguration.RegisterWellKnownServiceType(
        typeof( JobServerImpl ),
        "JobURI",
        WellKnownObjectMode.Singleton );
```

Choosing a Channel and a Port

As we stated in Chapter 2, the .NET Framework provides two stock channels, *HttpChannel* and *TcpChannel*. Selecting the proper channel transport is generally an easy choice because, in many environments, it makes no difference which transport you select. Here are some influencing factors on channel selection:

■   Whether your channel will transmit through a firewall

■   Whether sending data as plain text raises security concerns

■   Whether you require the .NET Remoting security features of IIS

In Chapter 4 we'll examine the message flow between client and server. To facilitate this, we'll use the *HttpChannel* (which by default uses the *SOAP-Formatter)* so that the messages will be in a human-readable form. The following snippet shows how easy it is to configure a channel:

```
HttpChannel oJobChannel = new HttpChannel( 4000 );
ChannelServices.RegisterChannel( oJobChannel );
```

First, we create an instance of the *HttpChannel* class, passing its constructor the value 4000. Thus, 4000 is the port on which the server listens for the client. Creating a channel object isn't enough to enable the channel to accept incoming messages. You must register the channel via the static method *Channel-Services.RegisterChannel*. Table 3-3 lists a subset of the public members of the *ChannelServices* class; the other public members are used in more advanced scenarios, which we'll cover in Chapter 7.

Table 3-3   Public Members of *System.Runtime.Remoting.Channels.ChannelServices*

Member	Member Type	Description
GetChannel	Method	Obtains an object of type *IChannel* for the registered channel specified by name
GetUrlsForObject	Method	Obtains an array of all the URLs at which a type is reachable
RegisterChannel	Method	Registers a channel for use in the application domain
RegisteredChannels	Read-only property	Gets an array of *IChannel* interfaces for all registered channels within the application domain
UnregisterChannel	Method	Unregisters a channel for use in the application domain

Choosing How Clients Will Obtain the Server's Metadata

A client of a remote type must be able to obtain the metadata describing the remote type. The metadata is needed for two main reasons:

■ To enable the client code that references the remote object type to compile

■ To enable the .NET Framework to generate a proxy class that the client uses to interact with the remote object

Several ways to achieve this result exist, the easiest of which is to use the assembly containing the remote object's implementation. From the perspective of a remote object implementer, allowing the client to access the remote object's implementation might not be desirable. In that case, you have several options for packaging metadata, which we'll discuss later in the "Metadata Dependency Issues" section. For now, however, the client will access the Job-ServerLib assembly containing the *JobServerImpl* type's implementation.

Configuring the Server for Remoting

At this point, we've programmatically configured the JobServer application for remoting. The following code snippet shows the body of the JobServer application's *Main* function:

```
{
// Register a listening channel.
HttpChannel oJobChannel = new HttpChannel( 4000 );
ChannelServices.RegisterChannel( oJobChannel );

// Register a well-known type.
RemotingConfiguration.RegisterWellKnownServiceType(
        typeof( JobServerImpl ),
        "JobURI",
        WellKnownObjectMode.Singleton );
}
```

This looks great, but what if you want to change the port number? You'd need to recompile the server. You might be thinking, "I could just pass the port number as a command-line parameter." Although this will work, it won't solve other problems such as adding new channels. You need a way to factor these configuration details out of the code and into a configuration file. Using a configuration file allows the administrator to configure the application's remoting behavior without recompiling the code. The best part of this technique is that you can replace all the previous code with a single line of code! Look at our new *Main* function:

```
{
RemotingConfiguration.Configure( @"..\..\JobServer.exe.config" );
}
```

Our new version of *Main* is a single line. All the .NET Remoting configuration information is now in the JobServer.exe.config configuration file.

> **Note**   By convention, the name of your configuration file should be the application's binary file name plus the string *.config*.

The following code listing shows the JobServer.exe.config configuration file:

```
<configuration>
    <system.runtime.remoting>
        <application name="JobServer">
            <service>
                <wellknown mode="Singleton"
                    type="JobServerLib.JobServerImpl, JobServerLib"
                    objectUri="JobURI" />
            </service>
            <channels>
                <channel ref="http"
                    port="4000" />
            </channels>
        </application>
    </system.runtime.remoting>
</configuration>
```

Notice the correlation between the configuration file and the remoting code added in the previous steps. The element *<channel>* contains the same information to configure the channel as we used in the original code snippet showing programmatic configuration. We've also replaced the programmatic registration of the well-known object by adding a *<wellknown>* element entry to the configuration file. The information for registering server-activated objects is under the *<service>* element. Both the *<service>* and *<channel>* elements can contain multiple elements. As you can see from this snippet, the power of configuration files is quite amazing.

Implementing the JobClient Application

We can now turn our attention to implementing a client application that makes remote method calls on the remote object hosted by the JobServer application. It's worth repeating that one of the great things about .NET Remoting is how unobtrusive it is. .NET's remoting capabilities just seem to exist in the background, without requiring a class implementer to write a large amount of extra "glue" code to benefit from the .NET Remoting architecture. Let's now detail the basic tasks that you must complete to enable a client application for remoting.

Choosing a Client Application Domain

We had several choices for hosting the *JobServerImpl* instance as a remote object. We have the same choices for implementing the client application.

We've chosen to implement the JobClient application as a Windows Forms application by using C#. The application is straightforward, consisting of a main form containing a *ListView* control. The *ListView* control displays a column for each *JobInfo* struct member: *JobID*, *Description*, *User*, and *Status*.

The form also contains three buttons that allow the user to perform the following actions:

■ Create a new job.

■ Assign a job.

■ Complete a job.

The remainder of this discussion assumes that you've created a new Microsoft Visual Studio .NET C# Windows Application project. After creating the project, add a *System.Windows.Forms.ListView* control and three *System.Windows.Forms.Button* controls to the Form1 form so that it resembles Figure 3-1.

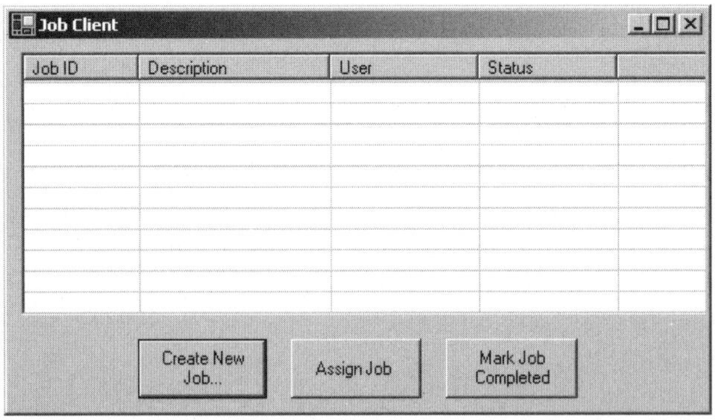

Figure 3-1   The JobClient application's main form

The JobClient application interacts with an instance of the *JobServerImpl* class that we developed in the previous section. Therefore, you need to add a reference to the JobServerLib.dll assembly so that the client can use the *IJobServer* interface, the *JobServerImpl* class, the *JobInfo* struct, and the *JobEventArgs* class.

Because the *Form1* class will interact with the *JobServerImpl* class instance, add a *JobServerImpl* type member and a method named *GetIJobServer* to the *Form1* class in the Form1.cs file:

```
using JobServerLib;

public class Form1 : System.Windows.Forms.Form
{
    :

    // This member holds a reference to the IJobServer interface
    // on the remote object.
    private IjobServer m_IJobServer;

    private IJobServer GetIJobServer()
    {
        return (IJobServer)new JobServerImpl();
    }

    :

}
```

Although the *JobServerImpl* type is remotable because it derives from *MarshalByRefObject*, the *JobServerImpl* instance created by the *GetIJobServer* method is local to the JobClient application's application domain. To make *JobServerImpl* remote, we need to configure .NET Remoting services, which we'll do later in this section after we implement the client application logic. For now, however, we'll develop the entire client application by using a local instance of the *JobServerImpl* class. As we mentioned at the beginning of this section, doing so offers a number of benefits, one of which is allowing us to quickly develop the sample application without dealing with .NET Remoting issues.

The following code listing shows the *Form1* constructor:

```
public Form1()
{
    //
    // Required for Windows Form Designer support
    //
    InitializeComponent();

    // Get a reference to the remote object.
    m_IJobServer = GetIJobServer();

    // Subscribe to the JobEvent.
    m_IJobServer.JobEvent +=
            new JobEventHandler(this.MyJobEventHandler);
}
```

The last statement in this listing subscribes to the *JobEvent*. We'll unsubscribe from the *JobEvent* when the user terminates the application. The following listing shows the *Form.Close* event handler:

```
private void OnClosed(object sender, System.EventArgs e)
{
// Make sure we unsubscribe from the JobEvent.
m_IJobServer.JobEvent -= new JobEventHandler(this.MyJobEventHandler);
}
```

Recall from the previous section that the *JobServerImpl* instance raises the *IJobServer.JobEvent* whenever a client creates a new job or changes a job's status to "Assigned" or "Complete." The following code listing shows the implementation for the *MyJobEventHandler* method:

```
public void MyJobEventHandler(object sender, JobEventArgs args)
{
    switch(args.Reason)
    {
        case JobEventArgs.ReasonCode.NEW:
            AddJobToListView(args.Job);
            break;
        case JobEventArgs.ReasonCode.CHANGE:
            UpdateJobInListView(args.Job);
            break;
    }
}
```

The *MyJobEventHandler* method uses two helper methods, which we'll discuss shortly. Based on the value of the *JobEventArgs* instance's *Reason* property, the method either adds the job information conveyed in the *JobEventArgs* instance to the list view or updates an existing job in the list view.

Caution Declaring the *MyJobEventHandler* event handler method with private (nonpublic) access will result in the runtime throwing a *System.Runtime.Serialization.SerializationException* exception when the client application subscribes to the *JobEvent*. The associated error message states, "Serialization will not deserialize delegates to nonpublic methods." This makes sense from a security perspective because otherwise code could circumvent the method's declared nonpublic accessibility level.

Note that the callback will occur on a thread different from the thread that created the *Form1* control. Because of the threading constraints of controls, most methods on controls aren't thread-safe, and invoking a *Control.xxxxx* method from a thread other than the creating thread might result in undefined behavior, such as deadlocks. Fortunately, the *System.Windows.Forms.Control* type provides several methods (such as the *Invoke* method) that allow noncreating threads to cause the creating thread to call methods on a control instance. The *Invoke* method takes two parameters: the instance of the delegate to invoke, and an array of object instances to pass as parameters to the target method.

The *AddJobToListView* method uses the *ListView.Invoke* method to call the *ListView.Items.Add* method on the creating thread. Before using the *List-View.Invoke* method, you must define a delegate for the method you want to invoke. The following code shows how to define a delegate for the *List-View.Items.Add* method:

```
// Need a delegate to the ListView.Items.Add method.
delegate ListViewItem dlgtListViewItemsAdd(ListViewItem lvItem);
```

The *AddJobToListView* method uses *Invoke* to add job information to the list view, as the following listing shows:

```
// Add job to the list view.
void AddJobToListView(JobInfo ji)
{
    // Create a delegate targeting the listView1.Items.Add method.
    dlgtListViewItemsAdd lvadd =
    new dlgtListViewItemsAdd( listView1.Items.Add );

    // Package the JobInfo data in a ListViewItem instance.
    ListViewItem lvItem =
            new ListViewItem(new string[] { ji.m_nID.ToString(),
                                            ji.m_sDescription,
                                            ji.m_sAssignedUser,
                                            ji.m_sStatus } );

    // Use Invoke to add the ListViewItem to the list view.
    listView1.Invoke( lvadd, new object[]{lvItem});
}
```

The implementation of the *UpdateJobInListView* method follows the same model as the *AddJobToListView* method to invoke the *GetEnumerator* method of the *ListView.Items* collection class. The following code implements the *UpdateJobInListView* method:

```
// Update job in list view.
void UpdateJobInListView(JobInfo ji)
```

(continued)

```
{
    IEnumerator ie = (IEnumerator)listView1.Invoke(new
            dlgtItemsGetEnumerator(listView1.Items.GetEnumerator));
    while( ie.MoveNext() )
    {
        // Find the job in the list view matching this JobInfo.
        ListViewItem lvItem = (ListViewItem)ie.Current;
        if ( ! lvItem.Text.Equals(ji.m_nID.ToString()) )
        {
            continue;
        }

        // Found it. Now go through the ListViewItem's subitems
        // and update accordingly.
        IEnumerator ieSub = lvItem.SubItems.GetEnumerator();
        ieSub.MoveNext(); // Skip JobID.

        // Update the description.
        ieSub.MoveNext();
        if ( ((ListViewItem.ListViewSubItem)ieSub.Current).Text !=
            ji.m_sDescription )
        {
            ((ListViewItem.ListViewSubItem)ieSub.Current).Text =
                    ji.m_sDescription;
        }

        // Update the assigned user.
        ieSub.MoveNext();
        if ( ((ListViewItem.ListViewSubItem)ieSub.Current).Text !=
            ji.m_sAssignedUser )
        {
            ((ListViewItem.ListViewSubItem)ieSub.Current).Text =
                    ji.m_sAssignedUser;
        }

        // Update the status.
        ieSub.MoveNext();
        if ( ((ListViewItem.ListViewSubItem)ieSub.Current).Text !=
            ji.m_sStatus )
        {
            ((ListViewItem.ListViewSubItem)ieSub.Current).Text =
                    ji.m_sStatus;
        }
    } // End while
}
```

The *UpdateJobInListView* method enumerates over the *ListView.Items* collection, searching for a *ListViewItem* that matches the *JobInfo* type's job identifier field. When the method finds a match, it enumerates over and updates the subitems for the *ListViewItem*. Each subitem corresponds to a column in the details view.

So far, we've created an instance of the *JobServerImpl* class and saved a reference to its *IJobServer* interface. We've added event-handling code for the *JobEvent*. We've also looked at how using the *ListView.Invoke* method allows us to update the *ListView* control from a thread other than the thread that created the control instance. We must complete the following tasks:

■ Obtain a collection of all current jobs to populate the *ListView* when the form loads.

■ Implement the *Button.Click* event handlers to allow the user to create, assign, and complete jobs.

Before implementing the *Button.Click* handlers, it's useful to introduce a couple of helper functions. The following code implements a method named *GetSelectedJob* that returns a *JobInfo* instance corresponding to the currently selected *ListViewItem*:

```
private JobInfo GetSelectedJobInfo()
{
    JobInfo ji = new JobInfo();

    // Which job is selected?
    IEnumerator ie = listView1.SelectedItems.GetEnumerator();
    while( ie.MoveNext() )
    {
        // Our list view does not allow multiple selections, so we
        // should have no more than one job selected.
        ji =
            ConvertListViewItemToJobInfo( (ListViewItem)ie.Current );
    }
    return ji;
}
```

This method in turn utilizes another method named *ConvertListViewItem-ToJobInfo*, which takes a *ListViewItem* instance and returns a *JobInfo* instance based on the values of the *ListViewItem* subitems:

```
private JobInfo ConvertListViewItemToJobInfo(ListViewItem lvItem)
{
    JobInfo ji = new JobInfo();
    IEnumerator ieSub = lvItem.SubItems.GetEnumerator();
    ieSub.MoveNext();
    ji.m_nID =
        Convert.ToInt32(
            ((ListViewItem.ListViewSubItem)ieSub.Current).Text);
```

(continued)

```
        ieSub.MoveNext();
        ji.m_sDescription =
            ((ListViewItem.ListViewSubItem)ieSub.Current).Text;
        ieSub.MoveNext();
        ji.m_sAssignedUser =
            ((ListViewItem.ListViewSubItem)ieSub.Current).Text;
        ieSub.MoveNext();
        ji.m_sStatus =
            ((ListViewItem.ListViewSubItem)ieSub.Current).Text;
        return ji;
    }
```

With the helper functions in place, we can implement the handler methods for the Assign, Complete, and Create *Button.Click* events:

```
private void buttonAssign_Click(object sender, System.EventArgs e)
{
    // Which job is selected?
    JobInfo ji = GetSelectedJobInfo();
    m_IJobServer.UpdateJobState(ji.m_nID,
                                System.Environment.MachineName,
                                "Assigned");
}


private void buttonComplete_Click(object sender, System.EventArgs e)
{
    // Which job is selected?
    JobInfo ji = GetSelectedJobInfo();
    m_IJobServer.UpdateJobState(ji.m_nID,
                                System.Environment.MachineName,
                                "Completed");
}
```

The Assign button and Complete button *Click* event handlers simply get the selected job and call *IJobServer.UpdateJobState*. Calling the *IJobServer.UpdateJobState* method elicits two results:

- The *JobServerImpl* instance sets the job state information for the specified job ID to "Assigned" or "Completed."

- The *JobServerImpl* instance raises the *JobEvent*.

Finally, the following listing shows the implementation for the Create New Job button:

```
private void buttonCreate_Click(object sender, System.EventArgs e)
{
    // Show Create New Job form.
    FormCreateJob frm = new FormCreateJob();
    if ( frm.ShowDialog(this) == DialogResult.OK )
```

```
    {
        // Create the job on the server.
        string s = frm.JobDescription;
        if ( s.Length > 0 )
        {
            m_IJobServer.CreateJob(frm.JobDescription);
        }
    }
}
```

The *buttonCreate_Click* method displays another form named *FormCreate-Job*, which asks the user to enter a description for the new job. After the user closes the form, the *buttonCreate_Click* method obtains the description entered by the user (if any). Assuming the user enters a description, the code calls the *IJobServer.CreateJob* method on the *JobServerImpl* instance, which creates a new job and raises the *JobEvent*.

You can implement the FormCreateJob form by adding a new form to the project. Figure 3-2 shows the FormCreateJob form.

Figure 3-2   The JobClient application's Create New Job form

The following code listing shows the additional code necessary to implement the *FormCreateJob* class:

```
public class FormCreateJob : System.Windows.Forms.Form
{
    private System.Windows.Forms.Button button1;
    private System.Windows.Forms.Button button2;
    private System.Windows.Forms.TextBox textBox1;
    private System.Windows.Forms.Label label1;

    private string m_sDescription;
    public string JobDescription
    {
        get{ return m_sDescription; }
    }

    private void button1_Click(object sender, System.EventArgs e)
```

(continued)

```
    {
        m_sDescription = textBox1.Text;
    }

    private void button2_Click(object sender, System.EventArgs e)
    {
    this.Hide();
    }
}
```

Obtaining the Server's Metadata

Now you must obtain the metadata describing the remote type you want to use. As we mentioned in the "Implementing the JobServer Application" section, the metadata is needed for two main reasons: to enable the client code that references the remote object type to compile, and to enable the .NET Framework to generate a proxy class that the client uses to interact with the remote object. This sample references the JobServerLib assembly and thus uses the *JobServerImpl* type's implementation. We'll discuss other ways of obtaining suitable metadata for the remote object later in this chapter in the sections "Exposing the *JobServer-Impl* Class as a Web Service" and "Metadata Dependency Issues."

At this point, you should be able to compile and run the application and test it by creating, assigning, and completing several new jobs. Figure 3-3 shows how the JobClient application looks after the user creates a few jobs.

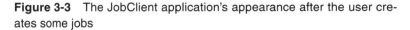

Figure 3-3 The JobClient application's appearance after the user creates some jobs

Let's recap what we've accomplished so far. We've implemented the Job-Client application as a C# Windows Forms application. If you run the sample application, the *GetIJobServer* method actually creates the *JobServerImpl* instance in the client application's application domain; therefore, the instance isn't remote. You can see this in the debugger, as shown in Figure 3-4.

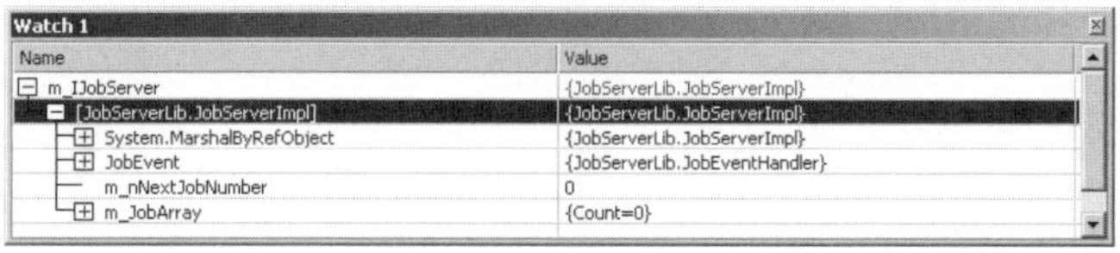

Figure 3-4   The *JobServerImpl* instance is local to the client application domain.

Recall from Chapter 2 that clients interact with instances of remote objects through a proxy object. Currently, the *m_IJobServer* member references an instance of the *JobServerLib.JobServerImpl* class. Because the *JobServerImpl* class derives from *System.MarshalByRefObject*, instances of it are *remotable*. However, this particular instance isn't remote because the application hasn't yet configured the .NET Remoting infrastructure. You can tell that it's not remote because the *m_IJobServer* member doesn't reference a proxy. In contrast, Figure 3-5 shows how the Watch window would look if the instance were remote.

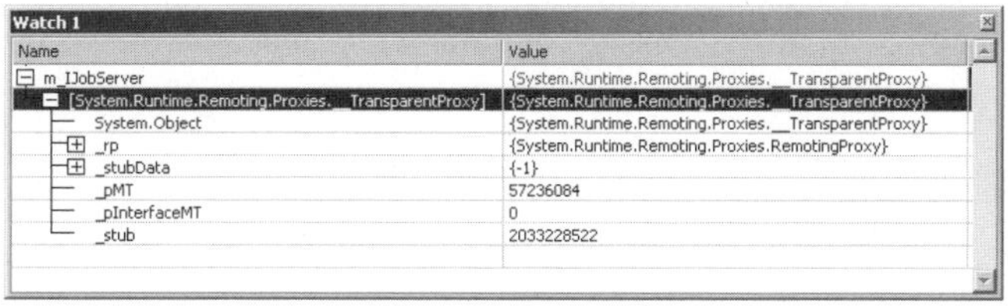

Figure 3-5   The *JobServerImpl* instance is remote to the client application domain.

You can easily see in Figure 3-5 how the *m_IJobServer* member references an instance of the *System.Runtime.Remoting.Proxies.__TransparentProxy* type. As discussed in Chapter 2, this type implements the transparent proxy, which forwards calls to the underlying type instance derived from *RealProxy*. This latter type instance can then make a method call on the remote object instance.

So far, we haven't dealt with any remoting-specific code for the JobClient application. Let's change that.

Configuring the JobClient Application for .NET Remoting

The second task necessary to enable remote object communication is to configure the client application for .NET Remoting. Configuration consists largely of registering a communications channel appropriate for the remote object and registering the remote object's type. You configure an application for .NET Remoting either programmatically or by using configuration files.

Programmatic Configuration

The .NET Framework provides the *RemotingConfiguration* class in the *System.Runtime.Remoting* namespace for configuring an application to use .NET Remoting. As discussed in the "Implementing the JobServer Application" section, this class provides various methods to allow programmatic configuration of the Remoting infrastructure. Let's look at the client-specific configuration methods that this class exposes.

You can configure the JobClient application for .NET Remoting by modifying the *GetIJobServer* method, as the following listing shows:

```
private IJobServer GetIJobServer()
{
    //
    // Register a channel.
    HttpChannel channel = new HttpChannel(0);
    ChannelServices.RegisterChannel(channel);

    //
    // Register the JobServerImpl type as a WKO.
    WellKnownClientTypeEntry remotetype =
                new WellKnownClientTypeEntry(typeof(JobServerImpl),
                                "http://localhost:4000/JobURI");
    RemotingConfiguration.RegisterWellKnownClientType(remotetype);

    return (IJobServer)new JobServerImpl();
}
```

In this listing, you create a new instance of the *HttpChannel* class, passing the value of 0 to the constructor. A value of 0 causes the channel to pick any available port and begin listening for incoming connection requests. If you use the default constructor (no parameters), the channel won't listen on a port and can only make outgoing calls to the remote object. Because the JobClient application subscribes to the *JobServerImpl* instance's *JobEvent* event, it needs to register a channel capable of receiving the callback when the *JobServerImpl* instance raises the *JobEvent* event. If you need to have the callback occur on a specific port, you can specify that port number instead of 0. When the constructor returns, the application is actively listening for incoming connections on either the specified port or an available port.

> **Note** The mscorlib.dll assembly defines most of the commonly used .NET Remoting types. However, another assembly named System.Runtime.Remoting.dll defines some other types, such as *HttpChannel* in the *System.Runtime.Remoting.Channels.Http* namespace.

After creating an instance of *HttpChannel*, you register the instance with *ChannelServices* via its *RegisterChannel* method. This method takes the *IChannel* interface from the *HttpChannel* instance and adds the interface to its internal data structure of registered channels for the client application's application domain. Once registered with the .NET Remoting infrastructure, the channel transports .NET Remoting messages between the client and the server. The channel also receives callbacks from the server on the *listening port*.

Note   You can register more than one channel if the channel names are unique. For example, you can expose a single remote object by using *HttpChannel* and *TcpChannel* at the same time. This way, a single host can expose the object to clients across firewalls (by using *HttpChannel*) and to .NET clients inside a firewall (by using the better-performing *TcpChannel*).

The next step is to configure the .NET Remoting infrastructure to treat the *JobServerImpl* type as a remote object that resides outside the JobClient application's application domain. The *RemotingConfiguration* class provides the *RegisterWellKnownClientType* method for configuring well-known objects on the client side. This method has two overloads. The one used in this sample takes an instance of a *System.Runtime.Remoting.WellKnownClientTypeEntry* class. You create an instance of this class by specifying the type of the remote object—in this case, *typeof(JobServerImpl)*—and the object's well-known URL.

Note   The *RemotingConfiguration* class provides an overloaded form of the *RegisterWellKnownClientType* method that takes two arguments, a *System.Type* instance specifying the type of the remote object, and a string specifying the URL, as shown here:

```
RemotingConfiguration.RegisterWellKnownClientType(
                       typeof(JobServerImpl),
                       http://localhost:4000/JobURI );
```

This form of the *RegisterWellKnownClientType* method uses these arguments to create an instance of *WellKnownClientType*, which it then passes to the other form of *RegisterWellKnownClientType*.

At this point, you've configured the JobClient application for remoting. The application can now connect to the *JobServerImpl* object hosted by the JobServer application without requiring any further changes in the original application code. It's not absolutely necessary to register the remote object's type with the *RemotingConfiguration* class. You need to do so only if you want to use the *new* keyword to instantiate the remote type. The other option is to use the *Activator.GetObject* method, which we'll look at later in the "Remoting the *IJobServer* Interface" section.

Configuration File

.NET Remoting offers a second method for configuring an application for .NET Remoting that uses configuration files. We introduced using configuration files earlier, in the section "Implementing the JobServer Application." You use different tags when configuring a client application for .NET Remoting. The following XML code shows the configuration file for the sample JobClient application:

```
<configuration>
   <system.runtime.remoting>
      <application name="JobClient">
         <client>
            <wellknown
               type="JobServerLib.JobServerImpl, JobServerLib"
               url="http://localhost:4000/JobURI" />
         </client>
         <channels>
            <channel ref="http" port="0" />
         </channels>
      </application>
   </system.runtime.remoting>
</configuration>
```

The client configuration file contains a *<client>* element, which you use to specify any remote objects used by the client application. In the previous listing, the *<client>* element contains a child element named *<wellknown>*, which you use to indicate any well-known server-activated objects this client uses. You can see how the *<wellknown>* element's attributes map closely to the parameters passed to the *WellKnownClientTypeEntry* constructor call that appeared in the earlier example showing programmatic configuration. The *<client>* element can also contain an *<activated>* element for specifying client-activated objects, which we'll discuss later in the "Extending the Sample with Client Activated Objects" section.

The elements for channel configuration are the same as those for the server configuration file. You specify the HTTP channel by using the *ref* property along with a port value of 0 to allow the .NET Remoting infrastructure to pick any available port. The following code listing shows how you can use the Job-Client.exe.config file to configure .NET Remoting by replacing the implementation of the *GetIJobServer* method with a call to the *RemotingConfiguration.Configure* method:

```
private IJobServer GetIJobServer()
{
    RemotingConfiguration.Configure( @"..\..\JobClient.exe.config" );
    return (IJobServer)new JobServerImpl();
}
```

Exposing the *JobServerImpl* Class as a Web Service

The JobServer and JobClient application designs are similar in many ways to traditional DCOM application designs. This example has a high degree of coupling in that we assume both client and server run under the common language runtime. Running all remoting pieces under the common language runtime means that we can take advantage of the full .NET Framework type system, choose the most efficient communication options, and enjoy a common environment for developing code. We also assume that a firewall doesn't separate the JobServer and JobClient applications (as a DCOM solution would require). These assumptions afford us a lot of freedom in making design decisions, and this flexibility is fine for intranet or private network solutions. If we design .NET Remoting applications with these assumptions in mind, we can gain the power and performance of DCOM with a far simpler and far more extensible programming model.

Over time, however, the requirements of the internal application might change, requiring that we expose all or part of the system to the outside world. This usually means introducing variables such as the Internet; firewalls; and unknown, uncontrolled clients that aren't necessarily running under the common language runtime. If the server application is implemented by using DCOM, making the transition isn't at all straightforward. The usual solution is to write Active Server Pages (ASP)—or now, ASP.NET—code to consume the DCOM objects and to provide an HTML-based interface for the outside world. However, outside parties might want to consume the services of the internal application directly, to integrate the services with their own application or to use their own visual interface. If the internal services are exposed only as human-readable HTML, integration with other applications is difficult and not resilient to change. The usual technique is for outside developers to resort to screen scraping or parsing the HTML that's meant only for visual communication. This technique is notoriously fragile because any revisions to the published HTML UI can break the application. Also, visual updates to Internet applications are very common. For many business-to-business scenarios and single business applications, exposing services directly is a far more powerful, flexible, and maintainable approach than hard-coding a visual HTML interface.

Herein lies the power of Web Services. Web Services provide a way to expose component services over the Internet rather than just present visual information. These services can be assembled to build larger applications that are similar to traditional software components. Web Services are high-level abstractions that accomplish this feat by using a number of collaborating technologies, such as SOAP; HTTP; XML; Web Service Description Language (WSDL); and Universal Description, Discovery, and Integration (UDDI). Basing Web Services on HTTP and SOAP makes the service communication firewall friendly. WSDL describes the Web Service public methods, parameters, and service location, and UDDI provides a directory for locating Web Services (WSDL files) on the Internet.

> **Note** WSDL is an XML grammar for describing Web Services in a platform-independent and language-independent manner. A WSDL document allows clients on any platform to locate a Web Service running on any platform and invoke its publicly exposed methods. Thus, WSDL is similar to Interface Definition Language (IDL), except that WSDL also specifies the location (URL) of the service. WSDL tools enable developers to generate a .wsdl file for a given Web Service and to automate creating client code to call those services. The .NET Framework provides two such tools: WSDL.exe and SOAPSuds.exe. SOAPSuds.exe is used with .NET Remoting–based Web Services, while WSDL.exe supports only ASP.NET-based Web Services.

All these underlying technologies are open and in various stages of draft or approval by the W3C. (See *http://www.w3c.org* for more information.) The Web Service vision dictates that as long as vendors comply with a set of open standards, anyone with standards-compliant tools can create a Web Service with any language on any platform and consume it with any language on any platform. Because of the flux in some of the nonfinalized underlying standards and the speed with which vendors update their tools, this universal interoperability has been realized only partially at the time of this writing. For more information about writing Web Services that have the best chance of interoperability, see the MSDN article "Designing Your Web Service for Maximum Interoperability."

Constraints of Web Services

As we've stated, Web Services can interoperate with clients running on any platform, written in virtually any language, and Web Services can get through firewalls. So why not use them all the time? The answer is that to achieve this interoperability, you lose some of the rich functionality .NET Remoting offers. Just as IDL or type libraries provide least-common-denominator descriptions of interface contracts and data types for COM objects, WSDL is a compromised description of calling syntax and data types for remotable objects. .NET Remoting provides full common language runtime type fidelity, while Web Services are limited to dealing with generic types that can more easily map to the type systems of many languages.

Because of WSDL's type description limitations, describing .NET remote objects by using WSDL requires us to avoid using properties. Although the object can still support properties for other .NET clients, Web Service clients must have another mechanism to get and set this data.

Being firewall friendly involves more than simply running over HTTP. Client callbacks can be problematic because they require initiating a connection to the client. Because the client becomes the server in callback scenarios, clients behind firewalls can't service connections made to ports that aren't open on the firewall. Although workarounds for these cases exist, these workarounds won't solve all issues when clients are behind Network Address Translation (NAT) firewalls. Furthermore, these workarounds aren't appropriate for most Web Service clients because of the proprietary nature of the required custom client code. Because these hardware firewalls can perform IP address translation, a server can't make a callback to a client based on its given IP address.

Changes to the Sample Application

To test the JobServer Web Service, we'll use a modified version of the JobClient Windows Forms application. Although our test client runs under the common language runtime, any non-.NET client with proper vendor tool support for creating callable client code from the Job Server's WSDL file should be able to access the JobServer Web Service.

This following discussion will summarize the changes to the job application design and implementation needed to fully support Web Services.

Removing Client Callback

Because our Web Service won't support client callbacks, we need another way to find out about job updates. To do this, we'll poll for the data by calling the *GetJobs* method every 5 seconds. This is a very common technique for Web-enabled client applications, and it's easy to set up by using the Windows Forms Timer control. Polling for data also simplifies the client application quite a bit. Instead of updating the *JobInfo* list with new jobs incrementally, we get the entire *JobInfo* list on every poll. Also, because no client event is exposed, there's no secondary thread and no need to update the UI by using the *Invoke* method.

Selecting an Activation Method

We usually implement Web Services as SingleCall-activated servers that manage state by using some persistent data store such as a database. As a simplifying assumption, we'll use the Singleton activation mode and retain state in memory. It's also possible to implement a stateful Web Service by using client-activated objects, but that might make it difficult or impossible for some non-.NET clients to use our service.

Now that the JobServer application is Web Service compliant, we need to properly configure IIS to host the *JobServerImpl* object. These steps aren't specific to exposing Web Services but are used in hosting any remote object in IIS.

Configuring the Virtual Directory

To configure the virtual directory, you first create a new Web application by running the IIS Microsoft Management Console (MMC) snap-in. Select the Default Web Site tree node, choose Action/New/Virtual Directory, and name the alias for the virtual directory *JobWebService*. After we finish configuring the wizard, we need to properly configure security for the Web application. By default, IIS configures newly created Web applications to use Windows Integrated authentication (NTLM authentication). This will make our application unreachable by non-Windows clients and users who don't have sufficient NTFS rights to the physical directory that JobWebService is aliasing. To make our Web Service available to all clients, we'll "turn off" security by configuring anonymous access. (We'll turn security on again in the section "Adding Security to the Web Service.") First, select the JobWebService application in the Default Web Site tree node. Choose Action/Properties. In the tabbed dialog box, choose Directory Security and click the Edit button. Uncheck Integrated Windows Authentication, and check Anonymous Access.

Configuring the Web.config File

Now we need to modify the configuration file details. You use the Web.config file located in the root of the hosting application's virtual directory to configure an IIS-hosted remote application, as the following listing shows:

```
<configuration>
  <system.runtime.remoting>
    <application>
      <service>
        <wellknown mode="SingleCall"
          type="JobServerLib.JobServerImpl,JobServerLib"
          objectUri="JobServer.soap" />
      </service>
    </application>
  </system.runtime.remoting>
</configuration>
```

The *<wellknown>* element is very similar to the same-named element used in the earlier applications' configuration files. The notable addition is that the *objectUri* attribute has the .soap extension. IIS-hosted well-known objects must have object URIs that end in either .rem or .soap.

Note that there's no *<channel>* element in this example, and recall that the previous examples used this tag to configure a channel type and set the port. The default channel for remoting objects hosted in IIS is *HttpChannel*, which is also required by Web Services. This *HttpChannel* automatically uses the same port IIS is configured to use (port 80 by default). To configure IIS to use a different port, run the IIS MMC snap-in, select Default Web Site, choose Action/Properties, and set the port under the Web Site tab.

Deployment

IIS-hosted remote objects must be placed in either the virtual directory's \bin directory or the global assembly cache (GAC). For simplicity, we'll deploy the *JobServerImpl* object to the \bin directory.

Using the SOAPSuds Tool

SOAPSuds is Microsoft's tool for extracting descriptions from .NET Remoting–based Web Services in a variety of formats. SOAPSuds can be run against a local assembly or an IIS-hosted .NET Remoting object endpoint. You have four main choices for output format:

- Assembly with implementation
- Metadata-only assembly

- XML schema (WSDL)

- Compilable class

Let's look at each of these formats now.

Assembly with Implementation

The following command generates an assembly containing the implementation of the JobServerLib assembly. First, you can run SOAPSuds directly against the local JobServerLib assembly by using the *–types* option:

```
Soapsuds -types:JobServerLib.JobServerImpl,JobServerLib →
         -oa:JobServerLib.dll
```

Here's the syntax for the *–types* option:

```
Namespace.ClassName,AssemblyName
```

The *–oa* option (short for *output assembly)* causes the tool to generate an assembly containing the implementation of the *JobServerImpl* class.

A more interesting case occurs when you run SOAPSuds against the IIS-hosted endpoint for the remote object:

```
Soapsuds -url:http://localhost/JobWebService/JobServer.soap?wsdl →
         -oa:JobServerLib.dll
```

Metadata-Only Assembly

SOAPSuds also provides a simple way to generate a metadata-only assembly. This is the syntax for doing so on the JobWebService application:

```
Soapsuds -url:http://localhost/JobWebService/JobServer.soap?wsdl →
         -oa:JobServerLib.dll
```

Many developers consider this technique the easiest way to generate an assembly containing only the minimum calling syntax needed for a .NET Remoting client.

XML Schema (WSDL)

Generating a .NET assembly of course is useful only for supporting .NET clients. We also need a way to create a WSDL description of our Web Service to support non-.NET clients. The *–os* flag tells SOAPSuds to output a schema file to describe the Web Service. Here's the syntax:

```
Soapsuds -url:http://localhost/JobWebService/JobServer.soap?wsdl →
         -os:JobServerLib.wsdl
```

For the record, you can obtain the same WSDL representation of the Web Service by browsing to the endpoint via Microsoft Internet Explorer. Simply enter this command into the browser's address bar:

```
http://localhost/JobWebService/JobServer.soap?wsdl
```

Next right-click the client area of the browser, and select View Source from the context menu. This file is functionally identical to the WSDL file generated by SOAPSuds. You can run this resulting file through a supporting tool to create a callable proxy wrapper. Non-.NET clients can use this technique to create client code to interoperate with .NET Remoting–based Web Services.

Compilable Class

SOAPSuds can also convert a WSDL file into compilable .NET source code by using the input schema flag (*–is*) and the generate code flag (*–gc*):

```
Soapsuds -is:JobServer.wsdl -gc
```

Or SOAPSuds can convert the WSDL file directly into an assembly:

```
Soapsuds -is:JobServer.wsdl -oa:JobServerLib.dll
```

> **Note**   You might recall from Chapter 2 that the *HttpChannel* serializes message objects by using a SOAP wire format by default. As its name implies, SOAPSuds is primarily intended to generate metadata for objects hosted within .NET Remoting servers that use *HttpChannel*. This is because SOAPSuds' default behavior is to generate what is known as a *wrapped proxy*. A wrapped proxy contains a hard-coded server URL and supports using only the *HttpChannel*, which is convenient for our Web Service client. However, SOAPSuds can also generate a nonwrapped proxy that supports the *TcpChannel* and allows the server URL to be explicitly set by calling code. You can generate a non-wrapped metadata assembly by using the *–nowp* option:
>
> ```
> Soapsuds -ia:InputAssemblyName -oa:OutputAssemblyName.dll -nowp
> ```
>
> When using the generated output metadata assembly, you must specify the server URL and desired channel either programatically or via a configuration file.

Adding Security to the Web Service

As we discussed earlier, easy security configuration is one of the best reasons to choose IIS as the hosting environment for .NET Remoting applications. You configure security for .NET Remoting–based Web Services the same way as you configure security for all IIS-hosted remote objects. Thus, you can follow these same steps to configure security for other IIS-hosting scenarios, such as client-activated objects and objects using formatters that aren't Web Service compliant, such as the binary formatter.

The following example shows how to configure the JobServer Web Service to use IIS NTLM. This way, IIS will authenticate the JobClient requests based on Windows NT credentials. In simple terms, the *JobServerImpl* object will be accessible only to clients that can supply credentials with sufficient NTFS rights to the JobWebService virtual directory. Note that NTLM is suitable only for intranet scenarios. This is because clients must have Windows credentials and NTLM authentication isn't firewall friendly or proxy-server friendly.

Changes to the Virtual Directory Settings

Select the JobWebService application in the Default Web Site tree node. Choose Action/Properties. In the tabbed dialog box, choose Directory Security and click Edit. This time, check Windows Integrated Authentication and uncheck Anonymous Access.

Changes to the Web.config File

Add the following lines to the JobWebService application's Web.config file:

```
<system.web>
  <authentication mode="Windows"/>
  <identity impersonate="true"/>
</system.web>
```

These options configure ASP.NET to use Windows authentication and to impersonate the browsing user's identity when making server-side requests.

Changes to the JobClient Application

.NET Framework clients can obtain credentials (user name, password, and domain name, if applicable) to submit to the server in two ways: default credentials and explicit credentials.

The default credentials concept is simply to obtain the user name and password of the currently logged-on user without requiring—or possibly allowing—the credentials to be explicitly specified. To configure the client to use default credentials via the client configuration file, add the *useDefaultCredentials* attribute to the HTTP channel, as shown here:

```
<channels>
  <channel ref="http" useDefaultCredentials="true"/>
</channels>
```

To specify default credentials at run time, set the *useDefaultCredentials* property of the channel in the channel constructor:

```
IDictionary props = new Hashtable();
props["useDefaultCredentials"] = true;

HttpChannel channel = new HttpChannel(
```

```
props,
null,
new SoapServerFormatterSinkProvider()
);
```

Instead of automatically passing the interactive user's credentials to the server, you might want to explicitly control the user name, password, and domain name. Because using explicit credentials also results in sending the supplied password across the wire in cleartext, this option should be used only in conjunction with some sort of encryption, such as Secure Sockets Layer (SSL).

You specify explicit credentials at run time by setting properties on the channel sink as follows. (We'll discuss channel sinks in more detail in Chapter 7, "Channels and Channel Sinks.")

```
IJobServer obj = (IJobServer)Activator.GetObject( typeof(IJobServer),
                "http://localhost/JobWebService/JobServer.soap" );

ChannelServices.GetChannelSinkProperties(obj)["username"] = "Bob";
ChannelServices.GetChannelSinkProperties(obj)["password"] = "test";
ChannelServices.GetChannelSinkProperties(obj)["domain"] = "";
```

Of course, in a real-world application you wouldn't want to hard-code credentials as shown here. Instead, you'd probably get the credentials from the user at run time or from a secure source.

This completes the steps necessary to secure the JobServer Web Service from unauthorized users. Although the Web Service is now secure, we can add an additional refinement to our authorization scheme. As configured, a user has either full access to the job assignment application or no access at all. However, we might want to support different access levels within our application, such as allowing only administrators to delete uncompleted jobs. The .NET Framework's role-based security allows us fine-grained control over which users can access server resources.

Using Role-Based Security with .NET Remoting

Anyone who's had the responsibility of managing Windows security for more than a trivial number of users is familiar with the usefulness of groups. Groups are powerful because access control to resources such as files and databases, as well as most operations, almost never needs to be as fine-grained as a per-user basis. Instead, users frequently share certain access levels that you can categorize into roles or groups.

Because this role-based or group-based approach is such a powerful abstraction for network administrators, it makes sense to use it to manage security in applications development. This is what role-based security is all about: it's an especially effective way to provide access control in .NET Remoting applications. Once you've authenticated a client, unless all authenticated clients have full access to the resources exposed by your application, you need to implement access control. As with all .NET Remoting security scenarios, using role-based security with .NET Remoting requires that you use IIS as the hosting environment.

When properly configured for security, a hosted remote object can use the current thread's *Principal* object to determine the calling client's identity and role membership. You can then allow or deny code to run based on the client's role. You can control access by using three programming methods:

- Declarative
- Imperative
- Direct principal access

Declarative programming means that you declare your intentions in code via attributes that are compiled into the metadata for the assembly. By using the *System.Security.Permissions.PrincipalPermissionAttribute* class and the *System.Security.Permissions.SecurityAction* enumeration, you can indicate that the calling client must be in a certain role to run a method:

```
[PrincipalPermissionAttribute(SecurityAction.Demand,
Role="BUILTIN\\Administrators")]
    public void MySecureMethod()
    {
        ⋮
    }
```

If the client calling *MySecureMethod* isn't in the BUILTIN\Administrators group, the system throws a *System.Security.SecurityException*.

Imperative programming is the traditional programming technique of putting the conditional role membership check in the method body, as shown here:

```
PrincipalPermission AdminPermission =
                new PrincipalPermission("Allen", "Administrator");
⋮
AdminPermission.Demand();
```

To use imperative role-based security, you create a *System.Security.Permissions.PrincipalPermission* object by passing in a user name and a role name. When you call the *PrincipalPermission* object's *Demand* method, code flow will continue if the client is a member of the specified role; otherwise, the system will throw a *System.Security.SecurityException*.

You might not want to throw exceptions when checking for role membership. Throwing exceptions can hurt the performance of a remote application, so you should throw them only in exceptional circumstances. For example, you wouldn't want test a user's role membership by instantiating several *Principal-Permission* objects and catching the inevitable exceptions. Instead, declarative and imperative security techniques are best used if you expect the user to have the requested permission and you are verifying this expectation.

If you need to test a principal for role membership and there's a high probability that the call will fail, you should use the *direct principal access* technique. Here's an example:

```
IPrincipal ClientPrincipal = Thread.CurrentThread.CurrentPrincipal;
If ( ClientPrincipal.IsInRole( "Administrator") )
{
    RunMe();
    ⋮
```

Thread.CurrentThread.CurrentPrincipal returns an *IPrincipal* interface that represents the client's identity. This interface provides an *IsInRole* method that will test the principal for role membership and return a Boolean value.

As we just mentioned, you must use IIS as the hosting environment to access role-based security. When you configure IIS to impersonate the client and to use a certain authentication scheme, the identity of the client will flow across the .NET Remoting boundary. Because you can't authenticate a .NET Remoting client by using a different host, such as a Windows service, *Thread.CurrentThread.CurrentPrincipal* will contain an empty *GenericIdentity*. Because you can't get the client's identity, you can't use access control. Therefore, when designing remote objects, you should think carefully about the expected hosting application type. You don't want to expose sensitive public remote methods to unauthenticated clients.

Effects of Code Access Security on Remoting

When you run a program on your computer, you fully trust that the code won't do anything malicious. Nowadays, code can come from many sources less trustworthy than the code you obtain from software purchased in shrink-wrapped packages, most notably from the Internet. What we really need are varying degrees of trust that depend on the code being accessed, rather than complete trust or no trust whatsoever. This is the purpose of .NET Code Access Security. The .NET Framework Code Access Security subsystem offers a flexible, full-featured way to control what permissions code requires to run, and it enforces constraints on code coming from various zones.

We won't spend any more time talking about Code Access Security in this book for the simple reason that Code Access Security doesn't work with .NET Remoting. Therefore, you should have a high degree of trust between client and server in a .NET Remoting application.

Extending the Sample with Client-Activated Objects

So far, this chapter has demonstrated various methods of hosting server-activated objects and shown the client code necessary to interact with them. As discussed in Chapter 2, the .NET Framework offers a second form of remote objects: client-activated objects. Client-activated objects are "activated" on demand from the client, exist on a per-client and per-reference basis, and can maintain state between method calls.

To demonstrate client-activated objects, let's extend the JobClient sample application by enabling users to add notes associated with a selected job. To support adding notes, we'll add a class derived from *MarshalByRefObject* named *JobNotes*, which we'll configure as a client-activated object. The stateful nature of client-activated objects will allow the notes to persist between method calls for as long as the *JobNotes* object instance remains alive.

The *JobNotes* Class

You implement a client-activated object in the same way that you implement a server-activated object: simply derive the class you want to be remotable from *System.MarshalByRefObject*. The way that the host application configures .NET Remoting determines whether a remote object is a client-activated object or a server-activated object.

The following code listing defines a new class named *JobNotes* that derives from *System.MarshalByRefObject*:

```
using System.Collections;

public class JobNotes : MarshalByRefObject
{
    private Hashtable m_HashJobID2Notes;

    public JobNotes()
    {
        m_HashJobID2Notes = new System.Collections.Hashtable();
    }

    public void AddNote(int id, string s)
    {
        // Defined later...
    }

    public ArrayList GetNotes(int id)
```

```
    {
        // Defined later...
    }

}
```

The *JobNotes* class allows clients to add textual notes for a specific job identifier. The class contains a *System.Collections.Hashtable* member that associates a given job identifier value to a *System.Collections.ArrayList* of strings that represent the notes for a particular job.

The *AddNote* method adds a note for the specified job ID, as shown in the following listing:

```
public void AddNote(int id, string s)
{
    // Look up notes list.
    ArrayList al = (ArrayList)m_HashJobID2Notes[id];
    if (al == null)
    {
        al = new ArrayList();
        m_HashJobID2Notes[id] = al;
    }

    // Insert a time stamp.
    s = s.Insert(0,Environment.NewLine);
    s = s.Insert(0,System.DateTime.Now.ToString());

    // Add s to the notes list.
    al.Add(s);
}
```

The following listing shows the implementation for the *GetNotes* method:

```
public ArrayList GetNotes(int id)
{
    // Look up notes for this job ID.
    ArrayList notes = (ArrayList)m_HashJobID2Notes[id];
    if (notes != null )
    {
        return notes;
    }
    return new ArrayList();
}
```

JobClient Application Changes

The client application needs a few code modifications to make use of the *Job-Notes* class. This application needs to provide the user with the ability to add a new note for the currently selected job. This entails adding another button that, when clicked, will display a form prompting the user to enter a new note for the selected job. For this sample application, we'll allow a user to add a note only if he or she is currently assigned to the selected job.

Let's implement the user interface changes necessary to allow a user to enter a note for the currently selected job. You can start by designing a new form named *FormAddNote* that displays a list of the current notes for the job and allows the user to enter a new note to the list. Go ahead and create a new form that resembles the one shown in Figure 3-6.

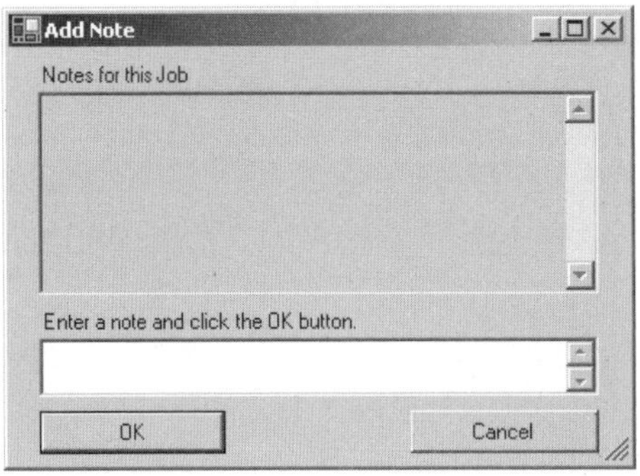

Figure 3-6 The *FormAddNote* form user interface

Add a *TextBox* control named *textBoxNotes* that shows the current notes for the job. This *TextBox* should be read-only. Add another *TextBox* control named *textBoxAddNote* that accepts input from the user. Finally, add the obligatory OK and Cancel buttons.

To allow the client code to display the current notes for a job as well as obtain a new note for a job, the client code sets the *Description* property of the *FormAddNote* class before displaying the form and gets the value of the *Description* property after the user closes the form. The following code listing defines the *Description* property:

```
private string m_sDescription;

public string Description
{
    get
    { return m_sDescription; }

    set
```

```
    { m_sDescription = value; }
}
```

When the form loads, it populates the *TextBox* referenced by the *textBox-Notes* member with the value of the *Description* property. The following code implements this behavior in the *Form.Load* event handler:

```
private void FormAddNote_Load(object sender, System.EventArgs e)
{
    this.textBoxNotes.Text = m_sDescription;
}
```

You also need to add *Button.Click* event handlers for each of the buttons. The following code implements the handler for the Cancel button's *Click* event:

```
private void button2_Click(object sender, System.EventArgs e)
{
    this.Hide();
}
```

The OK button *Click* event handler saves the text the user entered in *text-BoxAddNote* to the *m_sDescription* member so that the client code can then retrieve the text that the user entered through the *Description* property:

```
private void button1_Click(object sender, System.EventArgs e)
{
    m_sDescription = this.textBoxAddNote.Text;
}
```

Because each instance of the JobClient application will have its own remote instance of the *JobNotes* client-activated object, you can add a new member variable of type *JobNotes* to the *Form1* class and initialize it in the *Form1* constructor.

To allow the user to add a note to a selected job, you can add a button named *buttonAddNote* to *Form1* in Design view. The following code listing shows the implementation of the *buttonAddNote_Click* method:

```
private void buttonAddNote_Click(object sender, System.EventArgs e)
{
    // Instantiate a form for adding notes.
    FormAddNote frm = new FormAddNote();

    // Make sure the user is assigned to the selected job.
    JobInfo ji = GetSelectedJobInfo();
    if ( ji.m_sAssignedUser != System.Environment.MachineName )
    {
        MessageBox.Show("You are not assigned to that job");
        return;
    }
```

(continued)

```
    // Get the notes for the currently selected job and
    // display them in the dialog box.
    ArrayList notes = m_JobNotes.GetNotes(ji.m_nID);
    IEnumerator ie = notes.GetEnumerator();
    while(ie.MoveNext())
    {
        frm.Description += (string)ie.Current;
        frm.Description += Environment.NewLine;
        frm.Description += Environment.NewLine;
    }

    // Display the form and obtain the new note.
    if ( frm.ShowDialog(this) == DialogResult.OK )
    {
        string s = frm.Description;
        if ( s.Length > 0 )
        {
            m_JobNotes.AddNote(ji.m_nID, frm.Description);
        }
    }
}
```

At this point, you should be able to run the client and test the functionality of the *JobNotes* class even though the *JobNotes* instance created by the JobClient application isn't remote. Figure 3-7 shows the new form after a user has added some notes to a job.

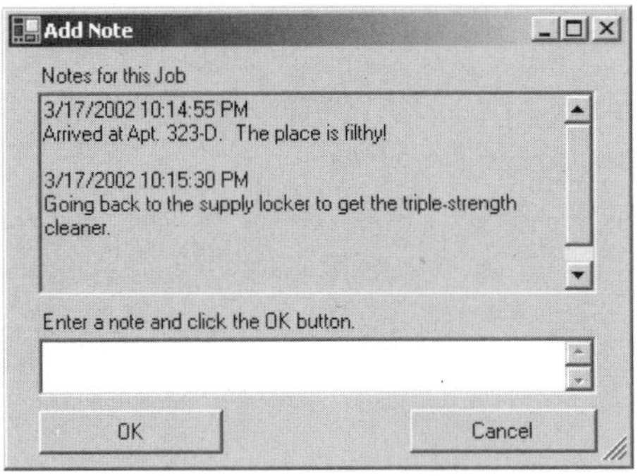

Figure 3-7   Adding some notes to a job

Configuring the Client for .NET Remoting Client-Activated Objects

To make instances of the *JobNotes* type remote, you have to instruct the run-time to treat the *JobNotes* type as a client-activated object. Let's do that now by configuring the JobClient application to consume the *JobNotes* type as a client-activated object.

Programmatic Configuration

The *RemotingConfiguration* class provides the *RegisterActivatedClientType* method to allow clients to register a type as client activated. You can add the following code to the *Form1* constructor just before creating a new instance of *JobNotes* to instruct the runtime that the *JobNotes* type is a client-activated object:

```
ActivatedClientTypeEntry acte =
        new ActivatedClientTypeEntry( typeof (JobNotes),
                                   "http://localhost:4000" );
RemotingConfiguration.RegisterActivatedClientType( acte );
```

You first instantiate the *ActivatedClientTypeEntry* type, passing two parameters to the constructor:

- The remote object type

- The URL of the endpoint where instances of the remote object type should be activated

You then pass the *ActivatedClientTypeEntry* instance to the *RegisterActivatedClientType* method, which registers the *JobNotes* type as a client-activated object. The *RegisterActivatedClientType* method is overloaded to also accept the same two parameters that the *ActivatedClientTypeEntry* constructor accepts.

Configuration File

As you saw earlier in the chapter, the alternative to programmatically configuring an application for .NET Remoting is to use a configuration file. You use the *<client>* element for registering both well-known objects and client-activated objects. Within this tag, you add an *<activated>* tag that specifies the same information required for programmatic configuration.

Let's modify the JobClient.exe.config file to specify the *JobNotes* type as a client-activated object:

```
<configuration>
  <system.runtime.remoting>
    <application name="JobClient">
      <client>
        <wellknown
          type="JobServerLib.JobServerImpl, JobServerLib"
          url="http://localhost:4000/JobURI" />
      </client>
      <client url = "http://localhost:4000">
        <activated type="JobServerLib.JobNotes, JobServerLib"/>
      </client>
      <channels>
        <channel ref="http" port="0" />
      </channels>
```

(continued)

```
    </application>
  </system.runtime.remoting>
</configuration>
```

You need to add a *<client>* element that specifies the URL of the activation endpoint by using the *url* attribute. The *<client>* element contains a child, the *<activated>* element. Because the JobClient application is using only one client-activated type, the configuration file contains only one *<activated>* element entry. If your application needs to activate several types at the same endpoint, you'll have several *<activated>* element entries—one for each type under the same *<client>* element. Likewise, if you need to activate different types at different endpoints, you'll have multiple *<client>* elements—one for each endpoint. You specify the type of the client-activated object by using the *<activated>* element's *type* attribute. In the previous code listing, we could have added the *<activated>* element to the existing *<client>* element that contains the *<wellknown>* element, but it's not necessary.

Configuring the Server for .NET Remoting Client-Activated Objects

Now we need to modify the JobServer application to configure the *JobNotes* type as a client-activated object. Once again, we can configure the application for .NET Remoting either programmatically or by using a configuration file.

Programmatic Configuration

The *RemotingConfiguration* class provides the *RegisterActivatedServiceType* method to allow you to programmatically configure a type for client activation. You use this method to configure the JobServer.exe host application to host *JobNotes* class instances as client-activated objects by adding the following line of code to the JobServer host application's *Main* method:

```
RemotingConfiguration.RegisterActivatedServiceType(typeof(JobNotes));
```

When the JobServer application executes this line of code, it registers the *JobNotes* type as a client-activated object. This means that the host will accept client activation requests for the *JobNotes* type. Upon receiving an activation request, the Remoting infrastructure instantiates an instance of the *JobNotes* class.

Configuration File

You can also use a configuration file to configure a server host application for client-activated objects. You use the *<activated>* element to register a specific type with the .NET Remoting infrastructure as a client-activated object. You can modify the JobServer.exe.config file to register the *JobNotes* class as a client-activated object by adding the *<activated>* tag, as shown in the following code listing:

```
<configuration>
  <system.runtime.remoting>
    <application name="JobServer">
      <service>
        <wellknown mode="Singleton"
          type="JobServerLib.JobServerImpl, JobServerLib"
          objectUri="JobURI" />
        <activated type="JobServerLib.JobNotes, JobServerLib" />
      </service>
      <channels>
        <channel ref="http" port="4000" />
      </channels>
    </application>
  </system.runtime.remoting>
</configuration>
```

Adding a Sponsor to the Lease

At this point, we've implemented and configured the *JobNotes* class as a client-activated object. It's now appropriate to consider the lifetime requirements for the *JobNotes* class.

Chapter 2 discussed how the .NET Remoting infrastructure uses a lease-based system to control the lifetime of remote objects. The System.Marshal-ByRefObject class provides a virtual method named InitializeLifetimeService that deriving classes can override to change the default lease values, thereby controlling how long the remote object instance lives.

The default implementation of the *InitializeLifetimeService* method returns an instance of an *ILease* implementation with default values. The default *Initial-LeaseTime* property value is 5 minutes, which means that the object's lease won't expire for 5 minutes. The default value for the *RenewOnCallTime* property is 2 minutes. If the lease is due to expire within the time specified by *RenewOnCall-Time*, calling a method extends the lease by setting its *CurrentLeaseTime* to the *RenewOnCallTime* property. This means that each time a method on this object is called, its lease can be extended to the value of the *RenewOnCallTime* property, provided the lease's remaining time is less than the value of the *RenewOnCallTime* property. The default value for the *SponsorshipTimeout* property is 2 minutes. Thus, if the lease has any sponsors when it expires, calls to the *ISponsor.Renewal* method will time out after 2 minutes if the sponsor doesn't respond.

To put this in perspective, recall that the *JobServerImpl* class provided an override for the *InitializeLifetimeService* method that returned *null*, indicating that the object instance should live indefinitely, until the host application terminated. For well-known objects in Singleton mode, such as *JobServerImpl*, having an indefinite lifetime makes sense.

However, for client-activated objects such as *JobNotes*, having an indefinite lifetime doesn't make sense because instances of the *JobNotes* class don't need to hang around after the client application shuts down. But if we need to persist the notes data, we'll need to implement a mechanism allowing disconnected *JobNotes* instances to serialize their state to a persistent store before being garbage collected. Then when a client application activates a new instance of the *JobNotes* class, the constructor will deserialize the previously stored state information. In this case, we'll probably want to reimplement the *JobNotes* class to support a SingleCall well-known object activation model. But this requirement isn't necessary for this sample application.

Suppose, however, that you do want to make the *JobNotes* instances hang around for longer than the default lease time. To do so, you need to override the *InitializeLifetimeService* method to obtain and initialize the object's lease with values other than the default.

Initializing the Lease

The *JobNotes* class overrides the *InitializeLifetimeService* method inherited from *System.MarshalByRefObject*. As discussed in the "Implementing the JobServer Application" section, the .NET Remoting infrastructure calls this method to obtain lease information for a remote object. The *JobServerImpl* class implementation of this method returns *null*, telling the .NET Remoting infrastructure that the object instance should live indefinitely. However, for the *JobNotes* class, there's no need to allow the object to live indefinitely. The following code listing shows how the *JobNotes* class overrides the default implementation of the *InitializeLifetimeService* method to modify the initial lease values that control its lifetime:

```
public override Object InitializeLifetimeService()
{
    ILease lease = (ILease)base.InitializeLifetimeService();
    if ( LeaseState.Initial == lease.CurrentState )
    {
        lease.InitialLeaseTime   = TimeSpan.FromMinutes(4);
        lease.SponsorshipTimeout = TimeSpan.FromMinutes(1);
        lease.RenewOnCallTime    = TimeSpan.FromMinutes(3);
    }

    return lease;
}
```

In implementing the *JobNotes* version of the *InitializeLifetimeService* method, we obtain the lease for this instance by calling the base class's implementation of *InitializeLifetimeService*. To set the lease's values, the lease must be in the *LeaseState.Initial* state. If the lease isn't in this state, attempts to set the values will result in an exception.

Implementing the *ISponsor* Interface

To take full advantage of the lease-based lifetime mechanism provided by .NET Remoting, you can create a sponsor by implementing the *ISponsor* interface and registering the sponsor with the lease for a remote object. When the lease expires, the runtime will call the *ISponsor.Renewal* method on any registered sponsors, giving each sponsor an opportunity to renew the lease.

For the JobClient application, you can make the *Form1* class a sponsor by having it derive from and implement the *ISponsor* interface, as the following code shows:

```
public TimeSpan Renewal(ILease lease)
{
    return TimeSpan.FromMinutes(5);
}
```

The *ISponsor.Renewal* method returns a *System.TimeSpan* instance representing 5 minutes, which has the effect of renewing the lease for 5 minutes. Depending on your application needs, you might want to use a longer or shorter time span. Using a longer time span results in less frequent calls to the *ISponsor.Renewal* method and therefore less network traffic—especially if the client application sponsored many client-activated object instances. The trade-off, of course, is that the client-activated object instances can exist on the server for longer than needed—potentially monopolizing much-needed resources. Using a shorter time span reduces the amount of time these so-called *zombie objects* hang around but results in more frequent calls to the *ISponsor.Renewal* method and therefore produces more network traffic.

Registering the Sponsor

With the *ISponsor* implementation complete, you can now register the *Form1* instance as a sponsor for the *JobNotes* instance's lease. You do this by first obtaining the *ILease* reference on the remote object and then calling the *ILease.Register* method, which passes the *ISponsor* interface of the sponsor. To demonstrate this, add the following code to the *Form1* constructor:

```
ILease lease = (ILease) RemotingServices.GetLifetimeService(m_JobNotes);
lease.Register((ISponsor) this);
```

Now when the JobClient application starts and creates the *JobNotes* instance, the lease for the *JobNotes* instance will have an initial lease time of 4 minutes. This is because the *JobNotes* class overrides the *InitializeLifetimeService* method, setting the *InitialLease* time property to 4 minutes. If the client doesn't call any methods on the *JobNotes* instance for these first 4 minutes, the lease will expire and the runtime will call the *ISponsor.Renewal* method on the *Form1* class, which renews the lease, keeping the *JobNotes* instance alive for 5 more minutes.

Metadata Dependency Issues

Throughout this chapter, we've taken the easy approach to metadata dependency issues in that both the JobClient and JobServer applications depend on each other's metadata. Specifically, the JobClient needs the *JobServerImpl* class's metadata, along with its supporting types. Likewise, because the client subscribes to the *JobEvent*, the JobServer needs the metadata for the *Form1* class defined in the JobClient application. In essence, the JobClient acts as a server by receiving the callback from the *JobEvent*. This type of architecture is sometimes known as *server-to-server*.

Providing the required metadata in this fashion is fine for the sample application, but in the real world, you might not want to provide either the client's metadata to the server or the server's metadata to the client. In this section, we'll look at several strategies you can use in your projects to handle these scenarios.

Removing the JobServer's Dependency on the JobClient's Metadata

First, it's important that you understand why the JobServer application depends on the JobClient's metadata. The following line of code in the *Form1* constructor causes this dependency:

```
m_IJobServer.JobEvent += new JobEventHandler(this.MyJobEventHandler);
```

The only reason the JobServer application depends on the JobClient application's metadata is that the *Form1* class defined in the JobClient application subscribes to *JobServerImpl.JobEvent*. Obviously, one way to break this dependency is to avoid subscribing to *JobEvent* in the first place by utilizing a polling method. We did that in the "Exposing the *JobServerImpl* Class as a Web Service" section when we modified the JobClient to interact with the Web Service. Let's assume that this solution is unacceptable.

In this case, we need a type that acts as a link between the *Form1.MyEventHandler* and the *JobServerImpl.JobEvent* event. The following code defines a class that does just that:

```
public class JobEventRepeater : MarshalByRefObject
{
    //
    // Event to which clients subscribe
    public event JobEventHandler JobEvent;

    //
    // Handler method for the IJobServer.JobEvent
    public void Handler(object sender, JobEventArgs args)
    {
        if (JobEvent != null)
        {
            JobEvent(sender, args);
        }
    }


    //
    // Prevent lifetime services from destroying our instance.
    public override object InitializeLifetimeService()
    {
        return null;
    }
}
```

The *JobEventRepeater* class acts as a repeater for the *JobEvent*. The class provides a *JobEvent* member and a *RepeatEventHandler* method that fires the *JobEvent*. To use this class, the client code creates a new instance of *JobEvent-Repeater* and subscribes to its *JobEvent* event instead of to the *JobServer-Impl.JobEvent* event. The client then subscribes the *JobEventRepeater* instance to the *JobServerImpl.JobEvent* event so that when the server fires its *JobEvent*, it invokes the *JobEventRepeater.RepeatEventHandler* method.

Assuming you add a member of type *JobEventRepeater* named *m_JobEventRepeater* to the *Form1* class, you can modify the *Form1* constructor to make use of the *JobEventRepeater* class by using the following code:

```
m_JobEventRepeater = new JobEventRepeater();
m_JobEventRepeater.JobEvent +=
        new JobEventHandler(this.MyJobEventHandler);
m_IJobServer.JobEvent +=
        new JobEventHandler(m_JobEventRepeater.Handler);
```

Figure 3-8 shows the relationship between the *Form1* instance, the *JobEvent-Repeater* instance, and the *JobServerImpl* instance.

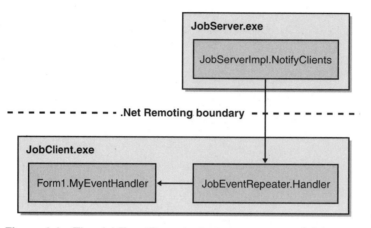

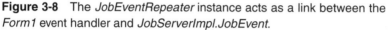

Figure 3-8   The *JobEventRepeater* instance acts as a link between the *Form1* event handler and *JobServerImpl.JobEvent*.

Now when the server fires *JobServerImpl.JobEvent* it invokes the handler for the *JobEventRepeater* instance. The *JobEventRepeater* instance, in turn, fires its *JobEvent*, which repeats (or forwards) the callback to the *Form1.MyJobEvent-Handler* method.

Of course, you'll also need to change the way that the *Form1* unsubscribes from the server's *JobEvent*. You can do so by replacing the original line of code in the *Form1.OnClosed* method with the following code:

```
// Make sure we unsubscribe from the JobEvent.
m_IJobServer.JobEvent -= new JobEventHandler(m_JobEventRepeater.Handler);
m_JobEventRepeater.JobEvent -= new JobEventHandler(this.MyJobEventHandler);
```

Developing a Stand-In Class to Publish in Place of *JobServerImpl* Metadata

There might be times when you're unable or unwilling to provide a client application with the remote object's implementation. In such cases, you can create what's known as a *stand-in class*, which defines the remote object's type but contains no implementation.

At present, the sample client application depends on the *JobServerImpl* type's metadata because it creates a new instance of *JobServerImpl* in the *GetI-JobServer* method of *Form1*. The client application references the JobServerLib assembly, which not only contains the definition of the *JobServerImpl* and *IJobServer* types but also contains the implementation of the *JobServerImpl* type.

The following code listing defines such a stand-in class for *JobServerImpl*:

```
public class JobServerImpl : MarshalByRefObject, IJobServer
```

```
{
    public event JobEventHandler JobEvent;

    public JobServerImpl()
    { throw new System.NotImplementedException(); }

    private void NotifyClients(JobEventArgs args)
    { throw new System.NotImplementedException(); }

    public void CreateJob( string sDescription )
    { throw new System.NotImplementedException(); }

    public void UpdateJobState( int nJobID, string sUser,
                                string sStatus )
    { throw new System.NotImplementedException(); }

    public ArrayList GetJobs()
    { throw new System.NotImplementedException(); }
}
```

The type name of the stand-in class and its assembly name must be the same as the actual implementation's type name and assembly name. You can use an assembly containing the stand-in class on the client side, while the server references the assembly containing the actual implementation. This way, the client application has the metadata necessary for the .NET Remoting infrastructure to instantiate a proxy to the remote object but doesn't have the actual implementation of the remote object. Figure 3-9 shows the dependency relationships between the applications and the JobServerLib assemblies.

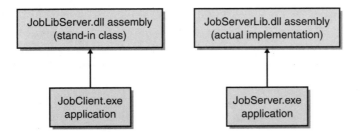

Figure 3-9   JobServerLib and stand-in assembly dependencies

Remoting the *IJobServer* Interface

Another way to remove the client's dependency on the remote object's implementation is by remoting an interface. The client interacts with the remote object through the interface type definition rather than through the actual remote object's class type definition. To remote an interface, place the interface definition along with any supporting types in an assembly that will be published to the client. You place the remote object's implementation of the interface in a separate assembly that you'll never publish to the client. Let's demonstrate this with the sample application by remoting the *IJobServer* interface.

Because the *JobServerImpl* class implements the *IJobServer* interface, you can provide the client with an assembly that contains only the *IJobServer* interface's metadata. First, you need to move the definition of the *IJobServer* interface as well as the *JobInfo, JobEventArgs, JobEvent,* and *JobEventHandler* type definitions and supporting data structures from the JobServerLib assembly into another assembly that we'll name JobLib. The JobServerLib assembly will then contain only the *JobServerImpl* class's metadata and therefore will be dependent on the new JobLib assembly. Figure 3-10 depicts the new dependencies.

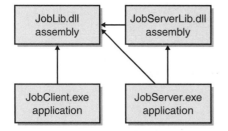

Figure 3-10 JobLib assembly dependencies

Now the JobClient application depends only on the JobLib assembly, which contains the *IJobServer* interface and supporting data types but doesn't contain the *JobServerImpl* definition. The JobClient application doesn't need the metadata for the *JobServerImpl* class because it interacts with this metadata through the *IJobServer* interface. Because you can't create an instance of an interface, remoting interfaces in this manner requires you to use the *Activator.GetObject* method. This method allows you to specify the type of an object to be activated at a specific URL endpoint.

The following code snippet uses the *Activator.GetObject* method to obtain the *IJobInterface* from the endpoint specified in the configuration file:

```
WellKnownClientTypeEntry[] ClientEntries =
        RemotingConfiguration.GetRegisteredWellKnownClientTypes();

return (IJobServer)Activator.GetObject( typeof(IJobServer),
                                    ClientEntries[0].ObjectUrl );
```

This code assumes the presence of the following entry in the JobClient.exe.config configuration file:

```
<wellknown type="JobServerLib.IJobServer, JobLib"
  url="http://localhost:4000/JobURI" />
```

Summary

In this chapter, we showed you how to build a simple distributed application by using .NET Remoting. We covered each of the major tasks that you need to perform for any distributed application that uses .NET Remoting. By now, you should have a good understanding of how to take advantage of the .NET Remoting infrastructure in your application development. The remainder of this book will show you how to take advantage of the more advanced .NET Remoting features by developing a custom proxy, channel, and formatter.

4

SOAP and Message Flows

By now, you should be well on your way to understanding how to use .NET Remoting to develop distributed applications. To further your understanding, this chapter will look at the actual messages exchanged among the objects within the JobClient and JobServer applications. Examining these messages will give you insight into the kind of information that .NET Remoting exchanges among distributed objects. However, before we look at these messages, we need to briefly discuss SOAP. If you're already familiar with SOAP, feel free to skip ahead to the "Message Flows" section of the chapter.

Simple Object Access Protocol

Much of the .NET Framework's interoperability hinges on SOAP. Although developers can choose more efficient protocols, none of these protocols has SOAP's flexibility. So what exactly is SOAP?

In broad terms, SOAP is an XML-based protocol that specifies a mechanism by which distributed applications can exchange both structured and typed information in a platform-independent and language-independent manner. In addition, SOAP specifies a mechanism for expressing remote procedure calls (RPC) as SOAP messages. SOAP specifies an envelope format for XML data wrapping, simple addressing, as well as data encoding and type encoding. This data-encoding scheme is especially interesting because it standardizes type descriptions independent of platform or programming language. Although many people assume that SOAP relies on HTTP for its transport, SOAP can theoretically use any transport, such as Simple Mail Transfer Protocol (SMTP) or Microsoft Message Queuing (MSMQ). In fact, you could put a SOAP message in a file on a floppy disk and carry it to a server for processing. You can find the complete specification for SOAP 1.1 at *http://www.w3.org/TR/SOAP/*.

SOAP has made such a big impact on the industry for many reasons, including the following:

- SOAP is simple. Because SOAP leverages existing technologies such as HTTP and XML, implementing SOAP is easy.

- SOAP is ubiquitous. Because it's simple to implement, it's also widely available. At the time of this writing, more than 30 SOAP implementations are available for a variety of programming languages and platforms.

- SOAP is built for the Internet. The SOAP RPC specification deals with the necessary HTTP headers for transporting SOAP messages. Because they integrate tightly with HTTP, SOAP messages are firewall friendly and easily supported by existing systems. SOAP also describes a simpler message-based scheme, but we'll discuss only the more full-featured SOAP RPC because this is what .NET Remoting uses.

One of SOAP's biggest advantages is also its biggest disadvantage. Because it's text based, SOAP is easy to read and is portable. However, converting data structures into verbose tag descriptions takes processing time and results in a larger payload. Still, the extra processing time is fairly minimal and shouldn't be an issue if your application needs the benefits that SOAP provides.

Why Should We Care About SOAP?

These days, most developers don't write SOAP directly. SOAP has become such a standard protocol that it's now part of the plumbing and vendors provide toolkits for its use. This is exactly what the .NET Framework gives developers. With .NET, developers can write .NET Remoting applications and choose *Soap-Formatter* via configuration, write XML Web Services that naturally use SOAP, or use the *XmlSerializer* class to serialize native classes into SOAP messages.

So if the .NET Framework hides the SOAP details from us, why should we care about them? One of the best reasons is that examining these details allows us to peek beneath the covers of .NET Remoting application communications. In addition to all SOAP's benefits (such as being firewall friendly and platform independent), SOAP is text based, unencrypted, and therefore human readable. If you configure your .NET Remoting application to use *SoapFormatter*, you can spy on the traffic between client and server and learn a lot about the way .NET Remoting works.

HTTP-Based RPC

In its simplest form, the SOAP specification defines an XML schema for SOAP messages. But the SOAP specification goes further: it defines the headers for using HTTP as a transport mechanism. We're interested only in the HTTP transport binding of SOAP in this book. Therefore, we'll start with an example of a standard HTTP header for a SOAP message:

```
HTTP/1.1 /JobServer/JobURI POST
Content-Type: text/xml
SOAPAction: MyMethod
```

The HTTP Uniform Resource Identifier (URI) describes the RPC endpoint—in this case, */JobServer/JobURI*. The *Content-Type* header of *text/xml*, which is followed by a *SOAPAction* header, defines the SOAP header. Based on the *SOAPAction* value of *MyMethod*, we can presume that this HTTP request includes a SOAP message containing information to allow the recipient to invoke the *MyMethod* method on the object associated with */JobServer/JobURI*. In the "Message Flows" section of this chapter, you'll see that .NET Remoting uses the *SOAPAction* header to identify the name of the method to invoke.

RPC-based SOAP uses a request/response pattern. A client sends a one-way request message, and the server responds by creating a one-way response message. This pattern fits perfectly with HTTP's request/response scheme.

SOAP Message Elements

The fundamental unit of exchange SOAP defines is the SOAP message. The following template shows the order and nesting of the elements that comprise a SOAP message. An instance of this template directly follows the HTTP header we just described.

```
<SOAP-ENV: Envelope>
   <SOAP-ENV: Header>
      ... Header information (the Header element may be included)
   </SOAP-ENV: Header>
   <SOAP-ENV: Body>
      ... Body information (the Body element must be included)
   </SOAP-ENV: Body>
</SOAP-NEV: Envelope>
```

The SOAP Envelope

The *<Envelope>* element is the mandatory root of every SOAP message. In addition, every *<Envelope>* has the following characteristics:

- It *must* reference the SOAP *Envelope* namespace (*xmlns: SOAP-ENV="http://schemas.xmlsoap.org/soap/envelope/"*).

- It *may* contain a single *<Header>* element.

- It *must* contain exactly one *<Body>* element.

The full SOAP *<Envelope>* element produced by .NET Remoting typically looks like this:

```
<SOAP-ENV:Envelope
  xmlns:xsi="http://www.w3.org/2001/XMLSchema-instance"
  xmlns:xsd="http://www.w3.org/2001/XMLSchema"
  xmlns:SOAP-ENC="http://schemas.xmlsoap.org/soap/encoding/"
  xmlns:SOAP-ENV="http://schemas.xmlsoap.org/soap/envelope/"
  xmlns:clr="http://schemas.microsoft.com/soap/encoding/clr/1.0"
  SOAP-ENV:encodingStyle="http://schemas.xmlsoap.org/soap/encoding/">
```

Plenty of namespace identifiers are included in this code to scope various elements of the SOAP message. The first two attributes map the conventional alias identifiers *xsi* and *xsd* to the XML namepsaces *http://www.w3.org/2001/ XMLSchema-instance* and *http://www.w3.org/2001/XMLSchema*, respectively. The *xmlns:SOAP-ENC* attribute maps the *SOAP-ENC* alias identifier to the SOAP 1.1 encoding schema. The *xmlns:SOAP-ENV* attribute maps the *SOAP-ENV* alias identifier to the SOAP 1.1 envelope schema. Later in this section, you'll see that most elements in the SOAP message use the namespace alias identifier *SOAP-ENV* for the elements and attributes defined in the *<Envelope>* element. Also note that the *encodingStyle* attribute indicates that the SOAP message follows the encoding rules specified in Section 5 of the SOAP 1.1 specification.

The Soap Header

If present, the *<Header>* element must directly follow the opening *<Envelope>* tag and appear, at most, once. Header entries are child elements of the *<Header>* element and provide a mechanism for extending the SOAP message with application-specific information that can affect the processing of the message. Furthermore, a header entry can include header attributes that affect its interpretation. The SOAP 1.1 specification defines two header attributes: *actor* and *mustUnderstand*. Keep in mind that the SOAP message can travel along a chain of SOAP message processors en route to its destination. The *actor* attribute specifies which of these message processors should actually act upon the message. The *mustUnderstand* attribute indicates whether the recipient of the message absolutely must know how to interpret the header entry. If *mustUnderstand* has a value of 1 rather than 0, the recipient must understand the header entry or reject the message. The following code snippet shows a header entry element named *MessageID* that contains the *mustUnderstand* attribute:

```
<SOAP-ENV:Header>
   <z:MessageID
     xmlns:a="My Namespace URI"
     SOAP-ENV:mustUnderstand="1">
       "2EE0E496-73B7-48b4-87A6-2CB2C8D9DBDE"
   </z:MessageID>
</SOAP-ENV:Header>
```

In our example, the recipient must understand the *MessageID* header entry to process the message.

The SOAP Body

Exactly one *<Body>* element must exist within an *<Envelope>* element. The *<Body>* element contains the actual payload destined for the endpoint. This is where the interesting application-specific data is located. In .NET Remoting, the *<Body>* element contains method calls with parameters including XML versions of complex data types such as structures. Section 5 of the SOAP 1.1 specification describes how to serialize arrays, structures, and object graphs; many developers colloquially refer to this encoding scheme as *Section 5 encoding*. Here's an example of a typical SOAP *<Body>* element used for RPC:

```
<SOAP-ENV:Body>
    <myns:GetPopulationOfState xmlns:myns="my-namespace-uri">
       <state>Florida</state>
    </myns:GetPopulationOfState>
</SOAP-ENV:Body>
```

Child elements of the *<Body>* element's method name element will contain any input and will reference parameters of the method. In the example, the child element *<state>* specifies that the caller wants to retrieve the population for the state of Florida. A response message payload will then contain any output and will reference parameters for the method. The recipient of the *GetPopulationOfState* request message might respond with the following SOAP message:

```
<SOAP-ENV:Envelope
  xmlns:SOAP-ENV=http://schemas.xmlsoap.org/soap/envelope/
  SOAP-ENV:encodingStyle=
  "http://schemas.xmlsoap.org/soap/encoding/"/>
   <SOAP-ENV:Body>
      <myns:GetPopulationOfStateResponse
        xmlns:myns="my-namespace-uri">
```

(continued)

```
            <Population>15982378</Population>
          </myns:GetLastTradePriceResponse>
      </SOAP-ENV:Body>
  </SOAP-ENV:Envelope>
```

The SOAP Fault

If an error occurs on the server, the SOAP specification defines a *<Fault>* tag that must be a child of the *<Body>* element. The *<Fault>* element carries information describing why the operation failed on the server. Of course, the implication is that you'll see *<Fault>* tags in response messages only.

Document/Literal SOAP

Before we jump into some examples of SOAP message flows for the sample applications we developed in Chapter 3, "Building Distributed Applications with .NET Remoting," it's worth noting that another "flavor" of SOAP exists. We've already described the RPC/encoded form of SOAP that .NET Remoting uses. The other form of SOAP, which is known as document/literal, is the default SOAP style used by ASP.NET XML Web Services.

Document/literal SOAP messaging has no rules about what the *<Body>* element can contain. This is a more flexible scheme because the content can be anything agreed upon by the sender and receiver. Document/literal messaging serializes data based on XML schemas that handle data as XML rather than as objects or structures. Naturally, the two camps of SOAP messaging are waging a religious war. We'll stay out of that one and focus on RPC/encoded SOAP so that we can spy on .NET Remoting message flows.

> **Note** Nothing in the SOAP specification says that RPC must be paired with encoded serialization and that document messaging must be paired with literal serialization. However, nearly all existing SOAP stacks implement the specification this way.

Message Flows

Examining the message exchange between the JobClient and JobServer applications at various points of interaction can be quite instructive. Because we've chosen the HTTP channel with the default SOAP formatter, we can view the messages in a mostly human-readable form by using a tracing tool. Because the messages can be large, we'll try to break some of them into chunks that are easier to explain.

The JobClient application instantiates a proxy to the *JobServerImpl* type when the application first starts. Because the application configures the *JobServer-Impl* type as a well-known object, the client doesn't need to send a message to the server application until the client application accesses the remote object instance in some way—for example, via a property or a method call.

The *add_JobEvent* Request Message

The client first accesses the remote object instance when it subscribes to the *JobEvent* event, resulting in the following message exchange:

- JobClient sends an *add_JobEvent* request message to JobServer.

- JobServer sends an *add_JobEvent* response message to JobClient.

The compiler generates the *add_JobEvent* and *remove_JobEvent* methods on the *JobServerImpl* class because the class defines the *JobEvent* event member. The request message consists of an HTTP POST request message containing application data defining a SOAP message.

The following listing shows the HTTP header portion of the request message:

```
POST /JobServer/JobURI HTTP/1.1
User-Agent: Mozilla/4.0+(compatible; MSIE 6.0; Windows 5.0.2195.0;
MS .NET Remoting; MS .NET CLR 1.0.3705.0 )
Content-Type: text/xml; charset="utf-8"
SOAPAction: "http://schemas.microsoft.com/clr/nsassem/
JobServerLib.IJobServer/JobServerLib#add_JobEvent"
Content-Length: 6833
Expect: 100-continue
Connection: Keep-Alive
Host: localhost
```

Although it's not evident in the HTTP request message headers, the Job-Client application sends the message to the endpoint URL that we specified when configuring the *JobServerImpl* type as a server-activated object. Notice that the URL of the HTTP request message is */JobServer/JobURI*. This directly correlates to the URL that we specified when configuring the *JobServerImpl* type as a server-activated type. The server-side host application's .NET Remoting infrastructure uses this information to route the message to the associated object instance.

The *SOAPAction* header signifies that the HTTP request message contains a SOAP message in the body pertaining to the *add_JobEvent* method.

The following listing shows the SOAP *<Envelope>* element portion of the message, which remains the same for all messages:

```
<SOAP-ENV:Envelope
  xmlns:xsi=http://www.w3.org/2001/XMLSchema-instance
  xmlns:xsd=http://www.w3.org/2001/XMLSchema
  xmlns:SOAP-ENC=http://schemas.xmlsoap.org/soap/encoding/
  xmlns:SOAP-ENV="http://schemas.xmlsoap.org/soap/envelope/"
  xmlns:clr=http://schemas.microsoft.com/soap/encoding/clr/1.0
  SOAP-ENV:encodingStyle="http://schemas.xmlsoap.org/soap/encoding/">
```

The *<Body>* portion of the SOAP message follows:

```
<SOAP-ENV:Body>
  <i2:add_JobEvent id="ref-1"
    xmlns:i2="http://schemas.microsoft.com/clr/nsassem/
    JobServerLib.IJobServer/JobServerLib">
    <value href="#ref-3"/>
  </i2:add_JobEvent>
```

The *<i2:add_JobEvent>* element specifies that this SOAP message encapsulates an RPC on the *IJobServer.add_JobEvent* method. The element contains a *<value>* element that represents the value of the parameter passed to the method. The following listing shows the definition for the *<a1:DelegateSerialization-Holder>* element to which the *<value>* element refers:

```
<a1:DelegateSerializationHolder id="ref-3"
  xmlns:a1="http://schemas.microsoft.com/clr/ns/System">
  <Delegate href="#ref-4"/>
  <target0 href="#ref-5"/>
</a1:DelegateSerializationHolder>
```

The *<a1:DelegateSerializationHolder>* element is a serialized instance of the *System.DelegateSerializationHolder* class. The serialized instance contains two members, one of which is the *<Delegate>* element which references the following element:

```
<a1:DelegateSerializationHolder_x002B_DelegateEntry id="ref-4"
  xmlns:a1="http://schemas.microsoft.com/clr/ns/System">
  <type id="ref-6">JobServerLib.JobEventHandler</type>
  <assembly id="ref-7">JobServerLib, Version=1.0.807.36861,
    Culture=neutral, PublicKeyToken=null</assembly>
  <target id="ref-8" xsi:type="SOAP-ENC:string">target0</target>
  <targetTypeAssembly id="ref-9">JobClient, Version=1.0.807.36865,
    Culture=neutral, PublicKeyToken=null</targetTypeAssembly>
  <targetTypeName id="ref-10">JobClient.Form1</targetTypeName>
  <methodName id="ref-11">MyJobEventHandler</methodName>
  <delegateEntry xsi:null="1"/>
</a1:DelegateSerializationHolder_x002B_DelegateEntry>
```

This element defines the delegate's type and assembly information—in this case, *JobServerLib.JobEventHandler* in the JobServerLib assembly. The element also defines the target's type information: the *MyJobEventHandler* method of the *JobClient.Form1* class defined in the JobClient assembly.

The second member of the *<a1:DelegateSerializationHolder>* is the *<target0>* element, which specifies the target object instance of the delegate:

```
<a2:ObjRef id="ref-5" xmlns:a2="http://schemas.microsoft.com/
  clr/ns/System.Runtime.Remoting">
  <uri id="ref-12">
     /16e04fb4_ad6d_47ec_b584_22624cf6c808/96410280_1.rem
  </uri>
  <objrefFlags>0</objrefFlags>
  <typeInfo href="#ref-13"/>
  <envoyInfo xsi:null="1"/>
  <channelInfo href="#ref-14"/>
</a2:ObjRef>
```

Notice that the *<target0>* element refers to the *<a2:ObjRef>* element. The *<a2:ObjRef>* element is the serialized *System.ObjRef* instance representing the target object instance of the delegate. Recall from Chapter 2, "Understanding the .NET Remoting Architecture," that an *ObjRef* contains the type information for each type in the derivation hierarchy of the type derived from *MarshalByRef-Object*. Because *JobClient.Form1* is a *Windows.Forms.Form* type, the serialized *ObjRef* describes a number of interfaces and concrete types. The remainder of the message defines each of the elements contained by the *<a2:ObjRef>* element. These elements include the marshaled object instance's URI; context identifier, application domain identifier, and process identifier information for the *Marshal-ByRefObject*; and channel information such as transport type (HTTP), IP address, and listening ports:

```
<a2:TypeInfo id="ref-13" xmlns:a2="http://schemas.microsoft.com/
  clr/ns/System.Runtime.Remoting">
  <serverType id="ref-15">JobClient.Form1, JobClient,
    Version=1.0.807.36865, Culture=neutral, PublicKeyToken=null
  </serverType>
  <serverHierarchy href="#ref-16"/>
  <interfacesImplemented href="#ref-17"/>
</a2:TypeInfo>

<a2:ChannelInfo id="ref-14" xmlns:a2="http://schemas.microsoft.com/
  clr/ns/System.Runtime.Remoting">
  <channelData href="#ref-18"/>
</a2:ChannelInfo>
```

The following element is an array of strings that represent the complete derivation hierarchy up to—but not including—*System.MarshalByRefObject*:

```
<SOAP-ENC:Array id="ref-16" SOAP-ENC:arrayType="xsd:string[5]">
<item id="ref-19">System.Windows.Forms.Form, System.Windows.Forms,
Version=1.0.3300.0, Culture=neutral, PublicKeyToken=b77a5c561934e089
</item>
<item id="ref-20">System.Windows.Forms.ContainerControl,
System.Windows.Forms, Version=1.0.3300.0, Culture=neutral,
PublicKeyToken=b77a5c561934e089</item>
<item id="ref-21">System.Windows.Forms.ScrollableControl,
System.Windows.Forms, Version=1.0.3300.0, Culture=neutral,
PublicKeyToken=b77a5c561934e089</item>
<item id="ref-22">System.Windows.Forms.Control, System.Windows.Forms,
Version=1.0.3300.0, Culture=neutral, PublicKeyToken=b77a5c561934e089
</item>
<item id="ref-23">System.ComponentModel.Component, System,
Version=1.0.3300.0, Culture=neutral, PublicKeyToken=b77a5c561934e089
</item>
</SOAP-ENC:Array>
```

The next element is a string array containing all the interfaces that the marshaled type implements:

```
<SOAP-ENC:Array id="ref-17" SOAP-ENC:arrayType="xsd:string[18]">
<item id="ref-24">System.ComponentModel.IComponent, System,
Version=1.0.3300.0, Culture=neutral, PublicKeyToken=b77a5c561934e089
</item>
<item id="ref-25">System.IDisposable, mscorlib, Version=1.0.3300.0,
Culture=neutral, PublicKeyToken=b77a5c561934e089</item>
<item id="ref-26">
System.Windows.Forms.UnsafeNativeMethods+IOleControl,
System.Windows.Forms, Version=1.0.3300.0, Culture=neutral,
PublicKeyToken=b77a5c561934e089</item>
<item id="ref-27">
System.Windows.Forms.UnsafeNativeMethods+IOleObject,
System.Windows.Forms, Version=1.0.3300.0, Culture=neutral,
PublicKeyToken=b77a5c561934e089</item>
<item id="ref-28">
System.Windows.Forms.UnsafeNativeMethods+IOleInPlaceObject,
System.Windows.Forms, Version=1.0.3300.0, Culture=neutral,
PublicKeyToken=b77a5c561934e089</item>
<item id="ref-29">
System.Windows.Forms.UnsafeNativeMethods+IOleInPlaceActiveObject,
System.Windows.Forms, Version=1.0.3300.0, Culture=neutral,
PublicKeyToken=b77a5c561934e089</item>
<item id="ref-30">
System.Windows.Forms.UnsafeNativeMethods+IOleWindow,
System.Windows.Forms, Version=1.0.3300.0, Culture=neutral,
```

```
PublicKeyToken=b77a5c561934e089</item>
<item id="ref-31">
System.Windows.Forms.UnsafeNativeMethods+IViewObject,
System.Windows.Forms, Version=1.0.3300.0, Culture=neutral,
PublicKeyToken=b77a5c561934e089</item>
<item id="ref-32">
System.Windows.Forms.UnsafeNativeMethods+IViewObject2,
System.Windows.Forms, Version=1.0.3300.0, Culture=neutral,
PublicKeyToken=b77a5c561934e089</item>
<item id="ref-33">System.Windows.Forms.UnsafeNativeMethods+IPersist,
System.Windows.Forms, Version=1.0.3300.0, Culture=neutral,
PublicKeyToken=b77a5c561934e089</item>
<item id="ref-34">
System.Windows.Forms.UnsafeNativeMethods+IPersistStreamInit,
System.Windows.Forms, Version=1.0.3300.0, Culture=neutral,
PublicKeyToken=b77a5c561934e089</item>
<item id="ref-35">
System.Windows.Forms.UnsafeNativeMethods+IPersistPropertyBag,
System.Windows.Forms, Version=1.0.3300.0, Culture=neutral,
PublicKeyToken=b77a5c561934e089</item>
<item id="ref-36">
System.Windows.Forms.UnsafeNativeMethods+IPersistStorage,
System.Windows.Forms, Version=1.0.3300.0, Culture=neutral,
PublicKeyToken=b77a5c561934e089</item>
<item id="ref-37">
System.Windows.Forms.UnsafeNativeMethods+IQuickActivate,
System.Windows.Forms, Version=1.0.3300.0, Culture=neutral,
PublicKeyToken=b77a5c561934e089</item>
<item id="ref-38">System.ComponentModel.ISynchronizeInvoke, System,
Version=1.0.3300.0, Culture=neutral, PublicKeyToken=b77a5c561934e089
</item>
<item id="ref-39">System.Windows.Forms.IWin32Window,
System.Windows.Forms, Version=1.0.3300.0, Culture=neutral,
PublicKeyToken=b77a5c561934e089</item>
<item id="ref-40">System.Windows.Forms.IContainerControl,
System.Windows.Forms, Version=1.0.3300.0, Culture=neutral,
PublicKeyToken=b77a5c561934e089</item>
<item id="ref-41">System.Runtime.Remoting.Lifetime.ISponsor,
mscorlib, Version=1.0.3300.0, Culture=neutral,
PublicKeyToken=b77a5c561934e089</item>
</SOAP-ENC:Array>
```

Finally, the message contains information identifying the calling application domain, context, and process as well as information about channels that the sending application domain is publishing. This content enables the recipient of the message to establish a communications channel if needed:

```
<SOAP-ENC:Array id="ref-18" SOAP-ENC:arrayType="xsd:anyType[2]">
```

(continued)

```
      <item href="#ref-42"/>
      <item href="#ref-43"/>
</SOAP-ENC:Array>

<a3:CrossAppDomainData id="ref-42"
   xmlns:a3="http://schemas.microsoft.com/clr/ns/
   System.Runtime.Remoting.Channels">
   <_ContextID>1300872</_ContextID>
   <_DomainID>1</_DomainID>
   <_processGuid id="ref-44">
      20c23b9b_4d09_46a8_bc29_10037f04f46f
   </_processGuid>
</a3:CrossAppDomainData>

<a3:ChannelDataStore id="ref-43"
   xmlns:a3="http://schemas.microsoft.com/clr/ns/
   System.Runtime.Remoting.Channels">
   <_channelURIs href="#ref-45"/>
   <_extraData xsi:null="1"/>
</a3:ChannelDataStore>

<SOAP-ENC:Array id="ref-45" SOAP-ENC:arrayType="xsd:string[1]">
   <item id="ref-46">http://66.156.56.215:1958</item>
</SOAP-ENC:Array>

</SOAP-ENV:Body>
</SOAP-ENV:Envelope>
```

The *add_JobEvent* Response Message

Once the *add_Delegate* method finishes, the server-side .NET Remoting infrastructure will package the result of the method call into a response message
and return it to the client. The following listing shows the HTTP response
message for the *add_Delegate* method:

```
HTTP/1.1 200 OK
Content-Type: text/xml; charset="utf-8"
Server: MS .NET Remoting, MS .NET CLR 1.0.3705.0
Content-Length: 580

<SOAP-ENV:Envelope ...>
   <SOAP-ENV:Body>
      <i2:add_JobEventResponse id="ref-1"
         xmlns:i2="http://schemas.microsoft.com/clr/nsassem/
         JobServerLib.IJobServer/JobServerLib">
      </i2:add_JobEventResponse>
   </SOAP-ENV:Body>
</SOAP-ENV:Envelope>
```

The *GetJobs* Request Message

When the client calls the *IJobServer.GetJobs* method on the remote *JobServerImpl* instance, the .NET Remoting infrastructure sends a *GetJobs* request message to the server:

```
POST /JobServer/JobURI HTTP/1.1
User-Agent: Mozilla/4.0+(compatible; MSIE 6.0; Windows 5.0.2195.0;
MS .NET Remoting; MS .NET CLR 1.0.3705.0 )
Content-Type: text/xml; charset="utf-8"
SOAPAction: "http://schemas.microsoft.com/clr/nsassem/
JobServerLib.IJobServer/JobServerLib#GetJobs"
Content-Length: 554
Expect: 100-continue
Host: localhost

<SOAP-ENV:Envelope … >
  <SOAP-ENV:Body>
    <i2:GetJobs id="ref-1" xmlns:i2="http://schemas.microsoft.com/
       clr/nsassem/JobServerLib.IJobServer/JobServerLib">
    </i2:GetJobs>
  </SOAP-ENV:Body>
</SOAP-ENV:Envelope>
```

The *GetJobs* Response Message

In response to the *GetJobs* request message, the server sends a *GetJobs* response message to the client. This message contains the serialized return result, an *ArrayList* of *JobInfo* instances containing all currently defined jobs:

```
HTTP/1.1 200 OK
Content-Type: text/xml; charset="utf-8"
Server: MS .NET Remoting, MS .NET CLR 1.0.3705.0
Content-Length: 1991

<SOAP-ENV:Envelope ...>

  <SOAP-ENV:Body>

    <i2:GetJobsResponse id="ref-1"
      xmlns:i2="http://schemas.microsoft.com/clr/nsassem/
      JobServerLib.IJobServer/JobServerLib">
      <return href="#ref-3"/>
    </i2:GetJobsResponse>

    <a1:ArrayList id="ref-3"
      xmlns:a1="http://schemas.microsoft.com/clr/ns/
```

(continued)

```
        System.Collections">
         <_items href="#ref-4"/>
         <_size>3</_size>
         <_version>6</_version>
      </a1:ArrayList>

      <SOAP-ENC:Array id="ref-4"
        SOAP-ENC:arrayType="xsd:anyType[16]">

         <item xsi:type="a3:JobInfo"
           xmlns:a3="http://schemas.microsoft.com/clr/nsassem/
           JobServerLib/JobServerLib%2C%20
           Version%3D1.0.819.24637%2C%20Culture%3Dneutral%2C%20
           PublicKeyToken%3Dnull">
            <m_nID>0</m_nID>
            <m_sDescription id="ref-6">Wash Windows</m_sDescription>
            <m_sAssignedUser id="ref-7">
              Administrator</m_sAssignedUser>
            <m_sStatus id="ref-8">Assigned</m_sStatus>
         </item>

         <item xsi:type="a3:JobInfo"
           xmlns:a3="http://schemas.microsoft.com/clr/nsassem/
           JobServerLib/JobServerLib%2C%20
           Version%3D1.0.819.24637%2C%20Culture%3Dneutral%2C%20
           PublicKeyToken%3Dnull">
            <m_nID>1</m_nID>
            <m_sDescription id="ref-9">Fix door</m_sDescription>
            <m_sAssignedUser id="ref-10">
              Administrator</m_sAssignedUser>
            <m_sStatus id="ref-11">Assigned</m_sStatus>
         </item>

         <item xsi:type="a3:JobInfo"
           xmlns:a3="http://schemas.microsoft.com/clr/nsassem/
           JobServerLib/JobServerLib%2C%20
           Version%3D1.0.819.24637%2C%20Culture%3Dneutral%2C%20
           PublicKeyToken%3Dnull">
            <m_nID>2</m_nID>
            <m_sDescription id="ref-12">
              Clean carpets</m_sDescription>
            <m_sAssignedUser id="ref-13">
              Administrator</m_sAssignedUser>
            <m_sStatus id="ref-14">Completed</m_sStatus>
         </item>

      </SOAP-ENC:Array>
   </SOAP-ENV:Body>
</SOAP-ENV:Envelope>
```

The *CreateJob* Request Message

The client application sends a *CreateJob* request message to the server when the client calls the *IJobServer.CreateJob* method on the remote *JobServerImpl* instance. The *IJobServer.CreateJob* method takes one parameter, the description for the new job. The following message creates a job with the description *Wash Windows*:

```
POST /JobServer/JobURI HTTP/1.1
User-Agent: Mozilla/4.0+(compatible; MSIE 6.0; Windows 5.0.2195.0;
MS .NET Remoting; MS .NET CLR 1.0.3705.0 )
Content-Type: text/xml; charset="utf-8"
SOAPAction: "http://schemas.microsoft.com/clr/nsassem/
  JobServerLib.IJobServer/JobServerLib#CreateJob"
Content-Length: 612
Expect: 100-continue
Host: localhost

<SOAP-ENV:Envelope ...>
   <SOAP-ENV:Body>
      <i2:CreateJob id="ref-1"
        xmlns:i2="http://schemas.microsoft.com/clr/nsassem/
        JobServerLib.IJobServer/JobServerLib">
         <sDescription id="ref-3">Wash Windows</sDescription>
      </i2:CreateJob>
   </SOAP-ENV:Body>
</SOAP-ENV:Envelope>
```

The *CreateJob* Response Message

Because the *CreateJob* method's return type is void and doesn't define any output parameters, the *CreateJob* response message is essentially an acknowledgment to the sender that the method call has finished:

```
HTTP/1.1 200 OK
Content-Type: text/xml; charset="utf-8"
Server: MS .NET Remoting, MS .NET CLR 1.0.3705.0
Content-Length: 574

<SOAP-ENV:Envelope ...>
   <SOAP-ENV:Body>
      <i2:CreateJobResponse id="ref-1"
        xmlns:i2="http://schemas.microsoft.com/clr/nsassem/
        JobServerLib.IJobServer/JobServerLib">
      </i2:CreateJobResponse>
   </SOAP-ENV:Body>
</SOAP-ENV:Envelope>
```

The *UpdateJobState* Request Message

The following message results from the JobClient application calling the *UpdateJobState* method passing as parameters the values *2*, *Administrator*, and *Completed*:

```
POST /JobServer/JobURI HTTP/1.1
User-Agent: Mozilla/4.0+(compatible; MSIE 6.0; Windows 5.0.2195.0;
MS .NET Remoting; MS .NET CLR 1.0.3705.0 )
Content-Type: text/xml; charset="utf-8"
SOAPAction: "http://schemas.microsoft.com/clr/nsassem/
  JobServerLib.IJobServer/JobServerLib#UpdateJobState"
Content-Length: 670
Expect: 100-continue
Host: localhost

<SOAP-ENV:Envelope ...>
  <SOAP-ENV:Body>

      <i2:UpdateJobState id="ref-1"
        xmlns:i2="http://schemas.microsoft.com/clr/nsassem/
        JobServerLib.IJobServer/JobServerLib">
        <nJobID>2</nJobID>
        <sUser id="ref-3">Administrator</sUser>
        <sStatus id="ref-4">Completed</sStatus>
      </i2:UpdateJobState>

  </SOAP-ENV:Body>
</SOAP-ENV:Envelope>
```

The *UpdateJobState* Response Message

Like the *CreateJob* response message, the *UpdateJobState* response message is essentially an acknowledgment to inform the sender that the method call has finished:

```
HTTP/1.1 200 OK
Content-Type: text/xml; charset="utf-8"
Server: MS .NET Remoting, MS .NET CLR 1.0.3705.0
Content-Length: 584

<SOAP-ENV:Envelope ...>
  <SOAP-ENV:Body>
    <i2:UpdateJobStateResponse id="ref-1"
      xmlns:i2="http://schemas.microsoft.com/clr/nsassem/
      JobServerLib.IJobServer/JobServerLib">
    </i2:UpdateJobStateResponse>

  </SOAP-ENV:Body>
</SOAP-ENV:Envelope>
```

The *JobNotes* Activation Request Message

When the JobClient application creates an instance of a *JobNotes* class, the .NET Remoting infrastructure sends an *Activate* request message to the JobServer application:

```
POST /RemoteActivationService.rem HTTP/1.1
User-Agent: Mozilla/4.0+(compatible; MSIE 6.0; Windows 5.0.2195.0;
MS .NET Remoting; MS .NET CLR 1.0.3705.0 )
Content-Type: text/xml; charset="utf-8"
SOAPAction: "http://schemas.microsoft.com/clr/ns/
  System.Runtime.Remoting.Activation.IActivator#Activate"
Content-Length: 2126
Expect: 100-continue
Host: localhost

<SOAP-ENV:Envelope ...>

   <SOAP-ENV:Body>
      <i2:Activate id="ref-1"
         xmlns:i2="http://schemas.microsoft.com/clr/ns/
         System.Runtime.Remoting.Activation.IActivator">
         <msg href="#ref-3"/>
      </i2:Activate>

      <a1:ConstructionCall id="ref-3"
         xmlns:a1="http://schemas.microsoft.com/clr/ns/
         System.Runtime.Remoting.Messaging">
         <__Uri xsi:type="xsd:anyType" xsi:null="1"/>
         <__MethodName id="ref-4">.ctor</__MethodName>
         <__MethodSignature href="#ref-5"/>
         <__TypeName id="ref-6">JobServerLib.JobNotes, JobServerLib,
           Version=1.0.819.24637, Culture=neutral,
           PublicKeyToken=null</__TypeName>
         <__Args href="#ref-7"/>
         <__CallContext xsi:type="xsd:anyType" xsi:null="1"/>
         <__CallSiteActivationAttributes xsi:type="xsd:anyType"
           xsi:null="1"/>
         <__ActivationType xsi:type="xsd:anyType" xsi:null="1"/>
         <__ContextProperties href="#ref-8"/>
         <__Activator href="#ref-9"/>
         <__ActivationTypeName href="#ref-6"/>
      </a1:ConstructionCall>

      <SOAP-ENC:Array id="ref-5" SOAP-ENC:arrayType="a2:Type[0]"
         xmlns:a2="http://schemas.microsoft.com/clr/ns/System">
      </SOAP-ENC:Array>
```

(continued)

```
<SOAP-ENC:Array id="ref-7" SOAP-ENC:arrayType="xsd:anyType[0]">
</SOAP-ENC:Array>
<a3:ArrayList id="ref-8"
  xmlns:a3="http://schemas.microsoft.com/clr/ns/
  System.Collections">
  <_items href="#ref-10"/>
  <_size>0</_size>
  <_version>0</_version>
</a3:ArrayList>

<a4:ContextLevelActivator id="ref-9"
  xmlns:a4="http://schemas.microsoft.com/clr/ns/
  System.Runtime.Remoting.Activation">
  <m_NextActivator href="#ref-11"/>
</a4:ContextLevelActivator>
<SOAP-ENC:Array id="ref-10"
  SOAP-ENC:arrayType="xsd:anyType[16]">
</SOAP-ENC:Array>
<a4:ConstructionLevelActivator id="ref-11"
  xmlns:a4="http://schemas.microsoft.com/clr/ns/
  System.Runtime.Remoting.Activation">
</a4:ConstructionLevelActivator>
  </SOAP-ENV:Body>
</SOAP-ENV:Envelope>
```

The *JobNotes* Activation Response Message

After activating a *JobNotes* instance, the .NET Remoting infrastructure sends an *ActivateResponse* message to the JobClient application. The message contains a serialized *System.ObjRef* that represents the new *JobNotes* instance residing in the JobServer application domain:

```
HTTP/1.1 200 OK
Content-Type: text/xml; charset="utf-8"
Server: MS .NET Remoting, MS .NET CLR 1.0.3705.0
Content-Length: 2723

<SOAP-ENV:Envelope ...>
  <SOAP-ENV:Body>
    <i2:ActivateResponse id="ref-1"
      xmlns:i2="http://schemas.microsoft.com/clr/ns/
      System.Runtime.Remoting.Activation.IActivator">
      <return href="#ref-3"/>
    </i2:ActivateResponse>
    <a1:ConstructionResponse id="ref-3"
      xmlns:a1="http://schemas.microsoft.com/clr/ns/
      System.Runtime.Remoting.Messaging">
```

```
    <__Uri xsi:type="xsd:anyType" xsi:null="1"/>
    <__MethodName id="ref-4">.ctor</__MethodName>
    <__TypeName id="ref-5">JobServerLib.JobNotes, JobServerLib,
      Version=1.0.830.37588, Culture=neutral,
      PublicKeyToken=null</__TypeName>
    <__Return href="#ref-6"/>
    <__OutArgs href="#ref-7"/>
    <__CallContext xsi:type="xsd:anyType" xsi:null="1"/>
</a1:ConstructionResponse>
<a3:ObjRef id="ref-6"
  xmlns:a3="http://schemas.microsoft.com/clr/ns/
  System.Runtime.Remoting">
    <uri id="ref-8">
      /cf2825b9_2974_4f5c_9810_2f96945b529d/16921141_1.rem</uri>
    <objrefFlags>0</objrefFlags>
    <typeInfo href="#ref-9"/>
    <envoyInfo xsi:null="1"/>
    <channelInfo href="#ref-10"/>
    <fIsMarshalled>0</fIsMarshalled>
</a3:ObjRef>
<SOAP-ENC:Array id="ref-7" SOAP-ENC:arrayType="xsd:anyType[0]">
</SOAP-ENC:Array>
<a3:TypeInfo id="ref-9"
  xmlns:a3="http://schemas.microsoft.com/clr/ns/
  System.Runtime.Remoting">
    <serverType id="ref-11">JobServerLib.JobNotes, JobServerLib,
      Version=1.0.830.37588, Culture=neutral,
      PublicKeyToken=null</serverType>
    <serverHierarchy xsi:null="1"/>
    <interfacesImplemented xsi:null="1"/>
</a3:TypeInfo>
<a3:ChannelInfo id="ref-10"
  xmlns:a3="http://schemas.microsoft.com/clr/ns/
  System.Runtime.Remoting">
    <channelData href="#ref-12"/>
</a3:ChannelInfo>
<SOAP-ENC:Array id="ref-12"
  SOAP-ENC:arrayType="xsd:anyType[2]">
    <item href="#ref-13"/>
    <item href="#ref-14"/>
</SOAP-ENC:Array>
<a4:CrossAppDomainData id="ref-13"
  xmlns:a4="http://schemas.microsoft.com/clr/ns/
  System.Runtime.Remoting.Channels">
    <_ContextID>1299232</_ContextID>
    <_DomainID>1</_DomainID>
    <_processGuid id="ref-15">
      efbc85bf_b165_4953_ab00_f37d49bbffb4</_processGuid>
```

(continued)

```
       </a4:CrossAppDomainData>
       <a4:ChannelDataStore id="ref-14"
         xmlns:a4="http://schemas.microsoft.com/clr/ns/
         System.Runtime.Remoting.Channels">
          <_channelURIs href="#ref-16"/>
          <_extraData xsi:null="1"/>
       </a4:ChannelDataStore>
       <SOAP-ENC:Array id="ref-16" SOAP-ENC:arrayType="xsd:string[1]">
          <item id="ref-17">http://66.156.71.188:4000</item>
       </SOAP-ENC:Array>
     </SOAP-ENV:Body>
</SOAP-ENV:Envelope>
```

The *remove_JobEvent* Request Message

The last interaction that the JobClient application has with the remote *JobServer-Impl* instance is to unsubscribe the *JobClient.Form1* instance from the *JobEvent*. This results in a call to the *remove_JobEvent* method, which the .NET Remoting infrastructure converts into a *remove_JobEvent* request message. This message is essentially identical to the *add_JobEvent* request message because the methods have the same signatures. As with the *add_JobEvent* request message, the *remove_JobEvent* message contains a serialized delegate instance. In this case, the target of the delegate is an instance of the *JobClient.Form1* type, which is a type derived from *MarshalByRefObject*. Thus, the message includes a serialized *System.ObjRef* instance representing the *JobClient.Form1* class instance that unsubscribes from the event. The following listing shows the *remove_JobEvent* request message:

```
POST /JobServer/JobURI HTTP/1.1
User-Agent: Mozilla/4.0+(compatible; MSIE 6.0; Windows 5.0.2195.0;
MS .NET Remoting; MS .NET CLR 1.0.3705.0 )
Content-Type: text/xml; charset="utf-8"
SOAPAction: "http://schemas.microsoft.com/clr/nsassem/
  JobServerLib.IJobServer/JobServerLib#remove_JobEvent"
Content-Length: 6839
Expect: 100-continue
Host: localhost

<SOAP-ENV:Envelope ...>
   <SOAP-ENV:Body>
      <i2:remove_JobEvent id="ref-1"
        xmlns:i2="http://schemas.microsoft.com/clr/nsassem/
        JobServerLib.IJobServer/JobServerLib">
         <value href="#ref-3"/>
      </i2:remove_JobEvent>
```

```
<a1:DelegateSerializationHolder id="ref-3"
  xmlns:a1="http://schemas.microsoft.com/clr/ns/System">
    <Delegate href="#ref-4"/>
    <target0 href="#ref-5"/>
</a1:DelegateSerializationHolder>
<a1:DelegateSerializationHolder_x002B_DelegateEntry id="ref-4"
  xmlns:a1="http://schemas.microsoft.com/clr/ns/System">
    <type id="ref-6">JobServerLib.JobEventHandler</type>
    <assembly id="ref-7">JobServerLib, Version=1.0.819.24637,
      Culture=neutral, PublicKeyToken=null</assembly>
    <target id="ref-8" xsi:type="SOAP-ENC:string">
      target0</target>
    <targetTypeAssembly id="ref-9">JobClient,
      Version=1.0.829.36775, Culture=neutral,
      PublicKeyToken=null</targetTypeAssembly>
    <targetTypeName id="ref-10">JobClient.Form1</targetTypeName>
    <methodName id="ref-11">MyJobEventHandler</methodName>
    <delegateEntry xsi:null="1"/>
</a1:DelegateSerializationHolder_x002B_DelegateEntry>

<a2:ObjRef id="ref-5"
  xmlns:a2="http://schemas.microsoft.com/clr/ns/
  System.Runtime.Remoting">
    <uri id="ref-12">
      /295e2d43_876a_4511_a774_12e7a65d96bc/13636498_1.rem</uri>
    <objrefFlags>0</objrefFlags>
    <typeInfo href="#ref-13"/>
    <envoyInfo xsi:null="1"/>
    <channelInfo href="#ref-14"/>
</a2:ObjRef>
<a2:TypeInfo id="ref-13"
  xmlns:a2="http://schemas.microsoft.com/clr/ns/
  System.Runtime.Remoting">
<serverType id="ref-15">JobClient.Form1, JobClient,
  Version=1.0.829.36775, Culture=neutral,
  PublicKeyToken=null</serverType>
    <serverHierarchy href="#ref-16"/>
    <interfacesImplemented href="#ref-17"/>
</a2:TypeInfo>

<a2:ChannelInfo id="ref-14"
  xmlns:a2="http://schemas.microsoft.com/clr/ns/
  System.Runtime.Remoting">
    <channelData href="#ref-18"/>
</a2:ChannelInfo>
```

(continued)

```
<SOAP-ENC:Array id="ref-16" SOAP-ENC:arrayType="xsd:string[5]">
   <item id="ref-19">System.Windows.Forms.Form,
      System.Windows.Forms, Version=1.0.3300.0, Culture=neutral,
      PublicKeyToken=b77a5c561934e089</item>
   <item id="ref-20">System.Windows.Forms.ContainerControl,
      System.Windows.Forms, Version=1.0.3300.0, Culture=neutral,
      PublicKeyToken=b77a5c561934e089</item>
   <item id="ref-21">System.Windows.Forms.ScrollableControl,
      System.Windows.Forms, Version=1.0.3300.0, Culture=neutral,
      PublicKeyToken=b77a5c561934e089</item>
   <item id="ref-22">System.Windows.Forms.Control,
      System.Windows.Forms, Version=1.0.3300.0, Culture=neutral,
      PublicKeyToken=b77a5c561934e089</item>
   <item id="ref-23">System.ComponentModel.Component, System,
      Version=1.0.3300.0, Culture=neutral,
      PublicKeyToken=b77a5c561934e089</item>
</SOAP-ENC:Array>

<SOAP-ENC:Array id="ref-17"
   SOAP-ENC:arrayType="xsd:string[18]">
   <item id="ref-24">System.ComponentModel.IComponent, System,
      Version=1.0.3300.0, Culture=neutral,
      PublicKeyToken=b77a5c561934e089</item>
   <item id="ref-25">System.IDisposable, mscorlib,
      Version=1.0.3300.0, Culture=neutral,
      PublicKeyToken=b77a5c561934e089</item>
   <item id="ref-26">
      System.Windows.Forms.UnsafeNativeMethods+IOleControl,
      System.Windows.Forms, Version=1.0.3300.0,
      Culture=neutral, PublicKeyToken=b77a5c561934e089</item>
   <item id="ref-27">
      System.Windows.Forms.UnsafeNativeMethods+IOleObject,
      System.Windows.Forms, Version=1.0.3300.0,
      Culture=neutral, PublicKeyToken=b77a5c561934e089</item>
   <item id="ref-28">System.Windows.Forms.
      UnsafeNativeMethods+IOleInPlaceObject,
      System.Windows.Forms, Version=1.0.3300.0,
      Culture=neutral, PublicKeyToken=b77a5c561934e089</item>
   <item id="ref-29">System.Windows.Forms.
      UnsafeNativeMethods+IOleInPlaceActiveObject,
      System.Windows.Forms, Version=1.0.3300.0,
      Culture=neutral, PublicKeyToken=b77a5c561934e089</item>
   <item id="ref-30">
      System.Windows.Forms.UnsafeNativeMethods+IOleWindow,
      System.Windows.Forms, Version=1.0.3300.0,
      Culture=neutral, PublicKeyToken=b77a5c561934e089</item>
```

```
      <item id="ref-31">
        System.Windows.Forms.UnsafeNativeMethods+IViewObject,
        System.Windows.Forms, Version=1.0.3300.0,
        Culture=neutral, PublicKeyToken=b77a5c561934e089</item>
      <item id="ref-32">
        System.Windows.Forms.UnsafeNativeMethods+IViewObject2,
        System.Windows.Forms, Version=1.0.3300.0,
        Culture=neutral, PublicKeyToken=b77a5c561934e089</item>
      <item id="ref-33">
        System.Windows.Forms.UnsafeNativeMethods+IPersist,
        System.Windows.Forms, Version=1.0.3300.0,
        Culture=neutral, PublicKeyToken=b77a5c561934e089</item>
      <item id="ref-34">System.Windows.Forms.
        UnsafeNativeMethods+IPersistStreamInit,
        System.Windows.Forms, Version=1.0.3300.0,
        Culture=neutral, PublicKeyToken=b77a5c561934e089</item>
      <item id="ref-35">System.Windows.Forms.
        UnsafeNativeMethods+IPersistPropertyBag,
        System.Windows.Forms, Version=1.0.3300.0,
        Culture=neutral, PublicKeyToken=b77a5c561934e089</item>
      <item id="ref-36">
        System.Windows.Forms.UnsafeNativeMethods+IPersistStorage,
        System.Windows.Forms, Version=1.0.3300.0,
        Culture=neutral, PublicKeyToken=b77a5c561934e089</item>
      <item id="ref-37">
        System.Windows.Forms.UnsafeNativeMethods+IQuickActivate,
        System.Windows.Forms, Version=1.0.3300.0,
        Culture=neutral, PublicKeyToken=b77a5c561934e089</item>
      <item id="ref-38">System.ComponentModel.ISynchronizeInvoke,
        System, Version=1.0.3300.0, Culture=neutral,
        PublicKeyToken=b77a5c561934e089</item>
      <item id="ref-39">System.Windows.Forms.IWin32Window,
        System.Windows.Forms, Version=1.0.3300.0, Culture=neutral,
        PublicKeyToken=b77a5c561934e089</item>
      <item id="ref-40">System.Windows.Forms.IContainerControl,
        System.Windows.Forms, Version=1.0.3300.0, Culture=neutral,
        PublicKeyToken=b77a5c561934e089</item>
      <item id="ref-41">System.Runtime.Remoting.Lifetime.ISponsor,
        mscorlib, Version=1.0.3300.0, Culture=neutral,
        PublicKeyToken=b77a5c561934e089</item>
</SOAP-ENC:Array>

<SOAP-ENC:Array id="ref-18"
  SOAP-ENC:arrayType="xsd:anyType[2]">
    <item href="#ref-42"/>
    <item href="#ref-43"/>
</SOAP-ENC:Array>
```

(continued)

```
<a3:CrossAppDomainData id="ref-42"
  xmlns:a3="http://schemas.microsoft.com/clr/ns/
  System.Runtime.Remoting.Channels">
  <_ContextID>1300872</_ContextID>
  <_DomainID>1</_DomainID>
  <_processGuid id="ref-44">
     20c23b9b_4d09_46a8_bc29_10037f04f46f
  </_processGuid>
</a3:CrossAppDomainData>

<a3:ChannelDataStore id="ref-43"
  xmlns:a3="http://schemas.microsoft.com/clr/ns/
  System.Runtime.Remoting.Channels">
  <_channelURIs href="#ref-45"/>
  <_extraData xsi:null="1"/>
</a3:ChannelDataStore>

<SOAP-ENC:Array id="ref-45" SOAP-ENC:arrayType="xsd:string[1]">
  <item id="ref-46">http://66.156.56.215:1958</item>
</SOAP-ENC:Array>

    </SOAP-ENV:Body>
</SOAP-ENV:Envelope>
```

The *remove_JobEvent* Response Message

Once the *remove_JobEvent* method returns, the .NET Remoting infrastructure sends the following message to the JobClient application to indicate the method call has finished:

```
HTTP/1.1 200 OK
Content-Type: text/xml; charset="utf-8"
Server: MS .NET Remoting, MS .NET CLR 1.0.3705.0
Content-Length: 586

<SOAP-ENV:Envelope ...>   <SOAP-ENV:Body>
    <i2:remove_JobEventResponse id="ref-1"
       xmlns:i2="http://schemas.microsoft.com/clr/nsassem/
       JobServerLib.IJobServer/JobServerLib">
    </i2:remove_JobEventResponse>
  </SOAP-ENV:Body>
</SOAP-ENV:Envelope>
```

Summary

In this chapter, we discussed SOAP internals as they apply to .NET Remoting applications. Using this understanding of SOAP, we examined several message flows between the JobClient and JobServer applications. Although the .NET Framework does a great job of hiding the SOAP details from programmers performing higher-level tasks, understanding SOAP can give you a powerful tool for developing .NET Remoting applications. By watching SOAP traffic, you can see how the .NET Remoting infrastructure sends messages for constructing objects and renewing leases as well as viewing your own method-based messages on the wire. Because you now have a basic understanding of SOAP, we'll use SOAP message flows in this book to reinforce concepts as appropriate.

5

Messages and Proxies

So far, we've used only the out-of-the-box functionality of .NET Remoting. In this chapter, we'll begin customizing various elements of the .NET Remoting infrastructure, starting with proxies. Specifically, we'll look at creating a custom proxy that implements a simple load-balancing scheme. We'll develop another proxy that shows how *ProxyAttribute* can be used to intercept activation. We'll also show you how to use *call context* to transfer extra information with the method call. However, before we discuss customizing proxies, let's examine the various kinds of messages a proxy might encounter.

Messages

You'll see a lot of messages throughout the rest of this book because they're the fundamental unit of data transfer in .NET Remoting applications. Because .NET Remoting objects such as proxies and message sinks use messages extensively, let's discuss messages in more detail before we begin customizing those other objects.

Recall from Chapter 2, "Understanding the .NET Remoting Architecture," that all .NET Remoting messages derive from *IMessage*. *IMessage* merely defines a single *IDictionary* property named *Properties*. *IDictionary* defines an interface for collections of key-and-value pairs. Because both the keys and values of *IDictionary*-based collections contain elements of type object, you can put any .NET type into these collections. But the objects you use must be serializable in order to be transported across a remoting boundary. We'll look at serialization in depth in Chapter 8, "Serialization Formatters."

Construction Call Messages

When you make a method call (including a constructor call) on a remote object, the .NET Remoting infrastructure constructs a message describing the method call. For example, consider the following client code:

```
Object obj = new MyRemoteObject();
```

The instantiation of the *MyRemoteObject* results in the instantiation of a .NET Remoting message with the *IDictionary* entries shown in Table 5-1.

Table 5-1   Construction Call Messages

Dictionary Key	Dictionary Value Data Type	Dictionary Value
__Uri	String	null
__MethodName	String	.ctor
__TypeName	System.String	MyNameSpace.MyRemoteObject, MyAssembly, Version=1.0.882.27668, CultureNeutral, PublicKeyToken=null
__MethodSignature	Type[]	null
__Args	Object[]	null
__CallContext	LogicalCallContext	null
__ActivationType	Type	null
__CallSiteActivationAttributes	Object[]	null
__ActivationType	Type	null

The value of the __*MethodName* key identifies the method as *.ctor*, which corresponds to the *MyRemoteObject* constructor method. Because *MyRemote-Object*'s constructor has no arguments, the __*MethodSignature* and __*Args* values are *null*. Because call context can be set in the client's calling code, the dictionary contains a key named __*CallContext*. We'll discuss call context and how to use it in the next section of this chapter. Finally, the message has dictionary keys for custom activation properties, which the .NET Remoting infrastructure uses during activation.

Method Call Messages

Consider the following method on the remote object:

```
Obj.MyMethod("A string", 14);
```

This method call results in the generation of a message with the *IDictionary* entries shown in Table 5-2.

Table 5-2   Method Call Messages

Dictionary Key	Dictionary Value Data Type	Dictionary Value
__Uri	*String*	*null*
__MethodName	*String*	*MyMethod*
__TypeName	*System.String*	*MyNameSpace.MyRemoteObject, MyAssembly, Version=1.0.882.27668, CultureNeutral, PublicKeyToken=null*
__MethodSignature	*Type[]*	[0] = *System.String*
		[1] = *System.Int32*
__Args	*Object[]*	[0] = a string
		[1] = 14
__CallContext	*LogicalCallContext*	*null*

Note that the *__MethodName*, *__MethodSignature*, and *__Args* keys are populated to reflect the remote object's method. Because the object has already been activated, the activation keys aren't present.

Message Types

All .NET Remoting messages implement the *IMessage* interface so that they at least have a single *IDictionary* property. The .NET Remoting infrastructure derives many interfaces from *IMessage* that generally serve two purposes. First, each of these interfaces provides various properties and/or methods to make accessing the *IMessage* internal dictionary more convenient. Second, each interface's specific type serves as a marker so that you know how to handle the message. For example, you might want to differentiate between a message for constructing a client-activated object and a message generated from a regular method call. Although either of these messages could be conveyed via a simple *IMessage* class, by having different types the interfaces can inform you of the intent of a message. Table 5-3 summarizes the common message interfaces and classes that you might encounter.

Table 5-3 Common Remoting Message Types

Message Type	Member Name (Partial Listing)	Description
IMessage		Implemented by all .NET Remoting messages.
IMethodMessage		Implemented by all messages that describe stack-based methods. Specifies properties common to all methods.
	Args	Array of method arguments passed.
	MethodName	Name of the method that originated the message.
	Uri	Uniform Resource Identifier (URI) of the object that this message is destined for.
	TypeName	Full type name of the object that this message is destined for.
IMethodReturnMessage		Implemented by all messages returning to the client.
	Exception	Exception thrown by the remote object, if any.
	OutArgs	Array of *[out]* arguments.
	ReturnValue	Object containing the return value of the remote method, if any.
IMethodCallMessage		Implemented by all messages originating from method calls. Specifies properties common to all method calls.
	InArgs	Array of *[in]* arguments.
IConstructionCallMessage		Message implementing this interface is sent to a client-activated object when you call *new* or *Activator.CreateInstance*. Server-activated objects receive this message when you make the first message call. As its name implies, this is the first message sent to an object, and it specifies properties common to remote object construction.
	ActivationType	Gets the type of the remote object to activate.
	Activator	Gets or sets the activator used to activate the remote object.
	ContextProperties	Gets the list of context properties that define the object's creation context.

Table 5-3   **Common Remoting Message Types**   *(continued)*

Message Type	Member Name (Partial Listing)	Description
IConstructionReturnMessage		Message implementing this interface is sent back to the client in response to an *IConstructionCallMessage*.
ReturnMessage		Concrete class that implements *IMethodReturnMessage*. This class is documented so that you can conveniently construct your own return message if you want to intercept a method call to return a valid message without involving the remote object.

Now that we've discussed messages, we can start looking at the .NET Remoting objects that handle messages. We'll start at the client side, where remote object method calls originate and the .NET Remoting infrastructure creates the messages.

Proxies

In general programming terms, a *proxy object* is any object that stands in for another object and controls access to that other object. Controlling another object through a proxy can be useful for purposes such as delaying the creation of an object that has expensive startup costs or implementing access control. At a minimum, most remoting technologies—including .NET Remoting—use proxies to make remote objects appear to be local. These remoting technologies usually use proxies to perform a variety of tasks depending on the architecture.

The .NET Remoting proxy layers actually comprise two proxy objects: one implemented primarily in unmanaged code and the other implemented in managed code that you can customize. Splitting the proxy layer into two separate objects is a useful conceptual design that makes customizing this layer easier for complex scenarios. Before we start customizing the proxy layer, let's examine these two proxy objects.

TransparentProxy

Suppose you call *new* or *Activator.CreateInstance* to instantiate a remote object:

```
MyObj obj = new MyObj();
int Result = obj.MyMethod();
```

As soon as the line calling *new* returns, *MyObj* contains a reference to a type named *TransparentProxy*. The .NET Remoting infrastructure dynamically creates the *TransparentProxy* instance at run time by using reflection against the real object's metadata. .NET Framework reflection is a powerful technique for examining metadata at run time. Using reflection, the .NET Remoting infrastructure discovers the public interface of the real object and creates a *Transparent-Proxy* that mirrors this interface. (For more information about reflection, see Jeffrey Richter's book *Applied Microsoft .NET Framework Programming*.) The resulting *TransparentProxy* object implements the public methods, properties, and members of *MyObj*. The client code uses this local *TransparentProxy* object as a stand-in for the real remote object, which is located in another remoting subdivision, such as another context, application domain, process, or machine. Hereafter, you won't see any difference in the semantics of dealing with a local copy of *MyObj* and the *TransparentProxy* that mirrors the remote object.

The main job of the *TransparentProxy* is to intercept method calls to the remote object and pass them to the *RealProxy*, which does most of the proxy work. (We'll discuss *RealProxy* in a moment.) Using unmanaged code, *TransparentProxy* intercepts calls to what appears to the caller to be a local object and creates a *MessageData* struct, consisting mainly of pointers to unmanaged memory and thereby describing the method call. The *TransparentProxy* passes this struct to the *PrivateInvoke* method of the *RealProxy*. The *PrivateInvoke* method uses the *MessageData* struct to create the remoting messages that will be passed through the message sink chain and eventually delivered to the remote object.

Although *TransparentProxy* is the type of object that client code holds in lieu of the real remote object, you can't do anything to customize or extend *TransparentProxy*. *RealProxy* is the only proxy that you can customize.

RealProxy

RealProxy is a documented and extensible managed class that has a reference to the unmanaged black box named *TransparentProxy*. However, *RealProxy* is an abstract class and therefore isn't directly creatable. When the *Transparent-Proxy* instance hands off the *MessageData* object to the *RealProxy*, it's actually passing it to a concrete class that derives from *RealProxy* and is named *Remoting-Proxy*. *RemotingProxy* is an undocumented internal class, so we can't derive from it. Instead, we'll replace *RemotingProxy* and derive our own class from *RealProxy* so that we can seize control and customize remoting behavior. Although most extensions to remoting are done by using message sinks, some reasons to extend *RealProxy* exist. *RealProxy* affords us the first opportunity to intercept and customize both remote object construction and remote object method calls. However, because no corresponding customizable server-side proxy exists, you must use message sinks to perform tasks that require client-side processing and server-side processing, such as encryption and compression.

Extending *RealProxy*

To write a proxy to replace *RemotingProxy*, we need to derive a class from *RealProxy* and add a new constructor and private *MarshalByRefObject*, as shown here:

```
public class MyProxy : RealProxy
{
    MarshalByRefObject _target;
    public MyProxy(Type type, MarshalByRefObject target)
    : base(type)
    {
        _target = target;
    }
}
```

We need to capture the reference to the real *MarshalByRefObject* so that our proxy can forward calls to the real remote object. We also call the *RealProxy*'s constructor and pass the type of the remote object so that the .NET Remoting infrastructure can generate a *TransparentProxy* instance to stand in for the object.

Next we need to override the abstract *Invoke* method:

```
public override IMessage Invoke(IMessage msg)
{
    // Handle message
}
```

Invoke is the main extensibility point of *RealProxy*. Here we can customize and forward, refuse to forward, or ignore the messages sent by the *TransparentProxy* and destined for the real object.

Now that we have a compilable *RealProxy* derivative, the next step is to hook up this instance to a certain *MarshalByRefObject*, thereby replacing the *RemotingProxy* class. Two techniques exist for creating proxies: using a *ProxyAttribute* class and creating proxies directly. We'll explore both techniques in the examples discussed next.

Custom Proxies in Practice

Because the .NET Remoting infrastructure provides so many ways to extend the remoting architecture, you might find that you can perform certain customization tasks in more than one way. Although message sinks and channels tend to be the most useful remoting extensibility points, reasons to perform certain customizations by using proxies do exist. Because proxies don't have a customizable server-side companion layer, they're best used to perform client-centric interception work. On the other hand, if your customizations require both client intervention and server intervention, you'll need to use message sinks.

In this section, we'll look at three examples of custom proxies. First, we'll use a proxy to intercept the remote object activation process and demonstrate the differences between client activation and server activation. Next we'll use a proxy to switch between firewall-friendly channels and high-performing channels. We'll round out the proxy section by showing a load-balancing example that uses call context.

Activation Example

One interesting feature of proxies is that you can use them to intercept the activation of both client-activated and server-activated objects. By intercepting an object's activation, you can choose to activate another object (perhaps on another machine), modify client-activated object constructor arguments, or plug in a custom activator. Before we start, let's introduce the *ProxyAttribute* class.

The *ProxyAttribute* class provides a way to declare that we want the .NET Remoting framework to use our custom proxy instead of the default *Remoting-Proxy*. The only restriction to plugging in custom proxies this way is that the *ProxyAttribute* can be applied only to objects that derive from *ContextBound-Object*, which we'll examine along with contexts in Chapter 6, "Message Sinks and Contexts." Because *ContextBoundObject* derives from *MarshalByRefObject*, this limitation won't be a problem. To wire up a *ProxyAttribute*, first derive a class from *ProxyAttribute* and override the base *CreateInstance* method:

```
[AttributeUsage(AttributeTargets.Class)]
public class MyProxyAttribute : ProxyAttribute
{
    public override MarshalByRefObject CreateInstance(Type serverType)
    {
        MarshalByRefObject target = base.CreateInstance(serverType);
        MyProxy myProxy = new MyProxy(serverType, target);
        return (MarshalByRefObject)myProxy.GetTransparentProxy();
    }
}
```

Next attach the *ProxyAttribute* to the *ContextBoundObject*:

```
[MyProxyAttribute]
public class MyRemoteObject : ContextBoundObject
{
}
```

When you instantiate *MyRemoteObject*, the .NET Framework calls the over-ridden *CreateInstance* method, in which you instantiate the custom proxy. Next we instantiate our proxy and cast its *TransparentProxy* to *MarshalByRefObject* and return. By using this technique, the client can call *new* or *Activator.CreateInstance* as usual and still use the custom proxy.

To intercept activation, you need to perform the following tasks:

■   Define a *ProxyAttribute* class.

■   Define a *RealProxy* class, and override its *Invoke* method.

■   In the *Invoke* method, handle the *IConstructionCallMessage*.

■   Apply the *ProxyAttribute* to a *ContextBoundObject*.

Here's the *ProxyAttribute* listing for our activation example:

```
[AttributeUsage(AttributeTargets.Class)]
public class SProxyAttribute : ProxyAttribute
{
    public override System.MarshalByRefObject
                CreateInstance(System.Type serverType)
    {
        Console.WriteLine("SProxyAttribute.CreateInstance()");
        // Get a proxy to the real object.
        MarshalByRefObject mbr = base.CreateInstance(serverType);

        // Are we on the client side or the server side? This matters
        // because the .NET Remoting infrastructure on both sides of
        // the boundary will invoke this method. If we are on the
        // server side, we need to return the MBR provided by the
        // previous base.CreateInstance call, rather than our custom
        // proxy. If we return our custom proxy, the runtime throws
        // an exception when trying to invoke methods on it.
        //
        if ( RemotingConfiguration.IsActivationAllowed(serverType) )
        {
            return mbr;
        }
        else
        {
            WellKnownServiceTypeEntry[] wcte =
              RemotingConfiguration
              .GetRegisteredWellKnownServiceTypes();
            if ( wcte.Length > 0 )
            {
                foreach(WellKnownServiceTypeEntry e in wcte)
```

(continued)

```
            {
                if ( e.ObjectType == serverType )
                {
                    return mbr;
                }
            }
        }
    }

    // If we get here, we are running on the client side and we
    // can wrap the proxy with our proxy.
    if ( RemotingServices.IsTransparentProxy(mbr) )
    {
        // Wrap the proxy with our simple interception proxy.
        SimpleInterceptionProxy p =
            new SimpleInterceptionProxy(serverType, mbr);
        MarshalByRefObject mbr2 =
            (MarshalByRefObject)p.GetTransparentProxy();
        return mbr2;
    }
    else
    {
        // This is an actual MBR object.
        return mbr;
    }
}
```

Our overridden *ProxyAttribute.CreateInstance* method will be called when the remote object to which the attribute is attached is created. Inside *CreateInstance*, we first call the base *CreateInstance* to create a *TransparentProxy* to the real object. Next we need to be aware that *ProxyAttributes* are invoked for all remote object instances they attribute. This means that our *CreateInstance* method will run when the client instantiates the object reference and when the .NET Remoting infrastructure instantiates the object instance on the server. We want to handle only the client-side case, so we need to determine where this *ProxyAttribute* is running. To determine whether this attribute is running on the server, we first call *RemotingConfiguration.GetRegisteredWellKnownService-Types* to get an array of *WellKnownServiceTypeEntry*. If our type is in this array, we assume this code is running on the server and we can simply return the *TransparentProxy*. Otherwise, we assume we're running on the client, and we instantiate our interception proxy and return its *TransparentProxy*.

What happens next depends on whether the remote object is client activated or server activated. If the remote object is client activated, the .NET Remoting infrastructure will call our interception proxy's *Invoke* method before the client call to *new* or *Activator.CreateInstance* returns. If the remote object is server activated, the call to *new* or *Activator.GetObject* returns and our proxy's *Invoke* method isn't called until the first method call is made on the remote object.

Here's the code for our *SimpleInterceptionProxy*:

```
public override Invoke(IMessage msg)
{
    // Handle construction call message differently than other method
    // call messages.
    if ( msg is IConstructionCallMessage )
    {
        // Need to finish CAO activation manually.
        string url = GetUrlForCAO(_type);
        if ( url.Length > 0 )
        {
            ActivateCAO((IConstructionCallMessage)msg, url);
        }


        IConstructionReturnMessage crm =
            EnterpriseServicesHelper.CreateConstructionReturnMessage(
            (IConstructionCallMessage)msg,
            (MarshalByRefObject)this.GetTransparentProxy());
        return crm;
    }
    else
    {
        MethodCallMessageWrapper mcm =
            new MethodCallMessageWrapper((IMethodCallMessage)msg);
        mcm.Uri = RemotingServices.GetObjectUri(
            (MarshalByRefObject)_target);
        return RemotingServices.GetEnvoyChainForProxy(
            (MarshalByRefObject)_target).SyncProcessMessage(msg);
    }
}

private void ActivateCAO(IConstructionCallMessage ccm, string url)
{
    // Connect to remote activation service.
    string rem = url + @"/RemoteActivationService.rem";
    IActivator remActivator =
        (IActivator)RemotingServices.Connect(typeof(IActivator), rem);
    IConstructionReturnMessage crm = remActivator.Activate(ccm);

    //
    // The return message's ReturnValue property is the ObjRef for
    // the remote object. We need to unmarshal it into a local proxy
```

(continued)

```
        // to which we forward messages.
        ObjRef oRef = (ObjRef)crm.ReturnValue;
        _target = RemotingServices.Unmarshal(oRef);
}

string GetUrlForCAO(Type type)
{
    string s = "";
    ActivatedClientTypeEntry[] act =
      RemotingConfiguration.GetRegisteredActivatedClientTypes();
    foreach( ActivatedClientTypeEntry acte in act )
    {
        if ( acte.ObjectType == type )
        {
            s = acte.ApplicationUrl;
            break;
        }
    }
    return s;
}
```

Regardless of whether the remote object is client activated or server activated, the first message sent to the proxy's *Invoke* method is an *IConstruction-CallMessage*. As we'll discuss shortly, we must explicitly handle the activation of client-activated objects. We first determine the activation type by using our *GetUrlForCAO* method. This is similar to how we determined whether the *ProxyAttribute* was running on the client or the server. But instead of searching for registered server-activated types, we'll search the list of registered client-activated types by using the *RemotingConfiguration.GetRegisteredActivatedClient-Types* method. If we find the type of the remote object in the array of *ActivatedClientTypeEntry* objects, we return the entry's *ApplicationUrl* because we'll need this URL to perform client activation.

If the URL is empty, we assume that the object is server activated. Handling the construction message for a server-activated object is trivial. Recall that server-activated objects are implicitly created by the server application when a client makes the first method call on that object instance. If the URL isn't empty, we call *ActivateCAO* to handle client-activated object activation. This process is a bit more involved than the activation of server-activated objects because we must create a new instance of the remote object. When a client-activated object is registered on a server, the .NET Framework creates a server-activated object with the well-known URI *RemoteActivation.rem*. The framework then uses this server-activated object to create instances of the registered client-activated object. Because we've taken control of the activation process, we need to directly call the .NET Framework–created *RemoteActivation.rem* URI. First, we append *RemoteActivation.rem* to the *ActivatedClientTypeEntry*'s URL. Next, by using *RemotingServices.Connect*, we request an *Activator* for the desired client-activated object. We create the actual object instance by passing the *IConstruction-CallMessage* to the *Activator*'s *Activate* method, which returns an *IConstruction-ReturnMessage*. We then extract the *ObjRef* from *IConstructionReturnMessage* and unmarshal it to get our proxy to the remote object.

Finally, we decorate the *ContextBoundObject* with our *ProxyAttribute*:

```
[SProxyAttribute()]
public class CBRemoteObject : ContextBoundObject
{
    ⋮
}
```

Our custom proxy now properly handles the activation of both client-activated and server-activated objects. Next we'll examine a real-world example containing both the *IMethodCallMessage* and *IMethodReturnMessage* message types.

Channel Changer Example

Let's revisit the job assignment application from Chapter 3. Recall that while hosting the *JobLib* remote object under Microsoft Internet Information Services (IIS) made the job assignment application firewall friendly, performance suffered because IIS supports only *HttpChannel*. Suppose that some machines running the JobClient application are laptops whose users might be inside the firewall one day and outside it another. It would be nice to use the better-performing *TcpChannel* when working on the intranet and to switch back to *HttpChannel* when working on the Internet—all without the user's knowledge. Some distributed technologies do this by tunneling the TCP protocol over HTTP. We don't have to tunnel with .NET Remoting because we can solve the problem much more easily by using a custom proxy. Here are the basic steps we'll take to do this:

1. Register both TCP and HTTP channels on the server.

2. Host the remote object in a managed executable because IIS doesn't support *TcpChannel*.

3. Define a custom proxy.

4. Register an HTTP channel within the proxy.

5. Directly instantiate the proxy within the client code.

6. In the *Invoke* method, inspect the *Exception* property of *IMethod-ReturnMessage* and resend the message over HTTP if necessary.

JobServer Changes   We need to change JobServer so that it registers both a TCP channel and an HTTP channel:

```
// Register a listening channel.
TcpChannel oTcpJobChannel = new TcpChannel( 5556 );
ChannelServices.RegisterChannel( oTcpJobChannel );
HttpChannel oHttpJobChannel = new HttpChannel( 5555 );
ChannelServices.RegisterChannel( oHttpJobChannel );

// Register a well-known type.
RemotingConfiguration.RegisterWellKnownServiceType(
  typeof( JobServerImpl ), "JobURI", WellKnownObjectMode.Singleton );
```

The most interesting detail here is that no coupling exists between an object and the channel that accesses it. The single *JobServerImpl* object is accessible from all registered channels. Therefore, in this case, the client can make one method call over TCP and the next over HTTP.

JobClient Changes   Instead of using a *ProxyAttribute* to instantiate our custom proxy, we'll directly instantiate the proxy in the client code, as shown here:

```
MyProxy myProxy =
  new MyProxy(typeof(RemoteObject),  new RemoteObject());
RemoteObject foo = (RemoteObject)myProxy.GetTransparentProxy();
```

Although direct proxy creation is the simplest way to plug in a custom proxy, a couple of drawbacks to using this method exist:

■   The proxy can't intercept remote object activation. You might never need to customize the activation process, so this limitation generally isn't an issue.

■   The proxy can't be transparent to the client code. Because the client must directly instantiate the proxy, this creation must be hard-coded into the client code.

Custom Proxy Details   Our custom proxy contains all the interesting client-side logic for sending messages using either *TcpChannel* or *HttpChannel*. This class will register an *HttpChannel*, attempt to connect using *TcpChannel*, and, on failure, retry the connection using *HttpChannel*.

```
public class ChannelChangerProxy : RealProxy
{
    string _TcpUrl;
    string _HttpUrl;
    IMessageSink[] _messageSinks;
```

```csharp
public ChannelChangerProxy (Type type, string url)
: base(type)
{
    _TcpUrl = url;
    BuildHttpURL( url );
    _messageSinks = GetMessageSinks();
}


private void BuildHttpURL(string _TcpUrl)
{
    UriBuilder uBuilder = new UriBuilder(_TcpUrl);
    uBuilder.Port = 5555;
    uBuilder.Scheme = "http";
    _HttpUrl = uBuilder.ToString();
}


public override IMessage Invoke(IMessage msg)
{
    Exception InnerException;
    msg.Properties["__Uri"] = _TcpUrl;
    IMessage retMsg =
      _messageSinks[0].SyncProcessMessage( msg );
    if (retMsg is IMethodReturnMessage)
    {
        IMethodReturnMessage mrm = (IMethodReturnMessage)retMsg;
        if (mrm.Exception == null)
        {
            return retMsg;
        }
        else
        {
            InnerException = mrm.Exception;
        }
    }
    // On failure, retry by using the HTTP channel.
    msg.Properties["__Uri"] = _HttpUrl;
    retMsg = _messageSinks[1].SyncProcessMessage( msg );
    if (retMsg is IMethodReturnMessage)
    {
        IMethodReturnMessage mrm = (IMethodReturnMessage)retMsg;
    }
    return retMsg;
}


private IMessageSink[] GetMessageSinks()
{
    IChannel[] registeredChannels =
      ChannelServices.RegisteredChannels;
    IMessageSink MessageSink;
```

(continued)

```
string ObjectURI;
ArrayList MessageSinks = new ArrayList();
foreach (IChannel channel in registeredChannels )
{
    if (channel is IChannelSender)
    {
        IChannelSender channelSender =
          (IChannelSender)channel;
        MessageSink = channelSender.CreateMessageSink(
                  _TcpUrl, null, out ObjectURI);
        if (MessageSink != null)
        {
            MessageSinks.Add( MessageSink );
        }
    }
}
string objectURI;
HttpChannel HttpChannel = new HttpChannel();
ChannelServices.RegisterChannel(HttpChannel);
MessageSinks.Add(HttpChannel.CreateMessageSink(
                  _HttpUrl, HttpChannel, out objectURI));
if (MessageSinks.Count > 0)
{
    return (IMessageSink[])MessageSinks.ToArray(
                      typeof(IMessageSink));
}
// Made it out of the foreach block without finding
// a MessageSink for the URL.
throw new
  Exception("Unable to find a MessageSink for the URL:" +
          _TcpUrl);
    }
}
```

The *ChannelChangerProxy* constructor expects a URL with a TCP scheme as an argument. Next we call *BuildHttpUrl* to change the port and scheme to the URL of the JobServer's well-known HTTP channel. In this case, we hard-coded the HTTP port as 80, but you can read these values from a configuration file for greater flexibility. When we get a message within the *Invoke* method, we'll eventually forward it to the first message sink in the chain. We'll look at customizing message sinks in detail in Chapter 6, "Message Sinks and Contexts," but for now, we'll just create and use the default sinks.

In the *GetMessageSinks* method, we enumerate the registered channels. (In this case, we registered only the single TCP channel.) When we find the registered channel, we create the message sink that will forward messages to the given URL (in this case, *tcp://JobMachine:5555/JobURI*) and store it in the message sink *ArrayList*. Because the client knows nothing about the proxy's intentions to use HTTP, we need to register an HTTP channel and then create and store its message sink.

Because the JobServer hosts a server-activated object, there won't be a constructor call or any traffic to the remote server until the first method call. Our *Invoke* method will get its first message when the client calls the first method on JobServerLib. When this happens, the *TransparentProxy* calls our proxy's *Real-Proxy.PrivateInvoke* base class method, which constructs a message and then passes it to our *Invoke* method. We pass the message directly to the *TcpChannel's* message sink by using *SyncProcessMessage*. *SyncProcessMessage* returns an *IMethodReturnMessage* object that we'll inspect to determine the success of the remote method call. On failure, the .NET Remoting infrastructure won't throw an exception but instead will populate the *Exception* property of *IMethod-ReturnMessage*. If the server is running, if no firewall exists to prevent the TCP traffic, and if no other problems delivering the message occur, the *Exception* property is *null* and we simply return the *IMethodReturnMessage* from *Invoke*.

If an exception occurs, we retry the operation by using the *HttpChannel* and the HTTP-specific URL. But we have to change the *__Uri* property on the message to the HTTP URL before sending out the message. If this operation fails too, we return the *IMethodReturnMessage* so that the .NET Remoting infrastructure can throw an exception.

In this example, we used a custom proxy to equip the job assignment application to support both high-performance communications and firewall-friendly communications without requiring the client code to make this determination. Even better, the .NET Remoting infrastructure enabled us to perform the task at a high level and to avoid programming at the HTTP and TCP protocol level.

Now let's consider a more involved example of custom proxies: using a *ProxyAttribute* and call context.

Load-Balancing Example

Suppose that the JobServer needs to scale to support hundreds or thousands of users and must be available at all times for these users to get their work done. The current architecture of having a single JobServer doesn't support these requirements. Instead, we need to run redundant JobServer applications on different machines, all of which have access to the latest data for a JobClient. We also need a technique for balancing the load across the JobServers. We'll have to make several changes to the JobServer's design, yet by using a custom proxy, we can make the fact that the JobClient will be connecting to more than one JobServer transparent to the client code. Implementing a real-world multi-server example would require some way to share data, probably by using a database. We'll leave that as an exercise for you to pursue on your own. Instead, this example focuses on the proxy details.

Here's the list of tasks this example requires:

- Construct a discovery server located at an endpoint known to the client.

- Construct a proxy that intercepts the client's calls and then calls the discovery server to get a list of redundant servers that we can dispatch calls to.

- Create a separate proxy for each redundant server's remote object.

- In the proxy, intercept the client's method calls and dispatch the calls to the proxies in a round-robin fashion.

- Add call context to transparently support load balancing.

***LoadBalancingServer* Changes**   To support discovery of other redundant servers, we'll add those servers' well-known URLs to the *LoadBalancingServer*'s configuration file, as shown here:

```
<configuration>
<appSettings>
    <add key="PeerUrl1" value="tcp://localhost:5556/JobURI"/>
    <add key="PeerUrl2" value="tcp://localhost:5557/JobURI"/>
    <add key="PeerUrl3" value="tcp://localhost:5558/JobURI"/>
</appSettings>
⋮
```

***RemoteObject* Changes**   To support a discovery server *JobServerImpl*, we'll implement a new interface, as follows:

```
public interface IDiscoveryServer
{
    string[] GetPeerServerUrls();
}

public string[] GetPeerServerUrls()
{
    ArrayList PeerUrls = new ArrayList();
    bool UrlsFound = true;
    string BaseKeyString = "PeerUrl";
    string KeyString;
    int Count = 0;
    while(UrlsFound)
    {
        KeyString = BaseKeyString + (++Count).ToString();
        string PeerUrl = ConfigurationSettings.AppSettings[KeyString];
        if (PeerUrl != null)
```

```
    {
        PeerUrls.Add(PeerUrl);
    }
    else
    {
        UrlsFound = false;
    }
    }
    return (string[])PeerUrls.ToArray( typeof(string) );
}
```

The intent here is to return the configured list of servers on request. The JobServer example doesn't perform any time-consuming tasks, so we'll add a method and simulate the load by causing the server to sleep for anywhere from 1 to 6 seconds:

```
public bool DoExpensiveOperation()
{
    Random Rand = new Random();
    int RandomNumber = Rand.Next(1000, 6000);
    System.Threading.Thread.Sleep( RandomNumber );
}
```

Custom Proxy Details   Instead of using a round-robin approach in which the client has to know the location of all the servers, we can use a discovery server to tell us where the other servers are located. This way, we need to publish only a single well-known discovery server URL. Although we do introduce a single point of failure at discovery time, we can add more discovery servers to get around this problem.

Adding Call Context

Now suppose that you want to add data to a method call without modifying the argument list. Many reasons for doing this exist, including the following:

■ You don't want to change an object's interface, possibly because of versioning reasons.

■ You don't want the caller to know that this information is being sent, possibly for security reasons.

■ You want to send data with many varying method calls, and adding redundant arguments would pollute the method signatures. Web servers send such data by issuing cookies that browsers retain and then seamlessly piggyback on an HTTP request to the Web server. Most nonbrowser-based applications must send this cookie data as a parameter to every method call.

We could solve all these problems if we could pass a boilerplate method parameter to and from methods behind the scenes, just as browsers do with cookies. This is exactly the what call context does.

In our example, we could balance the load on the servers by using a simple round-robin scheme, but it would be better if the servers told us what their load was and sent the next message to the server that's the least loaded. We can solve this problem very nicely by using call context.

What Is Call Context?   *CallContext* is an object that flows between application domains and can be inspected by various intercepting objects (such as proxies and message sinks) along the way. *CallContext* is also available within the client and server code, so it can be used to augment the data that's passed between method calls—without changing the parameter list. You simply put an object into *CallContext* by using the *SetData* method and remove it by using the *GetData* method. To support *CallContext*, the contained object must be marked with the *Serializable* attribute and must inherit the *ILogicalThreadAffinative* interface. *ILogicalThreadAffinative* is simply a marker and doesn't require that the object implement any methods.

Here's the object we'll place into *CallContext*:

```
[Serializable]
public class CallContextData : ILogicalThreadAffinative
{
    int _CurrentConnections;
    public CallContextData(int CurrentConnections)
    {
        _CurrentConnections = CurrentConnections;
    }

    public int CurrentConnections
    {
        get
        {
            return _CurrentConnections;
        }
    }
}
```

CallContextData is merely a wrapper around an *int* that allows us to send this variable via *CallContext*. By using *CallContextData*, the server will return the total number of connected clients. Our proxy will use this value to prioritize the calling order of the redundant server proxies. Of course, this simple example doesn't really support real-world load balancing because the connection count likely won't be up to date by the time we make the next method call. However,

the example does show the power of using proxies and call context together—
the client code needn't be aware that its calls are dispatched to various servers
and that additional data that isn't part of any method's parameter list is flowing
between client and server.

Server Call Context   We add these lines to *DoExpensiveWork* to populate the
call context with the current client connection count:

```
_CurrentConnections++;
  ⋮
CallContextData ccd = new CallContextData(_CurrentConnections--);
CallContext.SetData("CurrentConnections", ccd);
```

Then we extract the value in the client-side proxy:

```
object oCurrentConnections =
  CallContext.GetData("CurrentConnections");
```

Proxy Changes   The following is the complete listing for our *LoadBalancing-
Proxy* class:

```
public class LoadBalancingManager
{
    ArrayList _LoadBalancedServers = new ArrayList();
    public class LoadBalancedServer
    {
        public MarshalByRefObject Proxy;
        public int CurrentConnections;
        public bool IsActive;
    }

    public void AddProxy(MarshalByRefObject Proxy)
    {
        LoadBalancedServer lbs = new LoadBalancedServer();
        lbs.Proxy = Proxy;
        lbs.CurrentConnections = 0;
        lbs.IsActive = true;
        _LoadBalancedServers.Add(lbs);
    }

    public void SetCurrentConnections(MarshalByRefObject Proxy,
                                      int CurrentConnections)
    {
        foreach (LoadBalancedServer lbs in _LoadBalancedServers)
        {
            if (lbs.Proxy == Proxy)
            {
```

(continued)

```
                lbs.CurrentConnections = CurrentConnections;
                return;
            }
        }
    }

    public MarshalByRefObject GetLeastLoadedServer()
    {
        LoadBalancedServer LeastLoadedServer = null;
        foreach (LoadBalancedServer CurrentServer
                in _LoadBalancedServers)
        {
            if (LeastLoadedServer == null)
            {
                LeastLoadedServer = CurrentServer;
                continue;
            }
            if (CurrentServer.CurrentConnections <
                LeastLoadedServer.CurrentConnections)
            {
                LeastLoadedServer = CurrentServer;
            }
        }

        if (LeastLoadedServer == null)
        {
            return null;
        }
        else
        {
            return LeastLoadedServer.Proxy;
        }
    }
}

public class LoadBalancingProxy : RealProxy
{
    LoadBalancingManager LoadManager;
    int MaxProxies;

    public LoadBalancingProxy (Type type, string DiscoveryUrl)
    : base(type)
    {
```

```
        MarshalByRefObject ftp =
          (MarshalByRefObject)RemotingServices.Connect(type,
                                                DiscoveryUrl,
                                                null);
        IDiscoveryServer discoveryServer = (IDiscoveryServer)ftp;
        string[] PeerUrls = discoveryServer.GetPeerServerUrls();
        LoadManager = new LoadBalancingManager();
        foreach( string Url in PeerUrls)
        {
            MarshalByRefObject PeerServer =
              (MarshalByRefObject)RemotingServices.Connect(type, Url,
                                                null);
            LoadManager.AddProxy(PeerServer);
        }
    }

    public override IMessage Invoke(IMessage msg)
    {
        MarshalByRefObject CurrentServer =
          LoadManager.GetLeastLoadedServer();
        if (CurrentServer == null)
        {
            throw new Exception(
              "No remote servers are responding at this time.");
        }
        RealProxy rp = RemotingServices.GetRealProxy(CurrentServer);
        IMessage retMsg = rp.Invoke(msg);
        if (retMsg is IMethodReturnMessage)
        {
            IMethodReturnMessage mrm = (IMethodReturnMessage)retMsg;
            if (mrm.Exception == null)
            {
                // Check for call context.
                object oCurrentConnections =
                  CallContext.GetData("CurrentConnections");
                if (oCurrentConnections == null)
                {
                    // Because the server didn't send back any load
                    // information, consider it least loaded.
                    LoadManager.SetCurrentConnections( CurrentServer,
                                                0);
                }
                else if (oCurrentConnections is CallContextData)
                {
                LoadManager.SetCurrentConnections( CurrentServer,
```

(continued)

```
                        ((CallContextData)oCurrentConnections)
                          .CurrentConnections);
                    }
                    return retMsg;
                }
            }
            return retMsg;
        }
}
```

We've added a *LoadBalancingManager* class to control the details of our load-balancing algorithm. This class's primary job is to maintain a prioritized list of proxies based on the smallest client connection load. Our custom proxy will call *GetLeastLoadedServer* to dispatch each new method call.

Call Context Message Flow

Call context data is piggybacked on a method call but isn't necessarily related to the specific method. In accordance, the .NET Remoting infrastructure sends our *CallContextData* object via the SOAP header rather than the SOAP *Body* element. Here's the response SOAP message for the *DoExpensiveWork* method call:

```
<SOAP-ENV:Header>
    <h4:__CallContext href="#ref-3"
      xmlns:h4="http://schemas.microsoft.com/
      clr/soap/messageProperties" SOAP-ENC:root="1">
    <a1:LogicalCallContext id="ref-3"
      xmlns:a1="http://schemas.microsoft.com/clr/ns/
      System.Runtime.Remoting.Messaging">
      <CurrentConnections href="#ref-6"/>
    </a1:LogicalCallContext>
    <a2:CallContextData id="ref-6"
      xmlns:a2="http://schemas.microsoft.com/clr/nsassem/
      LoadBalancing/DiscoveryServerLib%2C%20
      Version%3D1.0.871.14847%2C%20Culture%3Dneutral%2C%20
      PublicKeyToken%3Dnull">
      <_CurrentConnections>1</_CurrentConnections>
    </a2:CallContextData>
</SOAP-ENV:Header>

<SOAP-ENV:Body>
    <i7:DoExpensiveOperationResponse id="ref-1"
      xmlns:i7="http://schemas.microsoft.com/clr/nsassem/
      LoadBalancing.IJobServer/LoadBalancingLib">
      <return>true</return>
    </i7:DoExpensiveOperationResponse>
</SOAP-ENV:Body>
```

Summary

This completes our discussion of messages and proxies. After examining messages, we used a variety of message types in our custom proxy examples and message sinks. Because messages are the fundamental unit of data transfer in .NET Remoting applications, we'll use them extensively in Chapters 6, 7, and 8 of this book. Next we discussed custom proxies and their uses as a client-centric part of the .NET Remoting infrastructure. Understanding proxies is important because they generate messages and are the first layer exposed to the client code. We discussed three classes that comprise the .NET Remoting proxy layer and showed how you can create your own proxy to intercept activation and general method calls. Because proxies are the first customizable object in the .NET Remoting infrastructure, they're ideal for intercepting the activation process and controlling the dispatching of remote method calls. In Chapter 6, we'll discuss contexts in depth, after we cover message sinks.

6

Message Sinks and Contexts

In this chapter, we'll continue exploring the customization of the .NET Remoting architecture by customizing features of the context architecture and message sinks. A deeper understanding of contexts and message sinks can help you design more efficient and powerful .NET Remoting applications. We'll use message sinks and contexts to prevent a client of a remote object from making a remote method call if the client passes invalid parameters to a method, thus saving a round-trip to the remote object. We'll also look at how you can trace messages and log exceptions thrown across context boundaries.

Message Sinks

Message sinks are one of the most important elements contributing to the extreme flexibility of the .NET Remoting architecture. In Chapter 2, "Understanding the .NET Remoting Architecture," we discussed how the .NET Remoting infrastructure connects message sinks together to form message sink chains, which process .NET Remoting messages and move them through contexts and application domains. The .NET Remoting infrastructure uses message sinks in a variety of functional areas, including these:

- Contexts, which we'll discuss in the next section of this chapter

- Channels, which we'll discuss in Chapter 7, "Channels and Channel Sinks"

- Formatters, which we'll discuss in Chapter 8, "Serialization Formatters"

IMessageSink

Any type that implements the *IMessageSink* interface can participate in the .NET Remoting architecture as a message sink. Table 6-1 lists the members of the *IMessageSink* interface.

Table 6-1 Members of *System.Runtime.Remoting.Messaging.IMessageSink*

Member	Member Type	Description
NextSink	Read-only property	The next message sink in the chain, or *null* if this is the last sink in the chain
AsyncProcessMessage	Method	Processes the message asynchronously
SyncProcessMessage	Method	Processes the message synchronously

The following code defines a class that implements *IMessageSink*:

```
public class PassThruMessageSink : IMessageSink
{
    ImessageSink _NextSink;

    public IMessageSink NextSink
    {
        get
        {
            return _NextSink;
        }
    }

    public PassThruMessageSink( IMessageSink next )
    {
        _NextSink = next;
    }

    public virtual IMessage SyncProcessMessage ( IMessage msg )
    {
        try
        {
            return _NextSink.SyncProcessMessage(msg);
        }
        catch(System.Exception e)
        {
            return new ReturnMessage(e, (IMethodCallMessage) msg);
        }
    }
```

```
public virtual IMessageCtrl AsyncProcessMessage( IMessage msg,
                                    IMessageSink replySink )
{
    try
    {
        AsyncReplyHelperSink.AsyncReplyHelperSinkDelegate rsd =
            new AsyncReplyHelperSink.AsyncReplyHelperSinkDelegate(
                            this.AsyncProcessReplyMessage );

        replySink = (IMessageSink)new AsyncReplyHelperSink(
                                        replySink,
                                        rsd );

        // Pass message to next sink.
        return _NextSink.AsyncProcessMessage( msg, replySink );
    }
    catch(System.Exception e)
    {
        return null;
    }
}


//
// When the async call completes, our helper class will call
// this method, at which point we can process the return message.
public IMessage AsyncProcessReplyMessage( IMessage msg )
{
    // Process the return message, and return it.
    return msg;
}
} // End class PassThruMessageSink
```

The *PassThruMessageSink* class is a valid *IMessageSink* implementation, although it simply passes the *IMessage* to the next sink in the chain. However, this class does show the general way of implementing *IMessageSink*, so let's examine the more interesting methods in detail.

Synchronous Message Processing

IMessageSink.SyncProcessMessage looks simple enough. As its name implies, *IMessageSink.SyncProcessMessage* processes the request message in a synchronous manner by passing that message to the next sink's *SyncProcessMessage* method. Synchronous processing completes only after the .NET Remoting infrastructure receives and returns the response message from the method call on the remote object, in which case the return value of *SyncProcessMessage* is an *IMessage* that encapsulates the return value of the method call and any *out* parameters.

If an exception occurs during message processing, we wrap the exception in a *ReturnMessage*, which we return to the caller. This isn't the same thing as an exception occurring during execution of the remote object's method. In that case, the response message returned by the .NET Remoting infrastructure on the server side encapsulates the exception thrown on the server side.

Asynchronous Message Processing

The .NET Remoting infrastructure processes asynchronous method calls by invoking the *IMessageSink.AsyncProcessMessage* method. Unlike *SyncProcessMessage*, *AsyncProcessMessage* doesn't process both the request and response messages. Instead, *AsyncProcessMessage* processes the request message and returns. Later, when the asynchronous operation completes, the .NET Remoting infrastructure (ironically) passes the response message to the *IMessageSink.SyncProcessMessage* method of the sink referenced by the second parameter to the *AsyncProcessMessage* method, *replySink*. If you need to process the response message of an asynchronous call, you must add a message sink to the front of the *replySink* chain prior to passing the request message to the next sink in the chain.

To facilitate implementing *AsyncProcessMessage*, we've defined a helper class named *AsyncReplyHelperSink* that takes a delegate to a callback method that it invokes upon receiving an *IMessage* in *SyncProcessMessage*:

```
//
// Generic AsyncReplyHelperSink class - delegates calls to
// SyncProcessMessage to delegate instance passed in ctor.
public class AsyncReplyHelperSink : IMessageSink
{
    // Define a delegate to the callback method.
    public delegate IMessage AsyncReplyHelperSinkDelegate(IMessage msg);

    IMessageSink               _NextSink;
    AsyncReplyHelperSinkDelegate _delegate;

    public System.Runtime.Remoting.Messaging.IMessageSink NextSink
    {
        get
        {
            return _NextSink;
        }
    }

    public AsyncReplyHelperSink( IMessageSink next,
                                 AsyncReplyHelperSinkDelegate d )
    {
        _NextSink = next;
```

```
            _delegate = d;
    }

    public virtual IMessage SyncProcessMessage (IMessage msg )
    {
        if ( _delegate != null )
        {
            // Notify delegate of reply message. The delegate
            // can modify the message, so save the result and
            // pass it down the chain.
            IMessage msg2 = _delegate(msg);
            return _NextSink.SyncProcessMessage(msg2);
        }
        else
        {
            return new ReturnMessage(
                new System.Exception(
                    "AsyncProcessMessage _delegate member is null!"),
                (IMethodCallMessage)msg );
        }
    }

    public virtual IMessageCtrl AsyncProcessMessage (
        System.Runtime.Remoting.Messaging.IMessage msg ,
        System.Runtime.Remoting.Messaging.IMessageSink replySink )
    {
        // This should not be called in the reply sink chain. The
        // runtime processes reply messages to asynchronous calls
        // synchronously. Someone must be trying to use us in a
        // different chain!
        return null;
    }
}
```

The *PassThruMessageSink* class uses the helper class by instantiating a delegate that targets its *AsyncProcessReplyMessage* method, passing the delegate to a new instance of the helper class, and adding the instance of the helper class to the reply sink chain. We'll use the *AsyncReplyHelperSink* class in several examples in the next section.

Understanding Contexts

In Chapter 2, we introduced the concept of context. Now it's time to look at the role of contexts within the .NET Remoting infrastructure. A better understanding of context can help you design more efficient .NET Remoting applications. In this section, we'll look at how you can customize features of the context architecture to prevent the client from making a remote method call if it passes invalid parameters to a method, thus saving a round-trip to the remote object. We'll also look at how you can trace messages and log exceptions thrown across context boundaries.

Establishing a Context

The context architecture employed by .NET Remoting consists of context-bound objects, context attributes, context properties, and message sinks. Any type derived from *System.ContextBoundObject* is a context-bound type and indicates to the .NET Remoting infrastructure that it requires a special environment, or context, for its instances to execute within. During activation of a context-bound type, the runtime will perform the following sequence of actions:

1. Invoke the *IContextAttribute.IsContextOK* method on each attribute for the type.

2. If any attribute indicated that the context wasn't OK for activation, invoke the *IContextAttribute.GetPropertiesForNewContext* method on each attribute, passing the constructor call message for the type being activated.

3. Construct the context.

4. Notify each context property that the context is frozen by invoking the *IContextProperty.Freeze* method on each context property.

5. Ask each context property whether the new context is OK by invoking the *IContextProperty.IsNewContextOK* method.

6. Activate the object in the new context, passing the constructor call message to the proxy object's *RealProxy.Invoke* method.

Context Attributes and Properties

You define and establish a context by attributing the context-bound type with one or more attributes that implement the *IContextAttribute* interface. Table 6-2 shows the methods that *IContextAttribute* defines.

Table 6-2   Members of *System.Runtime.Remoting.Contexts.IContextAttribute*

Member	Description
IsContextOK	The runtime calls this method to determine whether the current context is OK for activation of the attributed type.
GetPropertiesForNewContext	The runtime calls this method after an attribute has indicated that the current context isn't OK for activation of the attributed type.

As an alternative, you can derive a type from *System.ContextAttribute,* which derives from *System.Attribute* and provides a default implementation of *IContextAttribute. System.ContextAttribute* also implements *IContextProperty,* which we'll discuss shortly.

A context attribute participates in the activation process and performs the following functions:

■   Indicates to the .NET Remoting infrastructure whether the current context meets the execution requirements of the attributed type.

■   Contributes to the context one or more properties that provide services and/or enforce execution requirements of the attributed type.

During activation of a type derived from *ContextBoundObject,* the runtime invokes the *IContextAttribute.IsContextOK* method on each of the type's context attributes to determine whether the current context supports the execution requirements of that type. An attribute indicates that the current context is unacceptable by returning *false* from the *IsContextOK* method.

If any attribute on a type derived from *ContextBoundObject* returns *false* from *IContextAttribute.IsContextOK,* the runtime will create a new context for the object instance and call the *IContextAttribute.GetPropertiesForNewContext* method on each attribute. This allows the attribute to contribute one or more context properties that enforce the type's execution requirements. Context properties implement *IContextProperty.* Table 6-3 shows the members of *IContextProperty.*

Table 6-3   Members of *System.Runtime.Remoting.Contexts.IContextProperty*

Member	Member Type	Description
Name	Read-only property	The name of the property. Used as a key in the property collection for the context.
Freeze	Method	The .NET Remoting infrastructure calls this method after allowing all attributes to add properties to the context. After freezing the context, the .NET Remoting infrastructure disallows the addition of more context properties.
IsNewContextOK	Method	The runtime calls this method after freezing the context to give each context property a chance to abort creation of the context.

For example, suppose we want to create a context that provides a common logging facility to all its objects. The idea is that any code executing within the context could obtain a logging object from the context properties and call a method that logs a message. To implement a solution for the logging context, we need to implement a context attribute that contributes a context property providing the logging service. The following code defines a context attribute named *ContextLogAttribute*:

```
using System.Runtime.Remoting.Contexts;

[AttributeUsage(AttributeTargets.Class)]
class ContextLogAttribute : Attribute,
                            IContextAttribute
{
    public bool IsContextOK(
        System.Runtime.Remoting.Contexts.Context ctx,
        System.Runtime.Remoting.Activation.IConstructionCallMessage
        msg)
    {
        // Force new context.
        return false;
    }

    public void GetPropertiesForNewContext(
        System.Runtime.Remoting.Activation.IConstructionCallMessage
        msg)
    {
        // Add our property to the context.
        msg.ContextProperties.Add(new ContextLogProperty());
    }
}
```

During activation of a type derived from *ContextBoundObject* that's attributed with *ContextLogAttribute*, the .NET Remoting infrastructure calls *GetPropertiesForNewContext*, passing it the *IConstructionCallMessage*. At this point, the object hasn't yet been instantiated. Thus, the object's constructor method hasn't yet been called. *GetPropertiesForNewContext* adds a new instance of the *ContextLogProperty* class defined in the following code snippet to the *ContextProperties* member of the *IConstructionCallMessage*:

```
[AttributeUsage(AttributeTargets.Class)]
class ContextLogProperty : Attribute,
                           IContextProperty
{
    public void Freeze(
        System.Runtime.Remoting.Contexts.Context newContext)
    {
        // At this point, no more properties will be added.
    }

    public bool IsNewContextOK(
        System.Runtime.Remoting.Contexts.Context newCtx)
```

```
    {
        // We could also inspect the other properties
        // for the context to make sure none conflict,
        // but for this example, we just report A-OK.
        return true;
    }

    public string Name
    {
        get
        {
            return "ContextLogProperty";
        }
    }

    public void LogMessage(string msg)
    {
        Console.WriteLine(msg);
    }
}
```

The *ContextLogProperty* class implements the logging functionality. Because it's a context property, any object instances within the context can obtain an instance of the property and use it to log messages:

```
[ContextLogAttribute()]
class MyContextBoundObject : System.ContextBoundObject
{
    public void Foo()
    {
        Context ctx = Thread.CurrentContext;
        ContextLogProperty lg =
          (ContextLogProperty)ctx.GetProperty("ContextLogProperty");
        lg.LogMessage("In MyContextBoundObject.Foo()");
    }
}
```

Contexts and Remoting

Recall that the context forms a .NET Remoting boundary around object instances within it. Figure 6-1 illustrates how the .NET Remoting infrastructure isolates an object instance within a context from object instances outside the context by using a special type of channel known as a *cross-context channel* and four chains of message sinks that separate inbound message processing from outbound message processing.

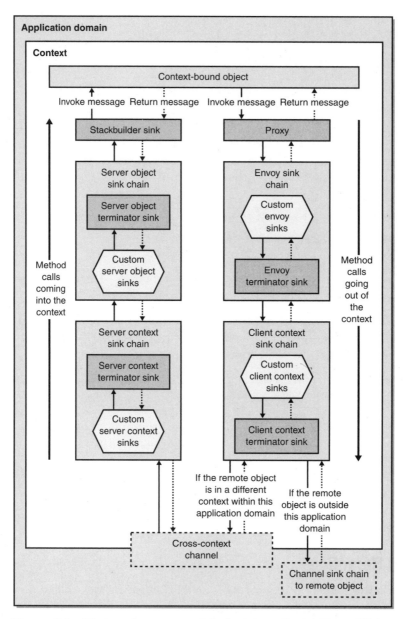

Figure 6-1 Chains of message sinks isolate a *ContextBoundObject* instance from objects outside the context.

All method calls entering the context enter as .NET Remoting messages, which flow through the cross-context channel, a contextwide server context sink chain, an object-specific server object sink chain, and the stackbuilder sink.

All method calls made to objects outside the context exit as .NET Remoting messages, which flow through a proxy and its associated envoy sink chain, a contextwide client context sink chain, and the channel (either cross context or application domain). Each sink chain consists of zero or more custom message sinks followed by a special terminator message sink that the .NET Remoting infrastructure defines.

As shown in Table 6-4, the message sink chain to which you add your message sink largely depends on when and where you want to enforce the context behavior for method call messages entering and exiting the context.

Table 6-4 Context Sink Chains

Sink Chain	Intercepts	Possible Usage
Client context	Method calls made by any object within the context on objects located outside the context.	■ Logging all method call messages exiting the context ■ Synchronization ■ Security ■ Transactions
Server context	Method calls made on any objects within the context from objects located outside the context.	■ Logging all method call messages entering the context ■ Synchronization ■ Security ■ Transactions
Server object	Method calls made on a specific context-bound object.	■ Interception of method call methods specific to an object instance ■ Might operate in conjuction with envoy sink to convey information from client context to server context
Envoy	Calls made by a client of the context-bound object. The envoy sink chain executes in the context of the client.	■ Validating method arguments prior to sending the method call message from the client to the server ■ Other method optimizations that are better performed in the context of the client

Before we discuss context sink chains in detail, let's examine the other kind of sink that's applicable to context but doesn't participate in sink chains: the dynamic context sink.

Dynamic Context Sinks

The .NET Remoting infrastructure supports the ability to programmatically register object instances of types implementing the *IDynamicMessageSink* into the context's message processing architecture at run time. Dynamic sinks aren't "true" message sinks because they don't implement *IMessageSink* and they aren't linked into chains. Dynamic sinks allow you to intercept method call messages at various points during message processing.

Creating a Custom Dynamic Sink

To create a custom dynamic context sink, you need to perform the following tasks:

- Define a dynamic message sink class that implements the *IDynamicMessageSink* interface.

- Define a dynamic property class that implements the *IDynamicProperty* and the *IContributeDynamicSink* interfaces.

- In the implementation of the *IContributeDynamicSink.GetDynamicSink* method, return an instance of the dynamic message sink class.

- Programmatically register and unregister the dynamic property by using the *Context.RegisterDynamicProperty* and *Context.UnregisterDynamicProperty* methods, respectively.

Table 6-5 shows how the parameters to the *Context.RegisterDynamicProperty* method dictate interception behavior. For each registered dynamic sink at a given interception level, the runtime calls the sink's *IDynamicMessageSink.ProcessMessageStart* method prior to processing a method call, passing it the *IMessage* representing the method call. Likewise, the .NET Remoting infrastructure calls the sink's *IDynamicMessageSink.ProcessMessageFinish* after a method call has returned, passing it the *IMessage* representing the response message of the method call.

Table 6-5   *Context.RegisterDynamicProperty* **Interception Behavior**

ContextBoundObject Parameter	*Context* Parameter	Interception Level
Reference to a proxy	*null*	Intercepts all method calls on the proxy
Reference to a real object	*null*	Intercepts all method calls on the real object
null	Reference to a context	Intercepts all method calls entering and leaving the context
null	*null*	Intercepts all method calls entering and leaving all contexts in the application domain

Client Context Sink Chain

As Figure 6-1 shows, the client context sink chain is the last sink chain through which messages flow on their way out of the context. However, the figure doesn't show that this chain is contextwide and that all outgoing method calls made by all objects within the context travel through this chain. You can implement behavior that applies to all outgoing method calls made by all object instances within the context by implementing a client context sink.

The .NET Remoting infrastructure inserts custom client context sinks at the front of the chain so that the last sink in the chain is the *System.Runtime.Remoting.Contexts.ClientContextTerminatorSink*. An application domain contains a single instance of this class that performs the following functions for all contexts within the application domain:

1. Notifies dynamic sinks that a method call leaving the context is starting.

2. Passes *IConstructionCallMessage* messages to any context properties implementing *IContextActivatorProperty* before calling the *Activator.Activate* method in the message to activate an instance of a remote object, and passes the *IConstructionReturnMessage* to any context properties implementing *IContextActivatorProperty* after *Activator.Activate* returns. Allows properties to modify the constructor call message and, on return, the constructor return message.

3. Passes non-*IConstructorCallMessage* messages onto either the *CrossContextChannel* or a suitable channel leaving the application domain, such as *HttpChannel* or *TcpChannel*.

4. Notifies any dynamic sinks that a method call leaving the context has finished. (For asynchronous calls, the *AsyncReplySink* handles this step when the call actually completes.)

Creating a Custom Client Context Sink

To create a custom client context sink, you need to perform the following tasks:

- Implement a message sink that performs the context-specific logic for all method calls leaving the context.

- Define a context property that implements the *IContributeClientContextSink* interface.

- Define a context attribute that contributes the context property defined in the previous step to the context properties in the construction call message during the call to *IContextAttribute.GetPropertiesForNewContext*.

- Apply the context attribute to the class declaration.

Server Context Sink Chain

The counterpart to the client context sink chain is the server context sink chain. As Figure 6-1 shows, the server context sink chain is the first sink chain through which messages flow on their way into the context. Like the client context sink chain, this chain is contextwide, and incoming method calls made by all objects outside the context travel through this chain. You can implement behavior that applies to all incoming method calls made by objects outside the context by implementing a server context sink.

The .NET Remoting infrastructure builds the server context sink chain by enumerating over the context properties in reverse order relative to the building of the client context sink chain. This is allows and preserves a symmetry of the order of operations performed during message sink processing between the two chains in the event that a property contributes a sink to both chains. The .NET Remoting infrastructure inserts custom server context sinks at the front of the chain so that the last sink in the chain is the *System.Runtime.Remoting.Contexts.Server-ContextTerminatorSink*. An application domain will contain a single instance of this class that performs the following functions for all contexts within the application domain:

■ Passes *IConstructionCallMessage* messages to any context properties implementing *IContextActivatorProperty* before calling the *Activator.Activate* method in the message to activate an instance of the server object, and passes the *IConstructionReturnMessage* to any context properties implementing *IContextActivatorProperty* after *Activator.Activate* returns. Allows properties to modify the constructor call message and, on return, the constructor return message.

■ Passes non-*IConstructionCallMessage* messages to the server object sink chain for the target server object specified in the message.

Creating a Custom Server Context Sink

To create a custom server context sink, you need to perform the following tasks:

■ Implement a message sink that performs the application-specific logic that you want to occur for all method calls coming into the context.

■ Define a context property that implements the *IContributeServer-ContextSink* interface.

■ Define a context attribute that contributes the context property defined in the previous step to the context properties in the construction call message during the call to *IContextAttribute.GetProperties-ForNewContext*.

■ Apply the context attribute to the class declaration.

Example: Exception Logging Context

To demonstrate the use of both the server context sink chain and the client context sink chain, let's define an exception logging context that performs the following tasks:

■ Logs all exceptions thrown as a result of method calls made on objects within the context by objects outside the context.

■ Logs all exceptions thrown as a result of method calls made by objects within the context on objects outside the context.

Let's first define a message sink class that inspects all messages it processes to determine whether the message contains an exception:

```csharp
public class ExceptionLoggingMessageSink : IMessageSink
{
    IMessageSink       _NextSink;
    static FileStream _stream;

    public IMessageSink NextSink
    {
        get
        {
            return _NextSink;
        }
    }

    public ExceptionLoggingMessageSink( IMessageSink next,
                                        string filename )
    {
        Trace.WriteLine("ExceptionLoggingMessageSink ctor");
        _NextSink = next;
        try
        {
            lock(this)
            {
                if ( _stream == null )
                {
                    _stream = new FileStream( filename,
                                              FileMode.Append );
                }
            }
        }
        catch( System.IO.IOException e )
        {
            Trace.WriteLine(e.Message);
        }
    }
```

As you can see, we've started defining a class named *ExceptionLogging-MessageSink*. The constructor allows chaining an instance into an existing sink chain by accepting the next sink in the chain. The constructor also accepts the name of the file the message sink uses to open a *FileStream* when logging exceptions.

Next we need to implement the *IMessageSink.SyncProcessMessage* method, which will pass the message to the next sink in the chain and utilize the services of a helper function to inspect the return message:

```
public IMessage SyncProcessMessage(IMessage msg)
{
    try
    {
        // Pass to next sink.
        IMessage retmsg = _NextSink.SyncProcessMessage(msg);

        // Inspect return message and log an exception if needed.
        InspectReturnMessageAndLogException(retmsg);

        return retmsg;
    }
    catch(System.Exception e)
    {
        return null;
    }
}

void InspectReturnMessageAndLogException(IMessage retmsg)
{
    MethodReturnMessageWrapper mrm =
        new MethodReturnMessageWrapper((IMethodReturnMessage)retmsg);

    if ( mrm.Exception != null )
    {
        lock(_stream)
        {
            Exception e = mrm.Exception;
            StreamWriter w = new StreamWriter(_stream,
                                                Encoding.ASCII);
            w.WriteLine();
            w.WriteLine("=========================");
            w.WriteLine();
            w.WriteLine(String.Format("Exception: {0}",
                                        DateTime.Now.ToString()) );
            w.WriteLine(String.Format("Application Name: {0}",
                                        e.Source));
            w.WriteLine(String.Format("Method Name: {0}",
                                        e.TargetSite.ToString()));
```

```
        w.WriteLine(String.Format("Description: {0}",
                                    e.Message));
        w.WriteLine(String.Format("More Info: {0}",
                                    e.ToString()));
        w.Flush();
    }
  }
}
```

The *InspectReturnMessageAndLogException* method wraps the message in a *System.Runtime.Remoting.Messaging.MethodReturnMessageWrapper* instance, which maps properties in the return message to properties defined by the *MethodReturnMessageWrapper* class to facilitate coding. The code checks the *Exception* property of the message, which won't be *null* if the message contains an exception. Because we're using this sink in a contextwide sink chain and multiple threads might be executing this code concurrently, we lock the stream before writing to it.

Next we need to implement the *IMessageSink.AsyncProcessMessage* method:

```
public IMessageCtrl AsyncProcessMessage(IMessage msg,
                                        IMessageSink replySink )
{
    try
    {
        //
        // Set up our reply sink with a delegate
        // to our callback method.
        AsyncReplyHelperSink.AsyncReplyHelperSinkDelegate rsd =
            new SyncReplyHelperSink.AsyncReplyHelperSinkDelegate(
            this.AsyncProcessReplyMessage);

        // We want to trace the response when we get it, so add
        // a sink to the reply sink.
        replySink =
            (IMessageSink) new AsyncReplyHelperSink( replySink,
                                                     rsd );

        return _NextSink.AsyncProcessMessage( msg, replySink );
    }
    catch(System.Exception e)
    {
        return null;
    }
}

//
// Trace the reply message and return it.
public IMessage AsyncProcessReplyMessage( IMessage msg )
```

(continued)

```
        {
            // Inspect reply message and log an exception if needed.
            InspectReturnMessageAndLogException(msg);
            return msg;
        }
    } // End class ExceptionLoggingMessageSink
```

The *AsyncProcessMessage* makes use of the *AsyncReplyHelperSink* that we defined earlier for handling asynchronous message processing. By instantiating an instance of *AsyncReplyHelperSink* with a delegate targeting the *ExceptionLogging-MessageSink.AsyncProcessReplyMessage* method and adding the helper sink to the reply sink chain, we can inspect the response message for asynchronous calls.

Now that we've developed a sink, we need to plug instances of it into the client context sink chain and the server context sink chain. We do this by creating a context property that implements the *IContributeClientContextSink* and *IContributeServerContextSink* interfaces:

```
[Serializable]
public class ExceptionLoggingProperty : IContextProperty,
                                        IContributeClientContextSink,
                                        IContributeServerContextSink
{
    private string _Name;

    IMessageSink _ServerSink;
    IMessageSink _ClientSink;
    string       _FileName;

    public ExceptionLoggingProperty(string name, string FileName)
    {
        _Name = name;
        _FileName = filename;
    }

    public void Freeze ( System.Runtime.Remoting.Contexts.Context
                         newContext )
    {
        // When this is called, we can't add any more properties
        // to the context.
    }

    public System.Boolean IsNewContextOK (Context newCtx )
    {
        return true;
    }

    public string Name
    {
        get
```

```
        {
            return _Name;
        }
    }

    public IMessageSink GetClientContextSink (IMessageSink nextSink )
    {
        Console.WriteLine("GetClientContextSink()");
        lock(this)
        {
            if ( _ClientSink == null )
            {
                _ClientSink =
                    new ExceptionLoggingMessageSink(nextSink,
                                                    _FileName);
            }
        }
        return _ClientSink;
    }

    public IMessageSink GetServerContextSink (IMessageSink nextSink )
    {
        Console.WriteLine("GetServerContextSink()");
        lock(this)
        {
            if ( _ServerSink == null )
            {
                _ServerSink =
                    new ExceptionLoggingMessageSink(nextSink,
                                                    _FileName);
            }
        }
        return _ServerSink;
    }
} // End class ExceptionLoggingProperty
```

The *ExceptionLoggingProperty* class implements the *IContextProperty* functionality that we saw in the beginning of this section. The interesting methods are *IContributeServerContextSink.GetServerContextSink* and *IContributeClient-ContextSink.GetClientContextSink*, each of which instantiate and return an instance of the *ExceptionLoggingMessageSink* we defined earlier. The runtime invokes the *GetServerContextSink* method during activation of an object instance within the context. Likewise, the runtime invokes the *GetClientContextSink* method upon the first occurrence of a method call out of the context.

Warning Each method returns a different instance of the *Exception-LoggingMessageSink*. If you try to use the same sink instance in both the client context sink chain and the server context sink chain, you'll end up with a problem if a method call into the context also ends up calling out of the context. The problem occurs because the *Exception-LoggingMessageSink* instance in the server context sink chain is also placed into the client context sink chain, creating a closed loop in the chain that prevents the message from leaving the context, resulting in an infinite recursion. Therefore, you need to design your sinks so that separate instances of the sink exist in each chain, as we've done here.

Note The client instantiates any context properties for a type in the context of the client during activation, prior to transmitting the constructor message to the remote object. This means that you should avoid placing code in context property constructors that depends on executing in the context of the remote object.

In our example, we could have created the *FileStream* in the *ExceptionLoggingProperty* and then passed the stream to the message sink constructor. This would be problematic in a remote application scenario in which the client and server objects exist in separate applications. In that case, the client application would have ownership of the exception log file because the *ExceptionLoggingProperty* would have opened a stream on that file. However, the message sinks would exist in the server application and might not be able to access it in a remote application.

Now we need to define a context attribute that adds the *ExceptionLogging-Property* to the context:

```
[AttributeUsage(AttributeTargets.Class)]
public class  ExceptionLoggingContextAttribute : ContextAttribute
{
    string _FileName;
```

```
public ExceptionLoggingContextAttribute(string filepath) :
    base("ExceptionLoggingContextAttribute")
{
    _FileName = filepath;
}


public override void GetPropertiesForNewContext (
    IConstructionCallMessage msg )
{
    // Add our property to the context properties.
    msg.ContextProperties.Add(
        new ExceptionLoggingProperty( this.AttributeName,
                                      _FileName));
}


public override System.Boolean IsContextOK (
    Context ctx, IConstructionCallMessage msg )
{
    // Does the context already have
    // an instance of this property?
    return (ctx.GetProperty( this.AttributeName ) != null);
}
} // End class ExceptionLoggingContextAttribute
```

The *ExceptionLoggingContextAttribute* class follows the general pattern for context attributes by deriving from *ContextAttribute* and overriding the *IsContextOK* and *GetPropertiesForNewContext* methods, which check for the existence of and add an instance of the *ExceptionLoggingContextProperty*, respectively.

Now we can attribute any class derived from *ContextBoundObject* by using the *ExceptionLoggingContextAttribute* like this:

```
[ ExceptionLoggingContextAttribute(@"C:\exceptions.log") ]
public class SomeCBO : ContextBoundObject
{
    ⋮
}
```

If any method calls made by object instances outside the context on an instance of *SomeCBO* throw an exception, or any calls made by an instance of *SomeCBO* on objects outside the context throw an exception, the *Exception-LoggingMessageSink* will log the exception information to the C:\exceptions.log file. Figure 6-2 shows an example of what the log might look like.

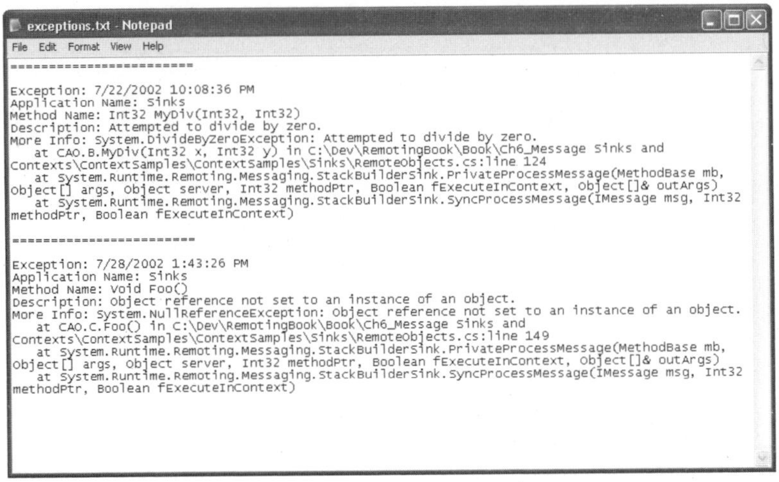

```
exceptions.txt - Notepad
File Edit Format View Help
========================

Exception: 7/22/2002 10:08:36 PM
Application Name: Sinks
Method Name: Int32 MyDiv(Int32, Int32)
Description: Attempted to divide by zero.
More Info: System.DivideByZeroException: Attempted to divide by zero.
   at CAO.B.MyDiv(Int32 x, Int32 y) in C:\Dev\RemotingBook\Book\Ch6_Message Sinks and
Contexts\ContextSamples\ContextSamples\Sinks\RemoteObjects.cs:line 124
   at System.Runtime.Remoting.Messaging.StackBuilderSink.PrivateProcessMessage(MethodBase mb,
Object[] args, Object server, Int32 methodPtr, Boolean fExecuteInContext, Object[]& outArgs)
   at System.Runtime.Remoting.Messaging.StackBuilderSink.SyncProcessMessage(IMessage msg, Int32
methodPtr, Boolean fExecuteInContext)

========================

Exception: 7/28/2002 1:43:26 PM
Application Name: Sinks
Method Name: Void Foo()
Description: Object reference not set to an instance of an object.
More Info: System.NullReferenceException: Object reference not set to an instance of an object.
   at CAO.C.Foo() in C:\Dev\RemotingBook\Book\Ch6_Message Sinks and
Contexts\ContextSamples\ContextSamples\Sinks\RemoteObjects.cs:line 149
   at System.Runtime.Remoting.Messaging.StackBuilderSink.PrivateProcessMessage(MethodBase mb,
Object[] args, Object server, Int32 methodPtr, Boolean fExecuteInContext, Object[]& outArgs)
   at System.Runtime.Remoting.Messaging.StackBuilderSink.SyncProcessMessage(IMessage msg, Int32
methodPtr, Boolean fExecuteInContext)
```

Figure 6-2 Output produced by the *ExceptionLoggingMessageSink* class

Server Object Sink Chain

As we mentioned earlier, both the server context sink chain and the client context sink chain intercept messages on a contextwide basis. If you want to implement context logic on a per-object-instance basis, you'll need to install a message sink into the server object sink chain, which allows you to intercept method call messages representing calls made on a context-bound object instance from objects outside the context. There's no corresponding per-object sink chain for intercepting calls made by an object instance within the context to objects outside the context.

The .NET Remoting infrastructure inserts custom server object sinks at the front of the chain so that the last sink in the chain is the *System.Runtime.Remoting.Contexts.ServerObjectTerminatorSink*. An application domain will contain a single instance of this class that performs the following functions for all contexts within the application domain:

- Notifies any dynamic sinks associated with the object instance that a method call on the object is starting.
- Passes the message to the *StackBuilderSink*, which ultimately invokes the method on the object instance.
- Notifies any dynamic sinks that a method call on the object instance has finished. (For asynchronous calls, the *AsyncReplySink* handles this step when the call actually completes.)

Creating a Custom Server Object Sink

To create a custom server object sink, you need to perform the following tasks:

- Implement a message sink that performs the context-specific logic for all method calls made on an object instance within the context.

- Define a context property that implements the *IContributeObjectSink* interface.

- Define a context attribute that contributes the context property defined in the previous step to the context properties in the construction call message during the call to *IContextAttribute.GetProperties-ForNewContext*.

- Apply the context attribute to the class declaration.

Example: Tracing All Method Calls Made on an Object

Earlier in the section, we developed a context property that exposed method call message logging functionality to all object instances within a context containing that property. In that example, an object instance could get the property from the context and call its *LogMessage* method to log a message. One drawback to that approach is that it requires the addition of extra logging functionality to every method of the class. In contrast to the context property, the interception capability of context sinks affords you the ability to provide the method call logging functionality as a tracing service that applies to all method calls on an object instance without requiring each method implementation to explicitly use the tracing functionality. You can use context to provide method call tracing functionality more conveniently by creating a message sink that performs the tracing and adding the message sink to the server object sink chain.

First, we need to implement a message sink that performs the message tracing functionality. The following code listing defines a class that provides diagnostic output for all messages that it receives:

```
public class TraceMessageSink : IMessageSink
{
    IMessageSink _NextSink;

    public IMessageSink NextSink
    {
        get
        {
            return _NextSink;
        }
    }
}
```

(continued)

```
public TraceMessageSink( IMessageSink next )
{
    _NextSink = next;
}

public virtual IMessage SyncProcessMessage ( IMessage msg )
{
    try
    {
        TraceMessage(msg);
        IMessage msgRet = _NextSink.SyncProcessMessage(msg);
        TraceMessage(msgRet);
        return msgRet;
    }
    catch(System.Exception e)
    {
        return new ReturnMessage(e, (IMethodCallMessage) msg);
    }
}
```

We've started defining a class named *TraceMessageSink*. The *SyncProcess-Message* method uses the following helper function to actually trace the message:

```
void TraceMessage(IMessage msg)
{
    Trace.WriteLine
    ("------------------------------------------------------");

    Trace.WriteLine( String.Format(
                "{0} :: TraceMessage() --- {1}",
                DateTime.Now.Ticks.ToString(),
                msg.GetType().ToString()) );

    Trace.WriteLine( String.Format("\tDomainID={0},
                ContextID={1}",
                Thread.GetDomainID(),

    Thread.CurrentContext.ContextID.ToString()));

    IDictionaryEnumerator ie = msg.Properties.GetEnumerator();
    while(ie.MoveNext())
    {
        Trace.WriteLine( String.Format("\tMsg[{0}] = {1}",
                    ie.Key, ie.Value));

        if ( ie.Value == null )
        {
            continue;
        }
```

```
        // Write out array elements if appropriate.
        if ( ! ie.Value.GetType().IsArray )
        {
            continue;
        }

        object[] ar = (object[])ie.Value;
        for(int i = 0; i<ar.Length; ++i )
        {
            Trace.WriteLine(.String.Format("\t\t[{0}] = {1}",
                            i, ar.GetValue(i)));
        }
    }
}
```

The *TraceMessage* method simply enumerates over the message properties, outputting each key-value pair by using *Trace.WriteLine*, which writes the output to the Output window of the debugger.

The following code completes the *TraceMessageSink* definition by defining the *AsyncProcessMessage* method:

```
public virtual IMessageCtrl AsyncProcessMessage (
    IMessage msg, IMessageSink replySink )
{
    try
    {
        // Trace the message before we send it down the chain.
        TraceMessage(msg);

        // We want to trace the response when we get it,
        // so add a sink to the reply sink helper.
        AsyncReplyHelperSink.AsyncReplyHelperSinkDelegate rsd =
            new AsyncReplyHelperSink.AsyncReplyHelperSinkDelegate
            (this.AsyncProcessReplyMessage);

        replySink =
            (IMessageSink)new AsyncReplyHelperSink( replySink,
                                                    rsd );

        // Pass to next sink.
        return _NextSink.AsyncProcessMessage( msg, replySink );
    }
    catch(System.Exception e)
    {
        return null;
    }
}
public IMessage AsyncProcessReplyMessage( IMessage msg )
```

(continued)

```
        {
            // msg is the reply message; go ahead and trace it.
            TraceMessage(msg);
            return msg;
        }
} // End class TraceMessageSink
```

The *AsyncProcessMessage* method traces the message before passing it to the next sink in the chain. Again, we use the *AsyncReplyHelperSink* defined earlier for handling asynchronous message processing. This time, we instantiate an instance of *AsyncReplyHelperSink* with a delegate that targets the *TraceMessage-Sink.AsyncProcessReplyMessage* method so that we can intercept the response message for asynchronous calls.

Now that we have a sink, we need to plug it into the server object sink chain. You do this by creating a context property that implements the *IContribute-ObjectSink* interface. Because the code implementing *IContextProperty* is largely boilerplate code, we'll show just the *IContributeObjectSink* implementation:

```
[Serializable]
public class TraceMessageSinkProperty : IContextProperty,
                                        IContributeObjectSink
{
    // IContextProperty implementation code removed for brevity.

    public IMessageSink GetObjectSink ( MarshalByRefObject obj,
                                        IMessageSink nextSink )
    {
        return new TraceMessageSink(nextSink);
    }
}
```

Nothing radical here: we just return an instance of *TraceMessageSink* from the *GetObjectSink* method. It's worth noting that one of the parameters to *Get-ObjectSink* is a *MarshalByRefObject*. The .NET Remoting infrastructure associates the message sink chain returned by *GetObjectSink* with the object referenced by the *obj* parameter. Although we don't utilize the *obj* parameter here, you might use it for some other informational purpose.

All we need now is an attribute that adds the *TraceMessageSinkProperty* to the constructor call message's context properties in the *GetPropertiesForNew-Context* method:

```
[AttributeUsage(AttributeTargets.Class)]
public class  TraceMessageSinkAttribute : ContextAttribute
{
    public TraceMessageSinkAttribute() :
        base("TraceMessageSinkAttribute")
    {
    }
```

```
public override void GetPropertiesForNewContext(
    IConstructionCallMessage msg )
{
    msg.ContextProperties.Add(
        new TraceMessageSinkProperty(this.AttributeName));
}

public override System.Boolean IsContextOK (
    Context ctx , IConstructionCallMessage msg )
{
    return (ctx.GetProperty(this.AttributeName) != null);
}
}
```

Now we can attribute any class derived from *ContextBoundObject* by using the *TraceMessageSinkAttribute* like this:

```
[TraceMessageSinkAttribute()]
public class C : ContextBoundObject
{
    void Foo(){ ... }
}
```

The *TraceMessageSink* class will intercept all method calls made by object instances outside the context to any object instances of the *C* class. Here's an example of possible trace output resulting from an invocation of the *C.Foo* method:

```
-------------------------------------------------------
631580307740445920 :: TraceMessage() ---
 System.Runtime.Remoting.Messaging.MethodCall
    DomainID=1, ContextID=1
    Msg[__Uri] = /fd062ced_1cc4_423b_949c_75acee5498bc/23509144_1.rem
    Msg[__MethodName] = Foo
    Msg[__MethodSignature] = System.Type[]
    Msg[__TypeName] = clr:CAO.C, Sinks
    Msg[__Args] = System.Object[]
    Msg[__CallContext] = System.Runtime.Remoting.Messaging.LogicalCallContext
    Msg[__ActivationTypeName] = CAO.C, Sinks, Version=1.0.876.29571,
Culture=neutral, PublicKeyToken=null
```

Envoy Sink Chain

Each of the context sinks we've discussed intercepts method call messages in the context of the server object instance. The envoy sink chain differs from the other context sink chains in that it executes in the context of the *client* object instance that's making method calls on the remote object. Figure 6-3 illustrates the relationship between a client object instance, proxy, and envoy sink chain in one application domain and a remote object instance.

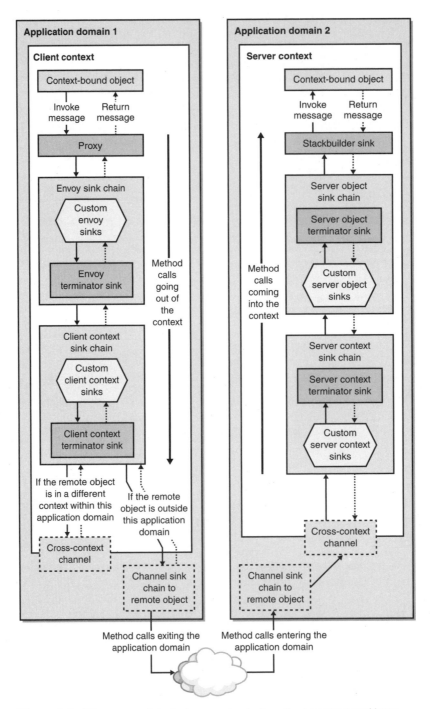

Figure 6-3 The envoy sink chain executes in the client context and intercepts method calls bound for the remote object instance.

The .NET Remoting infrastructure builds the envoy sink chain by enumerating over the context properties in reverse order relative to the building of the server object sink chain. Again, this enumeration allows and preserves a symmetry of the order of operations performed during message sink processing between the two chains in the event that a property contributes a sink to both chains. The .NET Remoting infrastructure inserts custom envoy sinks at the front of the chain so that the last sink in the chain is the *System.Runtime.Remoting.Contexts.EnvoyTerminatorSink*. One envoy sink chain exists for each proxy to a remote object instance and contains—at a minimum—the application domain–wide *EnvoyTerminatorSink* message sink instance.

After receiving the method call message from the transparent proxy, the real proxy (or a custom *RealProxy* derivative) passes the message on to the envoy sink chain. In Chapter 5, "Messages and Proxies," we used the *RemotingServices.GetEnvoyChainForProxy* method to obtain a reference to the first sink in this chain.

Because envoy sinks execute in the context of the client, they're the perfect sinks to use for validating method call arguments or performing other client-side optimization of the method call. By validating the method arguments on the client side, you can prevent method call messages from leaving the context, thus saving a round-trip to the server when you know the method call will ultimately result in an error because of invalid arguments.

As with the other terminator sinks, an application domain will contain a single instance of the *EnvoyTerminatorSink* class that performs the following functions for all contexts within the application domain:

- Validates the *IMessage* reference passed to *SyncProcessMessage* and *AsyncProcessMessage*, ensuring that it isn't *null*.

- Forwards a valid message to the client context sink chain.

Creating a Custom Envoy Sink

To create a custom envoy sink, you need to perform the following tasks:

- Implement a message sink that performs the application-specific logic that you want to occur in the client context whenever the client makes a method call on the server object.

- Define a context property that implements the *IContributeEnvoySink* interface.

- Define a context attribute that contributes the context property defined in the previous step to the context properties in the construction call message during the call to *IContextAttribute.GetPropertiesForNewContext*.

- Apply the context attribute to the class declaration.

> **Caution** The *ObjRef.EnvoyInfo* property carries the envoy sink chain across the .NET Remoting boundary during marshalling of the *ObjRef*, which always occurs during activation of client-activated objects. However, for well-known objects, the .NET Remoting infrastructure doesn't marshal an *ObjRef* to the client during activation. Therefore, the client won't receive the envoy sink chain. You can get a reference to a well-known object and its associated envoy sink chain if you force the marshaling of an *ObjRef* for the well-known object by either returning a reference to the well-known object as a return result of a method or as an *out* parameter of a method.

Example: Validating Method Parameters

To demonstrate envoy sinks, we'll implement a message sink that validates message parameters. To make the example more extensible, we've implemented a validation mechanism that allows the type implementer to create validation classes that implement the *IParamValidator* interface:

```
public interface IParamValidator
{
    bool Validate(object[] o);
}
```

The *IParamValidator.Validate* method takes an object array that represents the parameters passed to the method being validated. The first element in the array is parameter 1, the second is parameter 2, and so on. For example, the following method takes two parameters:

```
public void Foo(int x, int y)
{
    ⋮
}
```

The corresponding *IParamValidator.Validate* method implementation for *Foo* would expect an array of objects with a *Length* of 2. The first array element (at index 0) is the value of x, and the second array element is the value of y.

The following code defines a message sink that uses the *IParamValidator* interface to validate method call parameters in the *IMessage* received in *SyncProcessMessage* and *AsyncProcessMessage*:

```
[Serializable]
public class ParamValidatorMessageSink : IMessageSink
{
    Hashtable    _htValidators;
```

```
IMessageSink _NextSink;

public IMessageSink NextSink
{
    get
    {
        return _NextSink;
    }
}


//
// The constructor accepts a Hashtable of IParamValidator
// references keyed by the method name whose parameters
// they validate.
public ParamValidatorMessageSink( IMessageSink next,
                                    Hashtable htValidators)
{
    Trace.WriteLine("ParamValidatorMessageSink ctor");
    _htValidators = htValidators;
    _NextSink = next;
}

public IMessage SyncProcessMessage (IMessage msg )
{
    try
    {
        ValidateParams(msg);
    }
    catch ( System.Exception e )
    {
        return new ReturnMessage(e, (IMethodCallMessage)msg);
    }
    return _NextSink.SyncProcessMessage(msg);
}
```

Notice that the message sink is attributed with the *Serializable* attribute. This is so that the runtime can marshal the message sink instance during activation as part of the *EnvoyInfo* property of the *ObjRef*. Any message sink used in the envoy sink chain must be serializable so that it can flow across the .NET Remoting boundary into the client context. Also note that the constructor takes a *Hashtable* instance as a second parameter that hashes method names to the corresponding *IParamValidator* that validates the method parameters for the named method. The *SyncProcessMessage* method uses the following helper method to validate the parameters in the message:

```
//
// Validate the parameters in the message.
void ValidateParams(IMessage msg)
```

(continued)

```
        {
            // Make sure the msg is a method call message.
            if ( msg is IMethodCallMessage )
            {
                // Wrap the message to facilitate coding.
                MethodCallMessageWrapper mcm =
                    new MethodCallMessageWrapper((IMethodCallMessage)msg);

                // Look up the validator corresponding
                // to the called method.
                IParamValidator v =
                    (IParamValidator)_htValidators[mcm.MethodName];
                if ( v != null )
                {
                    // Use validator to validate the message parameters.
                    if ( ! v.Validate( mcm.Args ) )
                    {
                        throw new ArgumentException(
                            "IParamValidator.Validate() returned " +
                            "false indicating invalid parameter values");
                    }
                }
            }
        }
```

ValidateParams uses the method name contained in the message to look
up the associated *IParamValidator* reference, which the method then uses to
validate the message parameters by invoking *IParamValidator.Validate*. If the
parameters are invalid, *ValidateParams* throws an exception.

The *AsyncProcessMessage* method also uses the *ValidateParams* method:

```
public IMessageCtrl AsyncProcessMessage (
    IMessage msg, IMessageSink replySink )
{
    try
    {
        ValidateParams(msg);
        return _NextSink.AsyncProcessMessage( msg, replySink );
    }
    catch(System.Exception e)
    {
        replySink.SyncProcessMessage(
            new ReturnMessage( e, (IMethodCallMessage)msg) );
        return null;
    }
}
} // End class ParamValidatorMessageSink
```

Because we don't care about the response message, we don't need to add a message sink to the reply sink chain. Instead, we just validate the message parameters and pass the message to the next sink in the chain. If we find the parameters invalid, we send a *ReturnMessage* instance, encapsulating the exception, to the first sink in the reply sink chain.

The following code defines a context property that implements *IContribute-EnvoySink*:

```
[Serializable]
public class ParameterValidatorProperty : IContextProperty,
                                          IContributeEnvoySink
{
    private string _Name;
    Hashtable      _htValidators;

    public string Name
    {
        get
        {
            return _Name;
        }
    }

    public ParameterValidatorProperty( string name,
                                       Hashtable htValidator )
    {
        _Name = name;
        _htValidators = htValidators;
    }

    public IMessageSink GetEnvoySink( MarshalByRefObject obj,
                                      IMessageSink nextSink )
    {
        return new ParamValidatorMessageSink(nextSink,
                                             _htValidators);
    }

    public void Freeze ( Context newContext )
    {
        // When this is called, we can't add any more
        // properties to the context.
    }

    public Boolean IsNewContextOK ( Context newCtx )
    {
        return true;
    }
} // End class ParameterValidatorProperty
```

The *ParameterValidatorProperty* constructor takes a *Hashtable* parameter of *IParamValidator* references that the *IContributeEnvoySink.GetEnvoySink* method passes to the *ParameterValidatorMessageSink* constructor.

The following code defines an attribute that contributes the *Parameter-ValidatorProperty* to the context:

```
[AttributeUsage(AttributeTargets.Class)]
public class  ParameterValidatorContextAttribute : ContextAttribute
{
    string[]  _methodNames;
    Hashtable _htValidators;

    public ParameterValidatorContextAttribute(
        string[] method_names, params Type[] validators)
        : base("ParameterValidatorContextAttribute")
    {
        if ( method_names.Length != validators.Length )
        {
            throw new ArgumentException(
                "ParameterValidatorContextAttribute ctor",
                "Length of method_names and validators " +
                "must be equal");
        }

        _methodNames = method_names;
        _htValidators = new Hashtable(method_names.Length);

        int i = 0;
        foreach( Type t in validators )
        {
            _htValidators.Add(method_names[i++],
                Activator.CreateInstance(t) );
        }
    }

    public override void
        GetPropertiesForNewContext( IConstructionCallMessage msg )
    {
        msg.ContextProperties.Add(
            new ParameterValidatorProperty( this.AttributeName,
                                            _htValidators));
    }

    public override Boolean
        IsContextOK ( Context ctx , IConstructionCallMessage msg )
    {
        return (ctx.GetProperty(this.AttributeName) != null);
    }
}
```

The interesting code here is the *ParameterValidatorContextAttribute* constructor, which takes two parameters: an array of strings containing method names, and a variable-length *params* array of *Type* instances in which each *Type* is expected to implement the *IParamValidator* interface. The position of the elements in the arrays matches so that the method named by element 0 of the *string* array corresponds to the *Type* referenced by element 0 of the *Type* array. After verifying that the array lengths are the same, the constructor populates the *Hashtable* by mapping method names to a new instance of the matching *Type*.

We can use the *ParameterValidatorContextAttribute* like this:

```
[ ParameterValidatorContextAttribute(
  new string[] { "Bar", "Foo" },
  typeof(BarValidator), typeof(FooValidator))
]
public class SomeObject : ContextBoundObject
{
    public void Bar()
    {
        Console.WriteLine("ContextID={0}, SomeObject.Bar()",
            Thread.CurrentContext.ContextID);
    }

    public void Bar(int x)
    {
        Console.WriteLine("ContextID={0}, SomeObject.Bar(x={1})",
            Thread.CurrentContext.ContextID, x);
        return this;
    }

    public int Foo( int x, int y )
    {
        return x + y;
    }
}
```

Here's the listing for the *BarValidator*, which handles the fact that the *Bar* method is overloaded and limits input to an integer between 0 and 5000:

```
[Serializable]
class BarValidator : IParamValidator
{
    public bool Validate(object[] args)
    {
        // Bar is overloaded. We care about only the
        // version that has arguments.
        if ( args.Length != 0 )
```

(continued)

```
    {
        // First param is x. Limit to integer between 0 and 5000.
        int x = (int)args[0];
        if (!( 0 <= x && x <= 5000 ))
        {
            string err = String.Format(
                "BarValidator detected illegal 'x' parameter " +
                "value of '{0}'.\nLegal values: 0 <= x <= 5000.",
                x);
            throw new ArgumentException(err);
        }
    }
    return true;
    }
}
```

Figure 6-4 shows a screen shot of the exception message resulting from calling the *Bar* method and passing it the value 6500 for the *x* parameter.

Figure 6-4   Message box displayed as a result of passing invalid value for *x* to the *SomeObject.Bar* method

Here's the listing for the *FooValidator*, which validates both parameters passed to the *SomeObject.Foo* method:

```
[Serializable]
class FooValidator : IParamValidator
{
    public bool Validate(object[] args)
    {
        string e = "";

        // First parameter is x. Limit it to
        // an integer between 0 and 9999.
        int x = (int)args[0];
        if ( x > 9999 )
        {
            e = "parameter 'x' exceeds maximum allowed value " +
                "of '9999'";
        }
```

```
    // Second parameter is y. Limit it to
    // an integer less than 1000.
    int y = (int)args[1];
    if ( y > 1000 )
    {
        e = "parameter 'y' exceeds maximum allowed value " +
            "of '1000'";
    }

    if ( e.Length != 0 )
    {
        throw new ArgumentException
            ("FooValidator detected illegal parameter values\n\n"
            + e);
    }

    return true;
    }
}
```

Note that we declare the validator classes with the *Serializable* attribute. This is because the message sink holds a reference to these classes in its *_htValidators* member. Because the runtime marshals the envoy sink chain to the client in the *EnvoyInfo* property of the *ObjRef*, any message sink members must also be *Serializable*. You'll also want to keep them lightweight to minimize the transmission cost during marshaling across the .NET Remoting boundary.

Summary

Message sinks and contexts are key elements of the .NET Remoting infrastructure. As we saw in this chapter, message sinks allow you to intercept .NET Remoting messages at various points in both the client and server contexts. As we demonstrated, contexts allow the developer to define various services available to all objects executing within them. Examples of such services include message tracing and exception logging. Because the envoy sink chain executes in the client context, it's the perfect choice for validating method parameters prior to transmission. The .NET Remoting architecture allows for further customization via channels and channel sinks, which are the subject of the next chapter.

7

Channels and Channel Sinks

In this chapter, we'll continue showing you the various customizable features of .NET Remoting. To get a more detailed understanding of the channel architecture, we'll examine *HttpChannel* in depth. The next step will be to create a custom channel by using our own transport mechanism. Finally, we'll build a custom channel sink.

The .NET Framework has two types of channels: *HttpChannel* and *TcpChannel*. Although the overall structure of these two channels is very similar, they differ in the transport they use to transmit messages. Although HTTP and TCP will fulfill most transport needs, occasional problems that require a different transport will occur.

For example, you might need to access remote objects from a wireless device that supports the Wireless Application Protocol (WAP). To solve this problem, you'd create a custom channel that accepts incoming messages via WAP. When we look at the structure of channels later in the chapter, you'll see that once a message is reconstituted into the proper format, the channel framework is oblivious to the manner in which the message was received.

How Channels Are Constructed

To make it easier to understand the overall channel architecture when we create a custom channel, we'll show you the HTTP channel architecture. We benefit in several ways by discussing the construction of an existing channel. First, we get a more in-depth understanding of how the HTTP channel works. Second, we can introduce concepts at a higher level, making it easier to understand the overall channel architecture when we create a custom channel. We'll discuss the features of the HTTP channel that are relevant to creating our custom channel. The HTTP channel consists of six main classes that are relevant to us:

- *HttpChannel*
- *HttpServerChannel*
- *HttpServerTransportSink*
- *HttpClientChannel*
- *HttpClientTransportSinkProvider*
- *HttpClientTransportSink*

Channel Terminology

Table 7-1 introduces some channel terminology that will be necessary for understanding channels.

Table 7-1   Channel Terminology

Term	Description
Object URI	An object URI identifies a particular well-known object registered on the server.
Channel URI	A channel URI is a string that specifies the connection information to the server.
Server-activated URL	A server-activated URL is a unique string that the client uses to connect to the correct object on the server. In the URL *http://localhost:4000/SomeObjectUri*, *SomeObjectUri* is an object URI and *http://localhost:4000* is a channel URI.
Client-activated URL	A client-activated URL is a string that the client uses to connect to the correct object on the server. When using client-activated objects, you don't need to use a unique URL because the .NET Remoting infrastructure will generate one.

HttpChannel

The *HttpChannel* does little work. Its purpose is to wrap the functionality that's implemented in *HttpServerChannel* and *HttpClientChannel* into a single interface. Most of the methods in *HttpChannel* simply call their counterparts in either *HttpServerChannel* or *HttpClientChannel*. *HttpChannel* implements the interfaces *System.Runtime.Remoting.Channels.IChannel*, *System.Runtime.Remoting.Channels.IChannelSender*, and *System.Runtime.Remoting.Channels.IChannelReceiver*. Although *IChannel* is a required interface for channels,

IChannelSender and *IChannelReceiver* aren't required in all cases. If you just want a channel that receives messages, you must implement the *IChannelReceiver*; likewise, if your channel will just send messages, you need to implement only the *IChannelSender* interface. It's not necessary to inherit directly from the *IChannel* interface because both *IChannelSender* and *IChannelReceiver* handle this for you. Table 7-2 shows the interface for *IChannel*.

Table 7-2   Members of *System.Runtime.Remoting.Channels.IChannel*

Member	Member Type	Description
ChannelName	Property	Returns the name of the channel.
ChannelPriority	Property	Returns the priority of the channel. The default priority is 1.
Parse	Method	Extracts the channel URI and object URI from the URL.

ChannelName will generally be the name of the transport. For example, *HttpChannel* returns the lowercase string *http* for its name. The *ChannelPriority* property allows you to control the order in which channels attempt to connect to the remote object. For instance, if you have two channels registered on the server with different priorities and both channels registered on the client, the remoting infrastructure will select the channel with the higher priority. The *ChannelName* and *ChannelPriority* properties are read-only. *HttpChannel* has three constructors.

```
public HttpChannel();
public HttpChannel( int );
public HttpChannel( IDictionary,
                    IClientChannelSinkProvider,
                    IServerChannelSinkProvider );
```

The first constructor initializes the channel for both sending and receiving of messages, whereas the second constructor initializes the channel for receiving messages. The parameter for the second constructor sets the port on which the server will listen. The last constructor is a little more interesting. All channels that plan to use configuration files must implement a constructor with this signature. The .NET Remoting runtime throws an exception if this constructor isn't present. Because of the number of optional parameters that can be set for an *HttpChannel*, it wouldn't be practical to provide a constructor for all the combinations. To overcome this problem, channels use the *IDictionary* parameter to pass configuration information to the constructor. Table 7-3 lists the properties available for the *HttpChannel*.

Table 7-3 *HttpChannel* **Configuration Properties**

Name	Applies To	Description
name	Server and client	Used when you register multiple instances of *HttpChannel* because each channel must have a unique name.
priority	Server and client	Sets the channel priority.
clientConnectionLimit	Client	Sets the number of clients that can simultaneously be connected to the server. The default value is 2.
proxyName	Client	Allows setting of the proxy computer name.
proxyPort	Client	Allows setting of the proxy port.
port	Server	Sets the listening port.
suppressChannelData	Server	When this property is set, the *ChannelData* property will return *null*.
useIpAddress	Server	Specifies whether the channel should use the IP address. If this value is *false*, the channel will use the machine name retrieved from the static method *Dns.GetHostName*.
bindTo	Server	Allows you to specify the IP address of a network interface card that the server should bind to. This is particularly useful when you have multiple network interface cards in a machine.
machineName	Server	Allows you to override the machine name.

Channel properties can be set in two ways. The first way is programmatically. In the following snippet, we set the port and assign a new IP address to *bindTo*:

```
IDictionary ChannelProperties = new Hashtable();
ChannelProperties ["port"] = 4001;
ChannelProperties ["bindTo"] = "192.168.0.1";
HttpChannel channel = new HttpChannel( props,
                                       null,
                                       null );
```

The second way to set properties is in your configuration file:

```
<configuration>
  <system.runtime.remoting>
    <application>
      <service>
         ⋮
      </service>
```

```
      <channels>
        <channel ref="http" port="4001" bindTo="192.268.0.1"/>
      </channels>
    </application>
  </system.runtime.remoting>
</configuration>
```

The final two parameters of the constructor, *IClientChannelSinkProvider* and *IServerChannelSinkProvider*, allow you to specify a different formatter provider. The default formatter providers for *HttpChannel* are *SoapClientFormatterSink-Provider* and *SoapServerFormatterSinkProvider*.

We stated earlier that *HttpChannel* implements *IChannelReceiver*. Any channel that plans to receive messages must implement *IChannelReceiver*. Table 7-4 shows the members of *IChannelReceiver*. We'll cover these members in detail momentarily.

Table 7-4   Members of *System.Runtime.Remoting.Channels.IChannelReceiver*

Member	Member Type	Description
ChannelData	Property	Used to store channel information on an instance basis
GetUrlsForUri	Method	Returns an array of URLs that are used to uniquely identify remote objects
StartListening	Method	Tells the server channel to listen for incoming messages
StopListening	Method	Tells the server to stop listening for incoming messages

As we stated earlier, *HttpChannel* inherits from *IChannelSender*. *IChannel-Sender* provides the interface for client-side interaction with the channel. As you can see in Table 7-5, *IChannelSender* has only a single member.

Table 7-5   Member of *System.Runtime.Remoting.Channels.IChannelSender*

Member	Member Type	Description
CreateMessageSink	Method	Returns a channel message sink

HttpServerChannel

HttpServerChannel handles the server-side functionality for receiving messages. During construction, the *HttpChannel* class creates an instance of *HttpServer-Channel*. As with *HttpChannel*, *HttpServerChannel* has a constructor that takes an *IDictionary* object as its first parameter:

```
public HttpServerChannel( IDictionary properties,
                          IServerChannelSinkProvider provider );
```

HttpChannel removes client-side properties before passing the *IDictionary* object to *HttpServerChannel* constructor. At the time of construction, *HttpServer-Channel* performs the following operations:

- Extracts properties and sets corresponding member variables
- Initializes channel data
- Extracts channel data from the server sink providers
- Creates the server channel sink chain

We'll address each of these items in detail in the "Creating the Custom Channel *FileChannel*" section later in the chapter.

As stated earlier, *HttpServerChannel* handles the receiving of request messages; therefore, it must derive from *IChannelReceiver*. Let's take a closer look at the members in *HttpServerChannel* that implement the *IChannelReceiver* interface. The *ChannelData* property returns an object of type *ChannelDataStore*. The *ChannelDataStore* object is a private member variable named *_channelData*. The main purpose of *ChannelDataStore* is to store channel URIs that map to the channel. The channel URI for the *HttpChannel* is *http://<machine_name>:<port>*. The member function *GetUrlsForUri* uses *_channelData* to help generate its return value. *GetUrlsForUri* appends the object URI to the channel URI and returns the value in the 0 index of the string array.

The most interesting method in this group is *StartListening*. The responsibility of *StartListening* is to start a background thread that listens on a port for incoming messages. *StartListening* would look similar to the following pseudocode:

```
public void StartListening( Object data )
{
    ThreadStart ListeningThreadStart =
      new ThreadStart( this.Listen );
    _listenerThread = new Thread( ListeningThreadStart );
    _listenerThread.IsBackground = true;
    _listenerThread.Start();
}
```

In this snippet, *_listenerThread* is a member variable of type *Thread*. The *Listen* method sits in a loop, waiting for incoming messages. When *Listen* receives a message, it dispatches the message by calling the method *ServiceRequest* in the class *HttpServerTransportSink*. The *Listen* method then returns to a waiting state.

HttpServerTransportSink

The main responsibility of *HttpServerTransportSink* is to process request messages. *HttpServerTransportSink*, as with all server-side channel sinks, must derive from the interface *System.Runtime.Remoting.Channels.IServerChannelSink*. Table 7-6 presents the public members of this interface.

Table 7-6   Members of *System.Runtime.Remoting.Channels.IServerChannelSink*

Member	Member Type	Description
NextChannelSink	Property	Returns a reference to the next channel sink in the chain.
AsyncProcessResponse	Method	Returns the response payload from the process asynchronous message.
GetResponseStream	Method	Builds a *Stream* object that contains the *IMessage* object and any needed key/value pairs from the *ITransportHeaders* object.
ProcessMessage	Method	Used by the sink chain to handle incoming messages. Because the transport sink is the first sink in the chain, it doesn't need to perform any work.

During construction, *HttpServerTransportSink* receives a reference to the next sink in the sink chain. *HttpServerTransportSink* holds the reference in the member variable *_nextSink*. It's the responsibility of each sink in the chain to hold a reference to the next sink. Upon message receipt, each sink passes the request message down the sink chain by calling *_nextSink.ProcessMessage*. The return value for *ProcessMessage* is an enumeration of type *ServerProcessing*. Table 7-7 lists the enumeration values for *ServerProcessing*.

Table 7-7   *System.Runtime.Remoting.Channels. ServerProcessing* Enumeration Values

Value	Description
Complete	The request message was processed synchronously.
Async	The request message was dispatched asynchronously. Response data must be stored for later dispatching.
OneWay	The request message was dispatched and no response is permitted.

The request message contains two key items, an *ITransportHeaders* and a *Stream*. *ITransportHeaders* is a dictionary that allows key/value pairs of information to pass between the client and server. The .NET Framework provides a class named *System.Runtime.Remoting.Channels.CommonTransportKeys* that defines string keys for common data found in an *ITransportHeaders* object. *CommonTransportKeys* contains three public string fields:

■ *ConnectionId*

■ *IPAddress*

■ *RequestUri*

The *Stream* object contains the serialized .NET Remoting message—for example, a *ConstructionCallMessage* or a *MethodCallMessage*.

HttpClientChannel

HttpClientChannel handles the sending of request messages to the server. As with *HttpServerChannel*, *HttpChannel* creates an instance of *HttpClientChannel* in its constructor. *HttpClientChannel* has a multitude of constructors, but the most configurable one is this:

```
public FileClientChannel( IDictionary properties,
                          IClientChannelSinkProvider sinkProvider );
```

This constructor allows the client properties discussed in Table 7-3 to be set in the channel. It also allows you to specify an alternate sink provider. In a moment, we'll take a closer look at sink providers.

HttpClientChannel has one main purpose, to build an *IMessageSink* object. *CreateMessageSink* builds and returns the *IMessageSink* object. Recall that *CreateMessageSink* is a member of the *IChannelSender* interface. In the "Creating Custom Channels" section later in this chapter, we'll look at the details of *CreateMessageSink*, but for now it's sufficient to say that it returns an *HttpClientTransportSink*. *CreateMessageSink* doesn't directly create the new transport sink. It uses the class *HttpClientTransportSinkProvider*.

HttpClientTransportSinkProvider

The sole responsibility of *HttpClientTransportSinkProvider* is to create an instance of the *HttpClientTransportSink*. As with all client sink providers, *HttpClientTransportSinkProvider* derives from the interface *IClientChannelSinkProvider*. Table 7-8 shows the members of *System.Runtime.Remoting.Channels.IClientChannelSinkProvider*.

Table 7-8 Members of *System.Runtime.Remoting.Channels.IClientChannelSinkProvider*

Member	Member Type	Description
Next	Property	Gets or sets the next *IClientChannelSinkProvider* in the chain
CreateSink	Method	Creates and returns a new object that derives from the *IClientChannelSink*

The property *Next* always returns *null* because *HttpClientTransportSinkProvider* is the last provider in the chain. *CreateSink* returns a newly created *HttpClientTransportSink*.

HttpClientTransportSink

IClientChannelSink is the class that dispatches messages to the server. It implements the interface *System.Runtime.Remoting.Channels.IClientChannelSink*. Table 7-9 shows the members of this interface.

Table 7-9 Members of *System.Runtime.Remoting.Channels.IClientChannelSink*

Member	Member Type	Description
NextChannelSink	Property	Holds a reference to the next sink in the chain
AsyncProcessRequest	Method	Handles processing of asynchronous method calls
AsyncProcessResponse	Method	Handles asynchronous method calls that are returning from the server
GetRequestStream	Method	Builds a *Stream* object that contains the *IMessage* object and any needed key/value pairs from the *ITransportHeaders* object
ProcessMessage	Method	Handles processing of synchronous method calls

Because *HttpClientTransportSink* is the last sink in the chain, the only two methods that provide functionality are *ProcessMessage* and *AsyncProcessRequest*. The job of both *ProcessMessage* and *AsyncProcessRequest* is to package up the message and send it. The main difference between the two is that *ProcessMessage* waits for a response from the server, whereas *AsyncProcessRequest* sets up a callback method to watch for the return message from the server while the main thread of execution continues.

In this section, we took a high-level look at how channels are constructed. *HttpChannel* was our model for this discussion. Next we'll use this knowledge to build a custom channel.

Creating Custom Channels

The .NET Remoting infrastructure exposes interfaces and an architecture that allows us to plug our own custom channels into the runtime. Many reasons to create custom channels exist. For instance, you might want to make remote method calls between two computers that can communicate only over a phone line. A custom channel would be the perfect solution to this problem: you could configure the server and client channel sinks to connect and disconnect when they have messages to send. Here are some other examples of possible custom channels:

- User Datagram Protocol (UDP) channel

- Named-pipe channel

- File channel

- <insert obscure protocol> channel

You're probably thinking, "With the built-in channels, *HttpChannel* and *TcpChannel*, why would I need these?" Consider situations in which the client or server is on a system that doesn't support TCP or HTTP. On a system that doesn't have the .NET common language runtime, you'd have to generate the messages yourself. As long as the messages are in the proper format, the receiving or sending channel won't know the difference. This is incredibly powerful!

The Steps for Creating a Custom .NET Remoting Channel

This section introduces a set of steps that will guide you in creating a custom .NET Remoting channel. The steps are transport agnostic; therefore, you can apply them to the creation of any channel, regardless of the transport selected. For example, assume that our transport for the high-level steps is the hypothetical Widget transport. Armed with the Widget transport and following the naming convention of the stock .NET Remoting channels, we arrive at our channel name, *WidgetChannel*. Here is a list of steps that we'll follow in creating our channel:

1. Create the client-side channel classes. The client-side channel consists of three classes respectively derived from *IChannelSender*, *IClient-ChannelSinkProvider*, and *IClientChannelSink*:

```
public class WidgetClientChannel : IChannelSender
{
    ⋮
}
```

```
internal class
  WidgetClientChannelSinkProvider : IClientChannelSinkProvider
{
    ⋮
}
public class WidgetClientChannelSink : IClientChannelSink
{
    ⋮
}
```

2. Create the server-side channel classes. The server side contains two classes that respectively derive from *IChannelReceiver* and *IServer-ChannelSink*:

```
public class WidgetServerChannel : IChannelReceive
{
    ⋮
}
public class WidgetServerChannelSink : IServerChannelSink
{
    ⋮
}
```

3. Create a helper class named *WidgetChannelHelper*. This class houses the shared functionality between the server and client channel classes.

4. Create the main channel class that combines the functionality of both the server and client classes:

```
public WidgetChannel : IChannelSender, IChannelReceiver
{
    private WidgetClientChannel = null;
    private WidgerServerChannel = null;
    ⋮
}
```

Now that we've gone over the basic steps of creating a custom .NET Remoting channel, let's create one!

Creating the Custom Channel *FileChannel*

FileChannel is a .NET Remoting channel that uses files and directories to move messages between the server and client. The purpose of using something as rudimentary as files for the channel transport is to show the flexibility of .NET Remoting. For example, we could remote an object between two computers with a floppy disk! Now that's flexibility. Flexibility isn't the only benefit of *FileChannel*. Because file operations are so familiar, we can focus on the details of custom channel creation without the distraction of implementing a complex transport mechanism. Finally, *FileChannel* request and response messages remain in the server directory after processing. This leaves a chronological history of the message interaction between the server and client for diagnostic and debugging purposes.

FileChannel Projects

The sample code for the *FileChannel* has the following projects:

- **FileChannel**   Contains the implementation of the *FileChannel*.

- **DemonstrationObjects**   Contains a class named *Demo*. Our example client and server will be remoting an instance of the *Demo* class.

- **Server**   Registers the *FileChannel* with channel services. This project then simply waits for the user to terminate the server by pressing Enter. In the configuration file, the server is told to watch the directory C:\File.

- **Client**   Like the server project, this project registers the *FileChannel*. The project then demonstrates various types of method calls.

Implementing the *FileClientChannel* Class

Because *FileClientChannel* derives from the interface *IChannelSender*, we must implement the method *CreateSink*. In addition to *CreateSink*, we must add the *ChannelName* property, the *ChannelPriority* property, and the *Parse* method. These last three members are required because *IChannelSender* derives from *IChannel*. Adding these members will give us a basic starting point for *FileClientChannel*.

```
public class FileClientChannel : IChannelSender
{
    private String m_ChannelName = "file";
    private int m_ChannelPriority = 1;

    private IClientChannelSinkProvider m_ClientProvider = null;

    IClientChannelSinkProvider m_ClientProvider = null;
    public IMessageSink CreateMessageSink( String url,
                                           object remoteChannelData,
                                           out String objectURI )

    {
        ⋮
```

```
    }

    public String Parse( String url, out String objectURI )
    {
        return FileChannelHelper.Parse( url, out objectURI );
    }

    public String ChannelName
    {
        get { return m_ChannelName; }
    }

    public int ChannelPriority
    {
        get { return m_ChannelPriority; }
    }
}
```

Notice that we added two methods and two properties to our new class. All four of these members are required for channels that send request messages. To store the values returned by *ChannelName* and *ChannelPriority*, we added three new private fields: *m_ChannelName*, *m_ChannelPriority*, and *m_ClientProvider*. The *m_ChannelName* and *m_ChannelPriority* fields are initialized with default values that can be overridden by one of the constructors. The *m_ClientProvider* variable holds a reference to the sink provider. The *Parse* method calls the static method *Parse* on the class *FileChannelHelper*. The reason for moving the parse functionality into a separate class is to allow *FileClientChannel* and *FileServerChannel* to share the implementation. We'll take a closer look at *Parse* later in the chapter.

Next we need to add two constructors to *FileClientChannel*. The first constructor will set up a basic channel that uses SOAP as its formatter:

```
public FileClientChannel()
{
    ⋮
}
```

The second constructor allows you to customize the channel with an *IDictionary* object and to create the channel via a configuration file. To meet the requirements for configuration file support, the constructor must have a parameter that takes an instance of an *IClientChannelSinkProvider* object. The following constructor meets our requirements:

```
public FileClientChannel( IDictionary properties,
                          IClientChannelSinkProvider sinkProvider )
{
    if( properties != null )
```

(continued)

```
    {
        foreach (DictionaryEntry entry in properties)
        {
            switch ((String)entry.Key)
            {
                case "name":
                    m_ChannelName = ( String ) entry.Value;
                    break;
                case "priority":
                    m_ChannelPriority = ( int ) entry.Value;
                    break;
            }
        }
    }

    m_ClientProvider = sinkProvider;

    ⋮
}
```

This constructor extracts the information from the *IDictionary* object. The only two customizable parts of the *FileClientChannel* are the *ChannelName* and *ChannelPriority*. Because *ChannelName* and *ChannelPriority* are read-only properties, this constructor is the only place where you can change the member fields.

It's the responsibility of the *FileClientChannel* class to create the channel provider chain. Later, this provider chain will create the channel sink chain. *FileClientChannel* must also provide a default formatter for the instances in which the user of the class doesn't specify one. The following function will handle this for the *FileClientChannel*:

```
private void SetupClientChannel()
{
    if( m_ClientProvider == null )
    {
        m_ClientProvider = new SoapClientFormatterSinkProvider();
        m_ClientProvider.Next = new FileClientChannelSinkProvider();
    }
    else
    {
        AddClientProviderToChain(
                    m_ClientProvider,
                    new FileClientChannelSinkProvider( ));
    }
}
```

SetupClientChannel first checks to see whether a provider already exists by testing *m_ClientProvider* for *null*. If *m_ClientProvider* is *null*, we must build an *IClientChannelSinkProvider* chain. Part of building the provider chain is selecting a formatter provider for the channel. *FileChannel* will use *System.Runtime.Remoting.Channels.SoapClientFormatterSinkProvider*. Next we add our provider to the end of the chain. If *m_ClientProvider* isn't *null*, we must add our provider to the end of the chain. We do this by calling *AddClientProviderToChain*. This method is a replica of an internal remoting method of the same name found in the *CoreChannel* class.

```
private static void AddClientProviderToChain(
                        IClientChannelSinkProvider clientChain,
                        IClientChannelSinkProvider clientProvider )
{
    while( clientChain.Next != null )
    {
        clientChain = clientChain.Next;
    }

    clientChain.Next = clientProvider;
}
```

Because our provider must be last in the chain, *AddClientProviderToChain* must first move to the end of the chain. This is accomplished by calling the property *Next* until it returns *null*. At this point, we insert the new provider into the proper position in the chain.

Our final method to implement is *CreateMessageSink*. *CreateMessageSink* returns a reference to an *IMessageSink* object. At a minimum, this object will contain a formatter sink and our *FileClientChannelSink*. The remote object proxy then uses the chain to dispatch method calls. *CreateMessageSink* must be able to handle both client-activated and server-activated objects. When making a method call on a server-activated object, the *url* parameter will contain the URL that the channel was configured with. However, when making a call on a client-activated object, the *remoteChannelData* parameter will contain the URL.

```
public IMessageSink CreateMessageSink( String url,
                        object remoteChannelData,
                        out String objectURI )
{
    objectURI = null;
    String ChannelURI = null;

    if( url != null )
    {
        ChannelURI = Parse( url, out objectURI );
```

(continued)

```
        }
        else
        {
            if(( remoteChannelData != null ) &&
               ( remoteChannelData is IChannelDataStore ))
            {
                IChannelDataStore DataStore =
                    ( IChannelDataStore )remoteChannelData;

                ChannelURI = Parse( DataStore.ChannelUris[0],
                                    out objectURI );
                if( ChannelURI != null )
                {
                    url = DataStore.ChannelUris[0];
                }
            }
        }

        if( ChannelURI != null )
        {
            return ( IMessageSink ) m_ClientProvider.CreateSink( this,
                                             url, remoteChannelData );
        }

        objectURI = "";
        return null;
}
```

The majority of the code in *CreateMessageSink* is determining the correct server-activated or client-activated URL to pass to *CreateSink*. We first check the *url* parameter that's passed in to see whether it's *null*. If it's not *null*, we simply use the *Parse* function to extract the channel URI and the object URI. Calling *Parse* is also a sanity check to make sure that the URL is valid. If both the return value and the *objectURI* value are *null*, we don't have a proper URL for this channel. If the *url* parameter is *null*, we'll have to extract the information from the *remoteChannelData* parameter. The .NET Remoting infrastructure retrieves *remoteChannelData* from the server side of the channel. This object must be of the type *System.Runtime.Remoting.Channels.IChannelDataStore*. Before using this object, we must check its validity by using the *is* keyword. If the object is the correct type, we can cast it to a local variable of type *IChannelDataStore*. Recall from our *HttpChannel* discussion that an *IChannelDataStore* object contains an array of URIs that the server can process for this channel. As with the well-known object case, we'll check the channel URI that's returned from *Parse* to ensure we have a valid URL. Once we've reached this point, it's safe to call the *CreateSink* method on our *FileClientChannelSinkProvider*.

Implementing the *FileClientChannelSinkProvider* Class

The main purpose of *FileClientChannelSinkProvider* is to create our transport sink, *FileClientChannelSink*. Because *FileClientChannelSinkProvider* derives from the interface *IClientChannelSinkProvider*, we must implement the members *CreateSink* and *Next*. Because this is the last provider in the chain, *Next* will return only *null* and *CreateSink* will return only a reference to a new *FileClientChannelSink*.

```
internal class
    FileClientChannelSinkProvider : IClientChannelSinkProvider
{
    public IClientChannelSink CreateSink( IChannelSender channel,
                                          String url,
                                          Object remoteChannelData )
    {
        return new FileClientChannelSink( url );
    }

    public IClientChannelSinkProvider Next
    {
        get
        {
            return null;
        }
        set
        {
            throw new NotSupportedException();
        }
    }
}
```

As you can see, *CreateSink* simply creates a new *FileClientChannelSink* by passing in the URL.

Implementing the *FileClientChannelSink* Class

FileClientChannelSink handles the dispatching of method calls. It has the following responsibilities:

■   Handling synchronous method calls

■   Handling asynchronous method calls

■   Packaging and unpackaging the *ITransportHeaders* and *Stream* data into a file

■   Handling return messages from the server

FileClientChannelSink derives from the interface *IClientChannelSink*. Because we're the last sink in the chain, we'll add functionality to our implementation of *IClientChannelSink.ProcessMessage* and *IClientChannelSink.Async-ProcessRequest* only. *ProcessMessage* and *AsyncProcessRequest* are responsible for handling the first two items in the list. This is the basic layout for our new class:

```
internal class FileClientChannelSink : IClientChannelSink
{
    private String m_PathToServer = null;

    public delegate void AsyncDelegate( String fileName,
                                IClientChannelSinkStack sinkStack );

    public FileClientChannelSink( String url )
    {
        String ObjectURI;
        m_PathToServer = FileChannelHelper.Parse( url,
                                            out ObjectURI );
    }

    public void AsyncProcessRequest(
        IClientChannelSinkStack sinkStack,
        IMessage msg,
        ITransportHeaders requestHeaders,
        Stream requestStream )
    {
        ⋮
    }

    public void AsyncProcessResponse(
        IClientResponseChannelSinkStack sinkStack,
        object state,
        ITransportHeaders headers,
        Stream stream )
    {
        throw new NotSupportedException();
    }

    public Stream GetRequestStream( IMessage msg,
                                ITransportHeaders headers )
    {
        return null;
    }

    public void ProcessMessage( IMessage msg,
                                ITransportHeaders requestHeaders,
```

```
                               Stream requestStream,
                               out ITransportHeaders responseHeaders,
                               out Stream responseStream )
    {
        ⋮
    }

    public IClientChannelSink NextChannelSink
    {
        get
        {
            return null;
        }
    }

    public IDictionary Properties
    {
        get
        {
            return null;
        }
    }
}
```

ProcessMessage handles all synchronous methods calls. To do this, *Process-Message* must first bundle up the data necessary for the server to perform the method call. *ProcessMessage* then sends the request message to the server and waits for the return message. Upon receipt of the server's return message, *Process-Message* reconstitutes the response message into the appropriate variables.

```
public void ProcessMessage( IMessage msg,
                            ITransportHeaders requestHeaders,
                            Stream requestStream,
                            out ITransportHeaders responseHeaders,
                            out Stream responseStream )
{
    String uri = ExtractURI( msg );

    ChannelFileData data = new ChannelFileData( uri,
                                                requestHeaders,
                                                requestStream );
    String FileName = ChannelFileTransportWriter.Write(
                                     data,
                                     m_PathToServer,
                                     null );
    FileChannelHelper.WriteSOAPStream( requestStream,
                                       FileName + "_SOAP" );
```

(continued)

```
            FileName = ChangeFileExtension.ChangeFileNameToClientExtension(
                                               FileName );

            WaitForFile.Wait( FileName );

            ChannelFileData ReturnData =
                              ChannelFileTransportReader.Read( FileName );

            responseHeaders = ReturnData.header;
            responseStream = ReturnData.stream;
        }
```

ProcessMessage is the first method we have written that's specific to our transport. To remain transport agnostic as long as possible, we'll discuss the transport specifics of this method in more detail later.

AsyncProcessRequest handles asynchronous method calls against the remote object. *AsyncProcessRequest* will handle two types of request. Both requests package up and send the message in a similar manner as *ProcessMessage*. The difference is their actions after the message is delivered. The first request type is a *OneWay* asynchronous request. A *OneWay* method is marked with the *OneWayAttribute* and signals that we expect no return of data or confirmation of success. To check whether a method call is *OneWay*, we must inspect the *IMessage* object. The second request type is an ordinary asynchronous request. For this type of request, we'll invoke a delegate that waits for the return message.

```
public void AsyncProcessRequest( IClientChannelSinkStack sinkStack,
                                 IMessage msg,
                                 ITransportHeaders requestHeaders,
                                 Stream requestStream )
{
    String uri = ExtractURI( msg );

    ChannelFileData data = new ChannelFileData( uri,
                                                requestHeaders,
                                                requestStream );
    String FileName = ChannelFileTransportWriter.Write( data,
                                             m_PathToServer, null );
    FileChannelHelper.WriteSOAPStream( requestStream,
                                       FileName + "_SOAP" );

    if( !IsOneWayMethod( (IMethodCallMessage)msg ))
    {
        FileName =
            ChangeFileExtension.ChangeFileNameToClientExtension(
                                                    FileName );
        AsyncDelegate Del = new AsyncDelegate( this.AsyncHandler );
        Del.BeginInvoke( FileName, sinkStack, null, null );
    }
}
```

Our implementation of *AsyncProcessRequest* packages up the message and sends it to the server. We then use the private method *FileClientChannelSink.IsOneWayMethod* to check whether we need to wait for a return message:

```
private bool IsOneWayMethod( IMethodCallMessage methodCallMessage )
{
    MethodBase methodBase = methodCallMessage.MethodBase;
    return RemotingServices.IsOneWay(methodBase);
}
```

The static method *System.Runtime.RemotingServices.IsOneWay* returns a Boolean value indicating whether the method described by the supplied *MethodBase* parameter is marked with the *OneWayAttribute*.

When the method isn't a *OneWay* method, we invoke an *AsyncDelegate*. At construction, we pass *AsyncDelegate* the method *FileClientChannelSink.AsyncHandler*. The method alone isn't enough to complete the asynchronous call. We must also pass a sink stack object to *BeginInvoke*. The sink stack is used to chain together all the sinks that want to work on the returning message.

The job of *AsyncHandler* is to wait for the response message from the server. *AsyncHandler* will reconstitute the data into an *ITransportHeader* and *Stream* object before passing it up the sink chain:

```
private void AsyncHandler( String FileName,
                          IClientChannelSinkStack sinkStack )
{
    try
    {
        if( WaitForFile.Wait( FileName ))
        {
            ChannelFileData ReturnData =
                    ChannelFileTransportReader.Read( FileName );

            sinkStack.AsyncProcessResponse( ReturnData.header,
                                            ReturnData.stream );
        }
    }
    catch (Exception e)
    {
        if (sinkStack != null)
        {
            sinkStack.DispatchException(e);
        }
    }

}
```

After the invocation of the delegate, the thread of execution will continue. This allows the application to continue without waiting for the server response.

In this next step, we'll construct the server-side classes for *FileChannel*. We'll create two classes, *FileServerChannel* and *FileServerChannelSink*. These two classes will correspond with two server-side classes, *HttpServerChannel* and *HttpServerTransportSink*, which we discussed in the "How Channels Are Constructed" section of the chapter.

Implementing the *FileServerChannel* Class

FileServerChannel is the main class for our server-side processing. It has the following responsibilities:

- Listening for incoming messages

- Creating a formatter sink

- Creating a *FileServerChannelSink*

- Building the sink chain

As we discuss the construction of *FileServerChannel*, we'll take extra care in addressing these items.

FileServerChannel will be receiving messages; therefore, it must implement *IChannelReceiver*. Because *IChannelReceiver* implements *IChannel*, we must add three new members to *FileServerChannel*: *ChannelName*, *ChannelPriority*, and *Parse*. To support *IChannelReceiver* functionality, we must add the members *ChannelData*, *GetUrlsForUri*, *StartListening*, and *StopListening*. Let's start by examining the public interface of *FileServerChannel*:

```
public class FileServerChannel : IChannelReceiver
{
    public FileServerChannel( String serverPath ){ ... }

    public FileServerChannel( IDictionary properties,
                              IServerChannelSinkProvider provider )
        { ... }

    // IChannel members
    public String Parse( String url, out String objectURI ){ ... }

    public String ChannelName{ ... }

    public int ChannelPriority{ ... }

    // IChannelReceiver members
    public void StartListening( Object data ){ ... }
```

```
public void StopListening( Object data ){ ... }

public String[] GetUrlsForUri( String objectURI ){ ... }

public Object ChannelData{ ... }
}
```

As with *FileClientChannel*, *FileServerChannel* has two constructors. The first is a simple constructor that sets the private member variable *m_ServerPath* to the value passed into the constructor and calls the private method *Init*. The *m_ServerPath* variable designates which directory the server will watch for files.

The second constructor will allow for more granularity in the *FileServer-Channel* settings. Like the first constructor, it must also call *Init*.

```
public FileServerChannel( IDictionary properties,
                          IServerChannelSinkProvider provider )
{
    m_SinkProvider = provider;

    if( properties != null )
    {
        foreach (DictionaryEntry entry in properties)
        {
            switch ((String)entry.Key)
            {
                case "name":
                    m_ChannelName = ( String ) entry.Value;
                    break;
                case "priority":
                    m_ChannelPriority = ( int ) entry.Value;
                    break;
                case "serverpath":
                    m_ServerPath = ( String ) entry.Value;
                    break;
            }
        }
    }

    // Since the FileChannel constructor that calls this constructor
    // creates both the FileClientChannel and FileServerChannel
    // objects, we must check the m_ServerPath to see if we should
    // listen for incoming messages.
    if( m_ServerPath != null )
    {
        Init();
    }
}
```

Using this constructor is the only way to change the values returned by the get properties *ChannelName* and *ChannelPriority*. Both constructors call the *Init* method, which performs the following actions:

1. Creates a formatter

2. Initializes a *ChannelDataStore* object

3. Populates the *ChannelDataStore* object data from the provider chain

4. Creates the sink chain

5. Calls the method *StartListening*

When we built *FileClientChannel*, we chose *SoapClientFormatterSinkProvider* for our formatter provider; therefore, the server must use the corresponding provider—*SoapServerFormatterSinkProvider*.

```
private void Init()
{
    // If a formatter provider was not specified, we must create one.
    if( m_SinkProvider == null )
    {
        // FileChannel uses the SOAP formatter if no provider
        // is specified.
        m_SinkProvider = new SoapServerFormatterSinkProvider();
    }

    // Initialize the ChannelDataStore object with our channel URI.
    m_DataStore = new ChannelDataStore( null );
    m_DataStore.ChannelUris = new String[1];
    m_DataStore.ChannelUris[0] = "file://" + m_ServerPath;

    PopulateChannelData( m_DataStore, m_SinkProvider );

    IServerChannelSink sink =
        ChannelServices.CreateServerChannelSinkChain( m_SinkProvider,
                                                      this );

    // Add our transport sink to the chain.
    m_Sink = new FileServerChannelSink( sink, m_ServerPath );

    StartListening( null );
}
```

In the previous snippet, *m_DataStore* is populated with our channel URI. We use the private method *PopulateChannelData* to iterate the provider chain and collect data:

```
private void PopulateChannelData( ChannelDataStore channelData,
                                  IServerChannelSinkProvider provider)
```

```
{
    while (provider != null)
    {
        provider.GetChannelData(channelData);

        provider = provider.Next;
    }
}
```

The *GetChannelData* method extracts information from the provider's *IChannelDataStore* member. Because *GetChannelData* is a member of the *IServerChannelSinkProvider* interfaces, this member is present in all channel sink providers.

The next interesting part of *Init* is the call to *ChannelServices.CreateServerChannelSinkChain*. This static method builds the server-side sink chain. After we have the sink chain, we must add our sink, *FileServerChannelSink*, to the chain. The final responsibility for *Init* is to call the method *StartListening*.

StartListening is the first of the four members of the *IChannelReceiver* interface that we'll create. *StartListening* must create and start a thread that will watch a directory for incoming messages. After creating the thread, the function must not block on the main thread of execution but instead return from *StartListening*. This allows the server to continue to work while waiting to receive messages.

```
public void StartListening( Object data )
{
    ThreadStart ListeningThreadStart = new ThreadStart(
                            m_Sink.ListenAndProcessMessage );
    m_ListeningThread = new Thread( ListeningThreadStart );
    m_ListeningThread.IsBackground = true;
    m_ListeningThread.Start();
}
```

The *ThreadStart* delegate must be assigned a method that will be executed when our thread calls start. The method we'll be executing, *ListenAndProcessMessage*, is implemented as a public method on our sink. Once the thread is running, the server will accept request messages. The *StopListening* method simply ends the listening thread by calling *m_ListeningThread.Abort*.

```
public void StopListening( Object data )
{
    if( m_ListeningThread != null )
    {
        m_ListeningThread.Abort();
        m_ListeningThread = null;
    }
}
```

The final two *IChannelReceiver* members we need to implement are *ChannelData* and *GetUrlsForUri*. *ChannelData* is simply a read-only property that returns our *IChannelDataStore* member. *GetUrlsForUri* will take an object URI and return an array of URLs. For example, if the object URI *Demo.uri* is passed into *FileServerChannel.GetUrlsForUri*, the object URI should return *file:/ /<m_ServerPath>/Demo.uri*.

```
public String[] GetUrlsForUri( String objectURI )
{
    String[] URL = new String[1];

    if (!objectURI.StartsWith("/"))
    {
        objectURI = "/" + objectURI;
    }

    URL[0] = "file://" + m_ServerPath + objectURI;

    return URL;
}
```

The implementation for the *IChannel* members is straightforward. *Channel-Name* and *ChannelPriority* are read-only properties that return their respective member variables, *m_ChannelName* and *m_ChannelPriority*. *Parse* calls the shared implementation of *Parse* in the *FileChannelHelper* class.

Implementing the *FileServerChannelSink* Class

The job of *FileServerChannelSink* is to dispatch request messages from the client to the .NET Remoting infrastructure. *FileServerChannelSink* will implement the interface *IServerChannelSink*, so we must implement the members *NextChannel-Sink, AsyncProcessResponse, IServerChannelSink*, and *ProcessMessage*. Because we don't need to do any processing to the request message, we won't add any functionality to *ProcessMessage*. *IServerChannelSink* throws a *NotSupported-Exception* because we don't need to build a stream. The constructor for *FileServerChannelSink* must take a reference to the next sink in the chain. The read-only property *NextChannelSink* allows access to the reference. This is the basic layout of *FileServerChannelSink*:

```
internal class FileServerChannelSink : IServerChannelSink
{
    private IServerChannelSink m_NextSink = null;
    private string m_DirectoryToWatch;

    public FileServerChannelSink( IServerChannelSink nextSink,
                                  String directoryToWatch )
```

```
{
    m_NextSink = nextSink;
    m_DirectoryToWatch = directoryToWatch;
}

public ServerProcessing ProcessMessage(
                        IServerChannelSinkStack sinkStack,
                        IMessage requestMsg,
                        ITransportHeaders requestHeaders,
                        Stream requestStream,
                        out IMessage responseMsg,
                        out ITransportHeaders responseHeaders,
                        out Stream responseStream )
{
    throw new NotSupportedException();
}

public void AsyncProcessResponse(
                        IServerResponseChannelSinkStack sinkStack,
                        Object state,
                        IMessage msg,
                        ITransportHeaders headers,
                        Stream stream )
{
}

public Stream GetResponseStream(
                        IServerResponseChannelSinkStack sinkStack,
                        Object state,
                        IMessage msg,
                        ITransportHeaders headers )
{
    throw new NotSupportedException();
    return null;
}

public IServerChannelSink NextChannelSink
{
    get
    {
        return m_NextSink;
    }
}

public IDictionary Properties
{
    get
```

(continued)

```
        {
            return null;
        }
    }

    internal void ListenAndProcessMessage()
    {
        ⋮
    }
}
```

ListenAndProcessMessage is where all action takes place in *FileServer-ChannelSink. ListenAndProcessMessage* has the following responsibilities:

- Wait for messages
- Extract the *ITransportHeader* and *Stream* data from the message
- Pass the request to the sink chain
- Respond to the client

```
internal void ListenAndProcessMessage()
{
    while( true )
    {
        // Wait for client messages.
        String FileName = WaitForFile.InfiniteWait();

        // Server received a message; extract the data from
        // the message.
        ChannelFileData Data = ChannelFileTransportReader.Read(
                                                FileName );

        ITransportHeaders MessageHeader = Data.header;
        MessageHeader[ CommonTransportKeys.RequestUri ] = Data.URI;
        Stream MessageStream = Data.stream;

        // Add ourselves to the sink stack.
        ServerChannelSinkStack Stack = new ServerChannelSinkStack();
        Stack.Push(this, null);

        IMessage ResponseMsg;
        ITransportHeaders ResponseHeaders;
        Stream ResponseStream;

        // Start the request in the sink chain.
        ServerProcessing Operation = m_NextSink.ProcessMessage(
```

```
                                          Stack,
                                          null,
                                          MessageHeader,
                                          MessageStream,
                                          out ResponseMsg,
                                          out ResponseHeaders,
                                          out ResponseStream );

        // Respond to the client.
        switch( Operation )
        {
            case ServerProcessing.Complete:
                Stack.Pop( this );
                ChannelFileData data = new ChannelFileData( null,
                                        ResponseHeaders,
                                        ResponseStream );

                String ClientFileName = ChangeFileExtension.
                        ChangeFileNameToClientExtension( FileName );
                ChannelFileTransportWriter.Write( data,
                                        null,
                                        ClientFileName );
                FileChannelHelper.WriteSOAPMessageToFile(
                                ResponseStream,
                                ClientFileName + "_SOAP" );
                break;
            case ServerProcessing.Async:
                Stack.StoreAndDispatch(m_NextSink, null);
                break;
            case ServerProcessing.OneWay:
                break;


        }
    }
}
```

We'll discuss the transport toward the end of this section, so for now we'll gloss over those details. The first thing *ListenAndProcessMessage* does is infinitely wait on a message. Upon receipt of a request message, we extract the data. Before passing the data to the sink chain, we create a sink stack. To create a sink stack, we use the class *System.Runtime.Remoting.Channel.ServerChainSinkStack*. Once we have a new *ServerChainSinkStack*, we call its *Push* method. The first parameter takes an *IServerChannelSink* object, and the second parameter takes an object. The object parameter allows you to associate some state with your sink. This state comes into play only for channels that will be processing in *AsyncProcessResponse*, *ProcessMessage*, and *IServerChannelSink*, which our channel doesn't. *ProcessMessage* starts the processing of the request by the client. *ProcessMessage* returns a *ServerProcessing* object. With this object, we can determine the next action we must take. In the case of *ServerProcessing.Complete*, we remove our sink from the sink stack by using the *ServerChainSinkStack.Pop* method. *Pop* not only removes our sink, it removes any sink added after it.

So far, we have five classes that implement the majority of the custom channel functionality. The next class we must implement will tie together the server-side and the client-side classes.

Implementing the *FileChannel* Class

FileChannel is very simple. Its sole purpose is to provide a unified interface for both client and server, so it must implement both *IChannelSender* and *IChannelReceiver*. *FileChannel* has three constructors:

```
public FileChannel();
public FileChannel( String serverPath );
public FileChannel( IDictionary properties,
                    IClientChannelSinkProvider clientProviderChain,
                    IServerChannelSinkProvider serverProviderChain );
```

The first constructor creates a *FileClientChannel* object and assigns it to the private member *m_ClientChannel*. When using this constructor, *FileChannel* can send request messages only. The second constructor initializes the private member *m_ServerChannel* with a newly created *FileServerChannel*. This constructor requires a directory that we'll pass along to the *FileServerChannel*. The third constructor creates both a *FileServerChannel* and a *FileClientChannel*.

```
public FileChannel( IDictionary properties,
                    IClientChannelSinkProvider clientProviderChain,
                    IServerChannelSinkProvider serverProviderChain )
{
    m_ClientChannel = new FileClientChannel( properties,
                                             clientProviderChain );
    m_ServerChannel = new FileServerChannel( properties,
                                             serverProviderChain );
}
```

When configuring *FileChannel* via a configuration file, the .NET Remoting infrastructure will use this constructor. The remaining public members for *FileChannel* simply call their counterparts that have been implemented in either *FileServerChannel* or *FileClientChannel*.

```
public class FileChannel : IChannelSender, IChannelReceiver
{
    private FileClientChannel m_ClientChannel = null;
    private FileServerChannel m_ServerChannel = null;
```

```
// Constructors have been removed from this snippet.

public String Parse( String url, out String objectURI )
{
    return FileChannelHelper.Parse( url, out objectURI );
}

public String ChannelName
{
    get
    {
        if( m_ServerChannel != null )
        {
            return m_ServerChannel.ChannelName;
        }
        else
        {
            return m_ClientChannel.ChannelName;
        }
    }
}

public int ChannelPriority
{
    get
    {
        if( m_ServerChannel != null )
        {
            return m_ServerChannel.ChannelPriority;
        }
        else
        {
            return m_ClientChannel.ChannelPriority;
        }
    }
}

public Object ChannelData
{
    get
    {
        if( m_ServerChannel != null )
        {
            return m_ServerChannel.ChannelData;
        }

        return null;
    }
```

(continued)

```
    }

    public String[] GetUrlsForUri( String objectURI )
    {
        return m_ServerChannel.GetUrlsForUri( objectURI );
    }

    public void StartListening( Object data )
    {
        m_ServerChannel.StartListening( data );
    }

    public void StopListening( Object data )
    {
        m_ServerChannel.StopListening( data );
    }

    public IMessageSink CreateMessageSink( String url,
                                           object remoteChannelData,
                                           out String objectURI )
    {
        return m_ClientChannel.CreateMessageSink( url,
                                                  remoteChannelData,
                                                  out objectURI );
    }
}
```

Implementing the *FileChannelHelper* Class

The next step involves creating a helper class that will contain methods that share functionality between *FileClientChannel* and *FileServerChannel*. Because all these methods will be static, we made the constructor private. In the previous code snippets, we used the call to *FileChannelHelper.Parse* several times. Now we need to create the *Parse* method. As we've discussed, *Parse* is a member of the *IChannel* interface; therefore, the .NET Remoting infrastructure defines the method signature. *Parse* takes a URL as a parameter and returns a channel URI. In addition, *Parse* returns the object URI through an *out* parameter.

```
public static String Parse( String url, out String objectURI )
{
    objectURI = null;

    if( !url.StartsWith( "file://" ) )
    {
        return null;
```

```
    }

    int BeginChannelURI = url.IndexOf( "://", 0, url.Length ) + 3;
    int EndOfChannelURI = url.LastIndexOf( "/" );

    String ChannelURI;
    if( BeginChannelURI < EndOfChannelURI )
    {
        ChannelURI = url.Substring( BeginChannelURI,
                            EndOfChannelURI - BeginChannelURI );
        objectURI = url.Substring( EndOfChannelURI + 1 );
    }
    else
    {
        ChannelURI = url.Substring( BeginChannelURI );
    }

    return ChannelURI;
}
```

The key item to note in the snippet is the check for *file://* in the URI. This action allows *Parse* to identify whether *FileChannel* should be processing this URL. For example, if the URL starts with *http://*, we'd return *null* in both parameters.

The next method in *FileChannelHelper* is *WriteSOAPMessageToFile*. *WriteSOAPMessageToFile* writes a SOAP message stream to a file, thus providing a tool for diagnostic and educational purposes:

```
public static void WriteSOAPMessageToFile( Stream stream,
                                        String FileName )
{
    StreamWriter Writer = new StreamWriter( FileName );
    StreamReader sr = new StreamReader(stream);
    String line;
    while ((line = sr.ReadLine()) != null)
    {
        Writer.WriteLine(line);
    }
    Writer.Flush();
    Writer.Close();

    stream.Position = 0;
}
```

Creating the *FileChannel* Transport Class

Up until this point, we've avoided transport-specific discussions because we could show a clear separation between the mechanics of creating a channel and the transport. With the exception of configuration information, we see transport-specific code only in the following methods:

- *FileClientChannelSink.ProcessMessage*

- *FileClientChannelSink.AsyncProcessRequest*

- *FileClientChannelSink.AsyncHandler*

- *FileServerChannelSink.ProcessMessage*

Our transport will require a two-step process for both reading and writing messages. The first step is to load the class *ChannelFileData* with the data we'll need to send to the server. Once the data is contained in *ChannelFileData*, we'll use a *FileStream* to serialize it to the specified path. When reading data, we perform the steps in reverse.

The data contained in *ChannelFileData* consists of the request URI, *ITransportHeaders*, and the *Stream*:

```
[Serializable]
public class ChannelFileData
{
    private String m_URI = null;
    private ITransportHeaders m_Header = null;
    private byte[] m_StreamBytes = null;

    public ChannelFileData( String URI,
                            ITransportHeaders headers,
                            Stream stream )
    {
        String objectURI;
        String ChannelURI = FileChannelHelper.Parse( URL,
                                                out objectURI );
        if( ChannelURI == null )
        {
            objectURI = URL;
        }
        m_URI = objectURI;
        m_Header = headers;
        m_StreamBytes = new Byte[ (int)stream.Length ];
        stream.Read( m_StreamBytes, 0, (int) stream.Length );
        stream.Position = 0;
    }
```

```
public String URI
{
    get
    {
        return m_URI;
    }
}

public ITransportHeaders header
{
    get
    {
        return m_Header;
    }
}

public Stream stream
{
    get
    {
        return new MemoryStream( m_StreamBytes, false );
    }
}
}
```

First, notice that *ChannelFileData* has the *Serializable* attribute. This is integral for the next step. The only way to set data in *ChannelFileData* is through the constructor. To retrieve the data from the *ChannelFileData* object, we provide read-only properties.

Now that we have our data class to serialize, we need to create a class that writes the file to disk. This class, *ChannelFileTransportWriter*, will have a single method, named *Write*. For parameters, *Write* will take a *ChannelFileData* object, a path to write the file, and a name for the file.

```
public class ChannelFileTransportWriter
{
    private ChannelFileTransportWriter()
    {
    }

    public static String Write( ChannelFileData data,
                                String ServerPath,
                                String FileName )
    {
        // If FileName is null, generate a filename with Guid.NewGuid
        if( FileName == null )
```

(continued)

```
        {
            FileName = Path.Combine( ServerPath,
                                     Guid.NewGuid().ToString() +
                                     ".chn.server" );
        }

        // Append _Temp to the file name so the file is not accessed
        // by the server or client before we are finished writing the
        // file. After the data is written, we will rename the file.
        String TempFileName = FileName + "_Temp";
        IFormatter DataFormatter = new SoapFormatter();
        Stream DataStream = new FileStream( TempFileName,
                                            FileMode.Create,
                                            FileAccess.Write,
                                            FileShare.None );
        DataFormatter.Serialize( DataStream, data);
        DataStream.Close();

        File.Move( TempFileName, FileName );
        return FileName;
    }
}
```

ChannelFileTransportWriter has a few key items of note. First, *ChannelFile-TransportWriter* maintains no state, so we don't need instances of this class. This allows us to make the constructor private and the *Write* method static. Notice that we use *Guid.NewGuid* to generate unique names. This allows us to avoid naming conflicts when we use multiple channels to connect to the server.

Now that we can write request and response message files, we must be able to read them. To do this, we'll create a class named *ChannelFileTransportReader* that defines a single method named *Read* that will populate a *ChannelFileData* object:

```
public class ChannelFileTransportReader
{
    private ChannelFileTransportReader()
    {
    }

    public static ChannelFileData Read( String FileName )
    {
        IFormatter DataFormatter = new SoapFormatter();
        Stream DataStream = new FileStream( FileName,
                                            FileMode.Open,
                                            FileAccess.Read,
                                            FileShare.Read);
```

```
        ChannelFileData data =
            (ChannelFileData) DataFormatter.Deserialize(
                                            DataStream );
        DataStream.Close();
        File.Move( FileName, FileName + "_processed" );

        return data;
    }
}
```

Notice in the *Read* method that, after we're finished with a message, we append the string *_processed* to the end of the filename. This allows us to see a history of the messages that were sent between the server and client.

The final transport class we need to create is *WaitForFile*. *WaitForFile* will have two methods, *Wait* and *InfiniteWait*. *Wait*'s responsibility is to wait for some period for a file to appear.

```
public static bool Wait( String filename )
{
    int RetryCount = 120;

    while( RetryCount > 0 )
    {
        Thread.Sleep( 500 );

        if( File.Exists( filename ))
        {
            return true;
        }

        RetryCount--;
    }

    return false;
}
```

Wait checks for the file every half second for 1 minute. A more advanced version of *FileChannel* would allow you to set the retry count and the sleep time in the configuration file. *InfiniteWait* will wake up every half a second to see whether a file with an extension of *.server* is in the specified directory.

```
public static String InfiniteWait( String DirectoryToWatch )
{
    // Loop forever or until a file is found.
    while( true )
    {
        String[] File = Directory.GetFiles( DirectoryToWatch,
                                        "*.server" );
```

(continued)

```
        if( File.Length > 0 )
        {
            return File[0];
        }

        Thread.Sleep( 500 );
    }
}
```

Implementing a Custom Channel Sink

Request and response messages pass from one end of a sink chain to the other. During this traversal, sinks have the opportunity to do work based on the message information. By creating a custom sink, we can hook ourselves into the sink chain and gain access to every message before transmission and after receipt. But custom sinks aren't limited to just manipulating messages. A custom sink could perform some action based on the contents of the message. Finally, custom sinks don't have to be symmetric, so you're not required to have a sink on both the server and client. The following real-world uses for custom sinks should help you gain an understanding of their power:

■ **Encryption sink**   Would encrypt all messages that are transmitted between the sender and receiver. An encryption sink would require a sink at both the sender and receiver.

■ **Logging sink**   Would write a message to a database each time an object is created or a method is called. The sink could be located on the server only, the client only, or both.

■ **Access-time sink**   Would block calls on remote objects during certain periods. The sink could be located on the server only, client only, or both.

■ **Authentication sink**   Would disallow certain users based on information contained in the message sent from the client. In this case, a client channel sink and server channel sink would exist, but they would perform different operations. The client would add authentication data to the message, whereas the server would take that information and determine whether the method can be called.

In the first part of this chapter, we created a transport-specific custom channel. In doing so, we had to create a custom sink for the client and server.

In this section, we'll create a custom sink that allows us to modify the behavior of a sink chain. When we created the server-side channel classes, we didn't create a class that implemented *IServerChannelSinkProvider*. This was the only place where the server and client class weren't symmetric. It wasn't necessary for us to create a server sink provider because we were the first sink in the chain. To support placing a custom sink in the sink chain, we'll implement *IServerChannelSinkProvider*. Table 7-10 contains the members of *IserverChannelSinkProvider*

Table 7-10   Members of *System.Runtime.Remoting. Channel.IServerChannelSinkProvider*

Member	Member Type	Description
Next	Property	Allows you to set and get the next *IServerChannelSinkProvider* object
CreateSink	Method	Returns an *IServerChannelSink* for the beginning of a new sink chain
GetChannelData	Method	Returns the *IChannelDataStore* object for the current *IServerChannelSinkProvider* object

Creating the *AccessTime* Custom Sink

In the remainder of this chapter, we'll create a custom sink that allows us to block method calls on remote objects during a particular period. The process will entail three steps:

- Creating a sink named *AccessTimeServerChannelSink* that implements *IServerChannelSink*

- Creating a provider named *AccessTimeServerChannelSinkProvider* that implements *IServerChannelSinkProvider*

- Adding functionality for the custom implementation

The purpose of the *AccessTime* custom sink is to control the number of times method calls can be made on a remote object. During channel creation, you can set a starting and stopping time. If a method call is attempted between the starting and stopping time, this call won't be processed—it will return an error.

AccessTime Projects

The sample code for the *AccessTime* custom sink has the following projects:

- **AccessTimeSinkLib**   Contains the implementation of the sink and the sink provider.

- **DemonstrationObjects**   Contains a class named *Demo*. Our example client and server will be remoting an instance of the *Demo* class.

- **Server**   Registers *AccessTimeServerChannelSinkProvider* and *AccessTimeServerChannelSink* with channel services. This project then simply waits for the user to terminate the server by pressing Enter.

- **Client**   Like the server project, this project registers *AccessTimeServerChannelSinkProvider* and *AccessTimeServerChannelSink* with channel services. The project then demonstrates a method call on the remote object.

Implementing the *AccessTimeServerChannelSink* Class

Let's start by taking a high-level look at the public interface of *AccessTimeServerChannelSink*:

```
public class AccessTimeServerChannelSink : IServerChannelSink
{
    public AccessTimeServerChannelSink( IServerChannelSink nextSink,
                                        String blockStartTime,
                                        String blockStopTime,
                                        bool isHttpChannel )
    {
        ⋮
    }

    public ServerProcessing ProcessMessage(
        IServerChannelSinkStack sinkStack,
        IMessage requestMsg,
        ITransportHeaders requestHeaders,
        Stream requestStream,
        out IMessage responseMsg,
        out ITransportHeaders responseHeaders,
        out Stream responseStream )
    {
```

```
        ⋮
}

public void AsyncProcessResponse(
    IServerResponseChannelSinkStack sinkStack,
    Object state,
    IMessage msg,
    ITransportHeaders headers,
    Stream stream )
{
}

public Stream GetResponseStream(
    IServerResponseChannelSinkStack sinkStack,
    Object state,
    IMessage msg,
    ITransportHeaders headers )
{
    return null;
}

public IServerChannelSink NextChannelSink
{
    get
    {
        return m_NextSink;
    }
}

public IDictionary Properties
{
    get
    {
        return null;
    }
}
}
```

As you can see, the *AccessTimeServerChannel* sink is basic. Of the public members, the constructor and process message will perform the work. The constructor for *AccessTimeServerChannel* is as follows:

```
public AccessTimeServerChannelSink( IServerChannelSink nextSink,
                                    String blockStartTime,
                                    String blockStopTime,
                                    bool isHttpChannel )
{
```

(continued)

```
    m_NextSink = nextSink;

    if(( blockStartTime.Length > 0 ) && ( blockStopTime.Length > 0))
    {
        ParseHourAndMinute( blockStartTime,
                            out m_BlockStartTimeHour,
                            out m_BlockStartTimeMinute );
        ParseHourAndMinute( blockStopTime,
                            out m_BlockStopTimeHour,
                            out m_BlockStopTimeMinute );
    }
    m_IsHttpChannel = isHttpChannel;
}
```

The two parameters, *blockStartTime* and *blockStopTime*, appear in the format *HH:MM*, where *HH* is the hour and *MM* is the minute. We'll use the private method *ParseHourAndMinute* to populate our member time variables.

ProcessMessage is where we allow or deny method calls. If we aren't in a blocked time period, we call *ProcessMessage* on the next sink. If we are in a blocked time period, we must return and let the client know we couldn't fulfill its request. Here's the implementation of *ProcessMessage*:

```
public ServerProcessing ProcessMessage(
                        IServerChannelSinkStack sinkStack,
                        IMessage requestMsg,
                        ITransportHeaders requestHeaders,
                        Stream requestStream,
                        out IMessage responseMsg,
                        out ITransportHeaders responseHeaders,
                        out Stream responseStream )
{
    // If we are not in a blocked time period,
    // send the message down the chain.
    if( !IsBlockTimePeriod( ) )
    {
        return m_NextSink.ProcessMessage( sinkStack,
                                          requestMsg,
                                          requestHeaders,
                                          requestStream,
                                          out responseMsg,
                                          out responseHeaders,
                                          out responseStream );
    }
    else
    {
        if( m_IsHttpChannel )
        {
```

```
            responseMsg = null;
            responseStream = null;

            responseHeaders = new TransportHeaders();
            responseHeaders["__HttpStatusCode"] = "403";

            return ServerProcessing.Complete;
        }
        else
        {
            throw new RemotingException( "Attempt made to call a " +
                                "method during a blocked time" );
        }
    }
}
```

First, notice that we call the private method *IsBlockTimePeriod*. *IsBlock-TimePeriod* first checks to see whether we have nonzero time values in our member variables. If this condition is met, we compare the times and return *true* if we should block and *false* if the request message should be processed. If we aren't blocking, we pass the same parameters to *m_NextSink.ProcessMessage*. When we do block, we respond to the client in one of two ways, depending on the type of channel. If the transport channel we're using in this sink chain is *HttpChannel*, we'll respond with an HTTP status code of 403. Upon receipt of this HTTP status code, the client will throw an exception that will bubble up to the user of the channel's code. When the transport channel isn't *HttpChannel*, we throw a *RemotingException*. The exception will be packaged into a response message and rethrown on the client side. But before any of this can happen, *AccessTimeServerChannelSinkProvider* must create an *Access-TimeServerChannelSink* object.

Implementing the *AccessTimeServerChannelSinkProvider* Class

The main responsibility of *AccessTimeServerChannelSinkProvider* is to inject our sink into the sink chain. The secondary responsibility is to collect the data needed by the sink. *AccessTimeServerChannelSinkProvider* implements the interface *IServerChannelSinkProvider*:

```
public class AccessTimeServerChannelSinkProvider :
    IServerChannelSinkProvider
{
    private IServerChannelSinkProvider m_NextProvider;

    String m_BlockStartTime;
```

(continued)

```
String m_BlockStopTime;

public AccessTimeServerChannelSinkProvider(
    IDictionary properties,
    ICollection providerData )
{
    // Get the start and stop time.
    // An exception will be thrown if these keys are not found
    // in properties.
    m_BlockStartTime = ( String )properties["BlockStartTime"];
    m_BlockStopTime = ( String )properties["BlockStopTime"];
}

public IServerChannelSink CreateSink( IChannelReceiver channel )
{
    bool IsHttpChannel = channel is HttpServerChannel;

    IServerChannelSink nextSink = null;
    if( m_NextProvider != null )
    {
        nextSink = m_NextProvider.CreateSink( channel );
    }

    return new AccessTimeServerChannelSink( nextSink,
                                            m_BlockStartTime,
                                            m_BlockStopTime,
                                            IsHttpChannel );
}

public void GetChannelData( IChannelDataStore channelData )
{
}

public IServerChannelSinkProvider Next
{
    get
    {
        return m_NextProvider;
    }
    set
    {
        m_NextProvider = value;
    }
}
}
```

The most important method in *AccessTimeServerChannelSinkProvider* is *CreateSink*. *CreateSink* has three responsibilities:

■   Create the remainder of the sink chain.

■   Create *AccessTimeServerChannelSink*.

■   Test to see whether *IChannelReceiver* is an *HttpServerChannel* type.

To create the remainder of the sink chain, we call *CreateSink* on the next provider. The next provider is stored in the member *m_NextProvider*. This member is set by the .NET Remoting infrastructure by using the *Next* property. When the call to *m_NextProvider.CreateSink* returns, we'll have a reference to the first sink in this chain. We then pass the reference to the constructor of *AccessTimeServerChannelSink*, so our sink will be part of the chain.

Adding *AccessTimeServerChannelSink* to a Configuration File

The following configuration file demonstrates how to add a sink:

```
<configuration>
    <system.runtime.remoting>
        <application>
            <service>
                <wellknown mode="Singleton"
                        type="DemonstrationObjects.Demo,→
                                DemonstrationObjects"
                        objectUri="DemoURI" />
            </service>
            <channels>
                <channel ref="http" port="4000">
                    <serverProviders>
                        <provider type="AccessTimeSyncLib.→
                            AccessTimeServerChannelSinkProvider,→
                            AccessTimeSinkLib"
                            BlockStartTime="10:00" BlockStopTime="16:00"/>
                        <formatter ref="soap"/>
                    </serverProviders>
                </channel>
            </channels>
        </application>
    </system.runtime.remoting>
</configuration>
```

Notice that under the channel element, we added the element *serverProviders*. The *serverProviders* element contains two elements. The first is *provider*. The *provider* element is where our sink is added by using the *type* attribute. You'll also see the two attributes that define the time to disallow method calls.

The second element under *serverProviders* is *formatter*. Recall from the custom channel that the constructor for *FileServerChannel* added a formatter only when the *provider* parameter was *null*; therefore, we must specify a formatter when adding our sink.

Summary

In this chapter, we looked at *HttpChannel* to gain an understanding of the structure of channels. We then used this knowledge create our own channel by using the file system as our transport. Regardless of whether you'll ever need to create a custom channel, you should now have a greater understanding of what's happening behind the scenes when you use *HttpChannel* or *TcpChannel*. We wrapped the discussion up with the creation of a custom sink. In Chapter 8, "Serialization Formatters," we'll extend this knowledge when we create a formatter sink.

8

Serialization Formatters

In this chapter, we'll develop a custom serialization formatter capable of plugging into the .NET Remoting infrastructure. Before we do that, we'll examine the architecture that the .NET Framework uses to serialize object instances. We'll also look at several of the classes that the .NET Framework defines that facilitate building a serialization formatter. Finally, we'll develop a client formatter sink and a server formatter sink that we'll use to serialize the .NET Remoting messages exchanged between remote objects.

Object Serialization

Serialization is the process of converting an object instance's state into a sequence of bits that can then be written to a stream or some other storage medium. Deserialization is the process of converting a serialized bit stream to an instance of an object type. As we mentioned in Chapter 2, "Understanding the .NET Remoting Architecture," the .NET Remoting infrastructure uses serialization to transfer instances of marshal-by-value object types across .NET Remoting boundaries. In the next few sections, we'll discuss how serialization works in the .NET Framework so that you'll have a better understanding of it when we develop a custom serialization formatter later in the chapter.

> **Note** For more information about object serialization, consult the MSDN documentation and the excellent series of articles by Jeffrey Richter in his .NET column of *MSDN Magazine* in the April 2002 and July 2002 issues.

Serializable Attribute

The .NET Framework provides an easy-to-use serialization mechanism for object implementers. To make a class, structure, delegate, or enumeration serializable, simply attribute it with the *SerializableAttribute* custom attribute, as shown in the following code snippet:

```
[Serializable]
class SomeClass
{
    public int  m_public = 5000;
    private int m_private = 5001;
}
```

Because we've attributed the *SomeClass* type with the *SerializableAttribute*, the common language runtime will automatically handle the serialization details for us. To prevent the serialization of a field member of a type attributed with the *SerializableAttribute*, you can attribute the field member with the *NonSerializedAttribute*.

To serialize object instances of the *SomeClass* type, we need a serialization formatter to do the serialization and a stream to hold the serialized bits. As we discussed in Chapter 2, the .NET Framework provides the *SoapFormatter* and *BinaryFormatter* classes for serializing object graphs to streams. The following code serializes an instance of the *SomeClass* type to a *MemoryStream* by using the *SoapFormatter*:

```
// Create a memory stream and serialize a
// new instance of SomeClass to it using a formatter.
MemoryStream s = new MemoryStream();
SoapFormatter fm = new SoapFormatter();
fm.Serialize( s, new SomeClass() );

// Output the stream contents to the console.
StreamReader r = new StreamReader(s);
s.Position = 0;
Console.WriteLine( r.ReadToEnd() );
s.Position = 0;

// Deserialize the stream to an instance of SomeClass.
SomeClass sc = (SomeClass)fm.Deserialize(s);
```

Executing this code results in the *SomeClass* instance being serialized to the *MemoryStream* instance in a SOAP format. The following listing shows the contents of the memory stream after serialization of the *SomeClass* instance. (We've inserted spaces and new lines to help readability.)

```
<SOAP-ENV:Envelope
 xmlns:xsi=http://www.w3.org/2001/XMLSchema-instance
 xmlns:xsd="http://www.w3.org/2001/XMLSchema"
 xmlns:SOAP-ENC=http://schemas.xmlsoap.org/soap/encoding/
 xmlns:SOAP-ENV=http://schemas.xmlsoap.org/soap/envelope/
 xmlns:clr="http://schemas.microsoft.com/soap/encoding/clr/1.0"
 SOAP-ENV:encodingStyle="http://schemas.xmlsoap.org/soap/encoding/">
    <SOAP-ENV:Body>
        <a1:SomeClass id="ref-1" xmlns:
        a1="http://schemas.microsoft.com/clr/nsassem/RemoteObjects/
        RemoteObjects%2C%20Version%3D1.0.904.25890%2C%20
        Culture%3Dneutral%2C%20PublicKeyToken%3Dnull">
            <m_public>5000</m_public>
            <m_private>5001</m_private>
        </a1:SomeClass>
    </SOAP-ENV:Body>
</SOAP-ENV:Envelope>
```

After the *<SOAP-ENV:Envelope>* element, you can see that the *SoapFormatter* serialized the *SomeClass* instance as a child element of the *<SOAP=ENV:Body>* element. Notice that the *<a1:SomeClass>* element includes an *id* attribute equal to *ref-1*. As we'll discuss later in the chapter, during serialization of an object graph, formatters assign each serialized object an object identifier that facilitates serialization and deserialization. Following the *id* attribute, the *<a1:SomeClass>* element includes an *xml* namespace attribute alias that indicates the complete assembly name, version, culture, and public key token information for the assembly that contains the *SomeClass* type. Each of the child elements of the *<a1:SomeClass>* element corresponds to a class member and contains the member's value. The *m_public* member's value is 5000, while the *m_private* member's value is 5001.

Customizing Object Serialization

Although using *SerializableAttribute* is easy, it might not always satisfy your serialization requirements. The .NET Framework allows a type attributed with the *SerializableAttribute* custom attribute to handle its own serialization by implementing the *ISerializable* interface. This interface defines one method, *GetObjectData*:

```
void GetObjectData(
    SerializationInfo info,
    StreamingContext context
);
```

During serialization, when the formatter encounters an instance of a type that implements the *ISerializable* interface, the formatter calls the *GetObject-Data* method on the object instance, passing it a reference to a *Serialization-Info* instance and a reference to a *StreamingContext* instance. The *SerializationInfo* class is basically a specialized dictionary class that holds key-value pairs that the formatter will serialize to the stream. Table 8-1 lists some of the more significant public members of the *SerializationInfo* class.

Table 8-1 Significant Public Members of *System.Runtime. Serialization.SerializationInfo*

Member	Member Type	Description
AssemblyName	Read-write property	The full name of the assembly containing the type being serialized. Includes version information, culture, and public key token. You can modify this in *GetObjectData* to affect the assembly used during deserialization.
FullTypeName	Read-write property	Equivalent to *Type.FullName* of the type being serialized. You can modify this in *GetObjectData* to cause the type to be deserialized as a different type.
MemberCount	Read-only property	Indicates the number of members that have been added to the *SerializationInfo* instance.
AddValue	Method	Adds a named value to the *Serialization-Info* instance. This method has various overloads based on the type of the object being added.
GetValue	Method	Gets a named value from the *Serializa-tionInfo* instance based on the type of the object being retrieved.

The object implementing *GetObjectData* uses the *SerializationInfo* instance referenced by the first parameter, *info*, to serialize any information it requires for later deserialization. The *GetObjectData* method's second parameter, *context*, references an instance of *StreamingContext* and corresponds to the object referenced by the formatter's *Context* property. The *StreamingContext* instance exposes two properties, *Context* and *State*, that convey additional information that can affect the serialization operation. Both properties are read-only and specified as parameters to the *StreamingContext* constructor. The *State* property can be any bitwise combination of the *StreamingContextStates* enumeration type members: *All, Clone, CrossAppDomain, CrossMachine, CrossProcess, File, Other, Persistence,* and *Remoting.* The *Context* property can reference any object and conveys user-defined data to the serialization and deserialization operation.

The following code defines a class that implements the *ISerializable* interface:

```
[Serializable]
public class SomeClass2 : ISerializable
{
    public int m_public = 5000;
    private int m_private = 5001;

    public void GetObjectData( SerializationInfo info,
                               StreamingContext context)
    {
        //
        // Add a datetime value to the serialization info.
        info.AddValue( "TimeStamp", DateTime.Now );

        //
        // Serialize object members.
        info.AddValue( "m1", m_public );
        info.AddValue( "m2", m_public );
    }

    // Special deserialization ctor
    protected SomeClass2( SerializationInfo info,
                          StreamingContext context)
    {
        // Retrieve object members from
        // the SerializationInfo instance.
        m_public = info.GetInt32("m1");
        m_private = info.GetInt32("m2");

        // Retrieve time stamp.
        DateTime ts = info.GetDateTime("TimeStamp");
    }
}
```

The *SomeClass2* type implements the *ISerializable.GetObjectData* method. Using the *info* parameter, *SomeClass2* adds a new value named *TimeStamp* that contains the current system date and time. Notice that in addition to the implementation of *GetObjectData*, the *SomeClass2* type defines a special constructor that takes the same parameters as *GetObjectData*. The special constructor is an implicit requirement of implementing the *ISerializable* interface. If you fail to provide this form of the constructor, the runtime will raise an exception when deserializing an instance of the type. The following listing shows what a SOAP-formatted serialized instance of *SomeClass2* looks like:

```
<SOAP-ENV:Envelope
 xmlns:xsi=http://www.w3.org/2001/XMLSchema-instance
 xmlns:xsd=http://www.w3.org/2001/XMLSchema
 xmlns:SOAP-ENC=http://schemas.xmlsoap.org/soap/encoding/
 xmlns:SOAP-ENV=http://schemas.xmlsoap.org/soap/envelope/
 xmlns:clr=http://schemas.microsoft.com/soap/encoding/clr/1.0
 SOAP-ENV:encodingStyle="http://schemas.xmlsoap.org/soap/encoding/">
    <SOAP-ENV:Body>
        <a1:SomeClass2 id="ref-1" xmlns:
        a1="http://schemas.microsoft.com/clr/nsassem/RemoteObjects/
        RemoteObjects%2C%20Version%3D1.0.904.32400%2C%20
        Culture%3Dneutral%2C%20PublicKeyToken%3Dnull">
            <TimeStamp xsi:type="xsd:dateTime">
                2002-06-23T19:00:22.7003264-04:00
            </TimeStamp>
            <m1>5000</m1>
            <m2>5001</m2>
        </a1:SomeClass2>
    </SOAP-ENV:Body>
</SOAP-ENV:Envelope>
```

Notice that the *<a1:SomeClass2>* tag includes three child elements corresponding to the three values added to the *SerializationInfo* instance in *GetObjectData*. The name of each child element corresponds to the name specified for the *SerializationInfo.AddData* method. These names must be unique within the *SerializationInfo* instance.

Object Graph Serialization

In the earlier examples, the integer members appeared as child elements of the parent element. This is because the *SoapFormatter* serializes primitive types inline with the rest of the object. Let's look at an example in which the object being serialized has a member referencing another *object* instance. In this case, the formatter serializes a reference identifier rather than serializing the referenced object inline. The formatter will serialize the referenced object at a later position in the stream.

Figure 8-1 shows the object graph resulting from instantiation of a *SomeClass3* class, defined in the following code:

```
[Serializable]
public class SomeClass3
{
```

```
    public SomeClass2 m_sc3 = new SomeClass2();
    public int m_n = 2112;
}
```

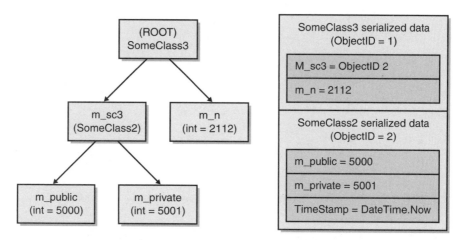

Figure 8-1   An object graph

Here's a SOAP-formatted serialized object instance of the *SomeClass3* type:

```
<SOAP-ENV:Envelope
 xmlns:xsi=http://www.w3.org/2001/XMLSchema-instance
 xmlns:xsd=http://www.w3.org/2001/XMLSchema
 xmlns:SOAP-ENC=http://schemas.xmlsoap.org/soap/encoding/
 xmlns:SOAP-ENV=http://schemas.xmlsoap.org/soap/envelope/
 xmlns:clr=http://schemas.microsoft.com/soap/encoding/clr/1.0
 SOAP-ENV:encodingStyle="http://schemas.xmlsoap.org/soap/encoding/">
    <SOAP-ENV:Body>
        <a1:SomeClass3 id="ref-1" xmlns:
         a1="http://schemas.microsoft.com/clr/nsassem/
         BasicSerialization/BasicSerialization%2C%20
         Version%3D1.0.905.37158%2C%20Culture%3Dneutral%2C%20
         PublicKeyToken%3Dnull">
            <m_sc2 href="#ref-3"/>
            <m_n>2112</m_n>
        </a1:SomeClass3>
        <a1:SomeClass2 id="ref-3" xmlns:
         a1="http://schemas.microsoft.com/clr/nsassem/
         BasicSerialization/BasicSerialization%2C%20
         Version%3D1.0.905.37158%2C%20Culture%3Dneutral%2C%20
         PublicKeyToken%3Dnull">
            <TimeStamp xsi:type="xsd:dateTime">
                2002-06-24T21:38:42.8411136-04:00
```

(continued)

```
          </TimeStamp>
          <m1>5000</m1>
          <m2>5001</m2>
        </a1:SomeClass2>
    </SOAP-ENV:Body>
</SOAP-ENV:Envelope>
```

Notice in this listing that the *<SOAP-ENV:Body>* element contains two child elements, each corresponding to a serialized object instance. The *SomeClass3* instance is the root of the object graph and appears as the first child element of the *<SOAP-ENV:Body>* element. The *<m_sc2>* child element of the *<a1:SomeClass3>* element contains an *href* attribute that references the element with *id* equal to *ref-3*, which is the identifier of the *SomeClass2* serialized instance in the *<a1:SomeClass2>* element.

Object Graph Deserialization

As the formatter deserializes an object graph, it will begin allocating and initializing object instances within the object graph as it reads the serialized data from the stream. During deserialization, the formatter keeps track of each object and the object's identifier. Each *object* member in the serialized object graph can reference one of the following:

■ An uninitialized object that hasn't yet been deserialized

■ A partially initialized object that has been deserialized

■ A fully initialized object that has been deserialized

The formatter might encounter an *object* member that references another object that the formatter hasn't yet deserialized, such as the *<m_sc2>* child element of the *<a1:SomeClass3>* element shown in the preceding example. In that case, the formatter updates an internal structure that associates the *object* member with the referenced object's identifier. Later, when the formatter deserializes the referenced object from the stream, it will initialize any *object* members referencing the object. For *object* members that reference an object that the formatter has deserialized, the formatter initializes the member with that object instance.

Knowing When Deserialization Has Completed

Whether you use the *SerializableAttribute* to allow the common language runtime to handle serialization details or you customize serialization by implementing the *ISerializable* interface, you might want to be notified when the formatter has finished deserializing the entire object graph. If so, you can implement the *IDeserializationCallback* interface. This interface has one method: *OnDeserializationCallback*. After a formatter has deserialized an entire object graph, it calls this method on any objects within the object graph implementing the *IDeserializationCallback* interface. When the formatter calls *OnDeserializationCallback* on an object, the object can be sure that all objects referenced by its members have been fully initialized. However, the object can't be sure that other objects that its members reference and that implement the *IDeserializationCallback* interface have had their *OnDeserializationCallback* methods called.

Serialization Surrogates and Surrogate Selectors

Sometimes you have a type that you want to serialize, but the type doesn't support serialization. Or maybe you need to augment the serialized information for a type with additional information. To provide extra flexibility in the serialization architecture, the .NET Framework makes use of *surrogates* and *surrogate selectors*. A surrogate is a class that can take over the serialization requirements for instances of other types. A surrogate selector is basically a collection of surrogates that, when asked, returns a suitable surrogate for a given type.

Surrogates

A surrogate implements the *ISerializationSurrogate* interface. This interface defines two methods: *GetObjectData* and *SetObjectData*. The signature of the *ISerializationSurrogate.GetObjectData* method is almost identical to that of *ISerializable.GetObjectData*. However, the *ISerializationSurrogate.GetObjectData* method takes one additional parameter of type *object*, which is the object to be serialized. The surrogate's implementation of *GetObjectData* can add members to the *SerializationInfo* instance prior to serializing the object members, or it can completely replace the serialization functionality of the given object.

The signature of *SetObjectData* is similar to that of *ISerializationSurrogate.GetObjectData* except that *SetObjectData* returns a populated object instance and takes an additional parameter of type *ISurrogateSelector*, which we'll discuss shortly. The surrogate's implementation of *SetObjectData* can read members from the *SerializationInfo* instance that were added during serialization of the object instance in the surrogate's *GetObjectData* implementation.

Surrogate Selectors

As we'll discuss in the "Serialization Formatters" section, one of the properties that a formatter exposes is the *SurrogateSelector* property. You can set the *SurrogateSelector* property to any object that implements the *ISurrogateSelector* interface. Formatters use the surrogate selector to determine whether the type currently being serialized or deserialized has a surrogate. If the type does, the formatter uses the surrogate to handle serialization and deserialization of instances of that type. We'll discuss the details of the serialization and deserialization process later in this chapter.

The .NET Framework defines the *System.Runtime.Serialization.Surrogate-Selector* class, which implements the *ISurrogateSelector* interface. The *Surrogate-Selector* class also defines the *Add* method that allows you to add a surrogate to its internal collection and the *Remove* method that allows you to remove a surrogate from this collection.

The *TimeStamper* Surrogate

The following example will demonstrate the use of serialization surrogates and surrogate selectors. We'll implement a surrogate that adds a time-stamp member to the *SerializationInfo* instance for an object and then serializes the object instance. The following code defines the *TimeStamperSurrogate* class:

```
class TimeStamperSurrogate : ISerializationSurrogate
{
    public void GetObjectData ( object obj,
                                SerializationInfo info,
                                StreamingContext context )
    {
        //
        // Add a datetime value to the serialization info.
        info.AddValue( "TimeStamperSurrogate.SerializedDateTime",
                DateTime.Now );

        //
        // Serialize the object.
        if ( obj is ISerializable )
        {
            ((ISerializable)obj).GetObjectData(info, context);
        }
        else
        {
            MemberInfo[]  mi  =
              FormatterServices.GetSerializableMembers(obj.GetType());

            object[] od  = FormatterServices.GetObjectData( obj,
                                                            mi );

            for( int i = 0; i < mi.Length; ++i )
            {
                info.AddValue( mi[i].Name, od[i] );
            }
        }
    }
}
```

```
public System.Object SetObjectData ( object obj,
                                      SerializationInfo info,
                                      StreamingContext context,
                                      ISurrogateSelector selector )
{

    // Get the values that this surrogate added in GetObjectData.
    DateTime dt = (DateTime)info.GetValue(
                      "TimeStamperSurrogate.SerializedDateTime",
                      typeof(DateTime) );

    if ( obj is ISerializable )
    {
        ObjectManager om = new ObjectManager(selector, context);
        om.RegisterObject(obj,1,info);
        om.DoFixups();
        obj = om.GetObject(1);
    }
    else
    {
        MemberInfo[]  mi  =
         FormatterServices.GetSerializableMembers(obj.GetType());

        object[] od  = FormatterServices.GetObjectData( obj,
                                                        mi );

        int i = 0;
        SerializationInfoEnumerator ie = info.GetEnumerator();
        while(ie.MoveNext())
        {
            if ( mi[i].Name == ie.Name )
            {
                od[i] = Convert.ChangeType( ie.Value,
                            ((FieldInfo)mi[i]).FieldType);
                ++i;
            }
        }

        FormatterServices.PopulateObjectMembers( obj, mi, od );
    }
    return obj;
}
}
```

The *TimeStamperSurrogate.GetObjectData* method adds a value with the current date and time to the *SerializationInfo* instance, *info*. The method then allows the object to add values to the *SerializationInfo* instance if this instance implements the *ISerializable* interface. Otherwise, the method uses the *FormatterServices* class to obtain the values for the object's serializable members and adds them to the *SerializationInfo* instance. We'll discuss the *FormatterServices* class in the "Serialization Formatters" section of the chapter.

The *TimeStamperSurrogate.SetObjectData* method reverses the process of the *GetObjectData* by first obtaining the time-stamp value from the *SerializationInfo* instance, *info*. If the object implements *ISerializable*, the *SetObjectData* makes use of the *ObjectManager* class, which we'll also discuss in the "Serialization Formatters" section of the chapter. For now, it's enough to know that these statements result in a call to the special constructor on the *ISerializable* object with the *SerializationInfo* instance, *info*, and the *StreamingContext* instance, *context*. If the object doesn't implement the *ISerializable* class, *SetObjectData* uses the *FormatterServices* class to obtain information about the object's serializable members and retrieves the member's values from the *SerializationInfo* instance.

RemotingSurrogateSelector

In addition to the *SurrogateSelector* class, the .NET Framework defines another surrogate selector, *RemotingSurrogateSelector*, which is used during serialization of .NET Remoting related types. Table 8-2 lists the various surrogate classes that the .NET Remoting infrastructure uses.

Table 8-2   .NET Remoting Surrogates

Class	Description
RemotingSurrogate	Handles serialization of marshal-by-reference object instances
ObjRefSurrogate	Handles serialization of *ObjRef* instances by adding a value named *fIsMarshalled* to the *SerializationInfo* instance indicating that the serialized *ObjRef* instance was passed as a parameter rather than the marshal-by-ref object it represents
MessageSurrogate	Handles serialization of the *MethodCall*, *MethodResponse*, *ConstructionCall*, and *ConstructionCall* messages by enumerating over the *IMessage.Properties* collection and adding each property to the *SerializationInfo* as appropriate
SoapMessageSurrogate	Handles special serialization requirements of SOAP messages

Serialization Formatters

As demonstrated earlier, serialization formatters serialize objects to streams. What we haven't discussed yet is how to write a custom serialization formatter that can be plugged into .NET Remoting. Writing a serialization formatter is largely an exercise in the following tasks, in no particular order:

■   Obtaining a list of an object type's serializable members

■   Traversing an object graph that's rooted at the object being serialized

■   Serializing the full type name of an object, its containing assembly, and the values of its serializable members

■   Serializing references to objects within the graph so that the graph can be reconstructed during deserialization

Fortunately, the .NET Framework provides several classes that you can use to facilitate coding solutions for each of these tasks. Table 8-3 lists the classes provided by the .NET Framework and the purpose each serves. We'll look at examples of using these classes shortly when we look at performing each of the tasks.

Table 8-3   Classes Useful for Writing Serialization Formatters

Class	Namespace	Description
FormatterServices	*System.Runtime.Serialization*	Serialization/deserialization
ObjectIDGenerator	*System.Runtime.Serialization*	Serialization
ObjectManager	*System.Runtime.Serialization*	Deserialization
Formatter	*System.Runtime.Serialization*	Can be used as base class for a formatter; provides methods helpful for object graph traversal and object scheduling

Let's examine using these classes in isolation first, to see what they can do. We'll put them all together when we write a custom formatter later in the section.

Obtaining a Type's Serializable Members

Table 8-4 lists some of the methods that the *FormatterServices* class provides that facilitate writing custom serialization formatters.

Table 8-4 Significant Public Methods of *System.Runtime.Serialization.FormatterServices*

Method	Description
GetSerializableMembers	Obtains the serializable members for a given type
GetObjectData	Obtains the values for one or more serializable members of an object instance
GetUninitializedObject	Obtains an uninitialized object instance during deserialization
PopulateObjectMembers	Initializes an uninitialized object instance's members with values

In an example in the previous section, we defined the *SomeClass2* type. The following code snippet demonstrates using each of the *FormatterServices* methods listed in Table 8-4 to obtain the serializable members and their values for a serializable instance of the *SomeClass2* type:

```
SomeClass2 sc = new SomeClass2();

// Obtain the serializable members and their values.
MemberInfo[] mi =
    FormatterServices.GetSerializableMembers(sc.GetType());

object[] vals = FormatterServices.GetObjectData(sc,mi);

// Obtain an uninitialized object and populate its members.
SomeClass2 sc2 =
    (SomeClass2)FormatterServices.GetUninitializedObject(typeof
    (SomeClass2));

FormatterServices.PopulateObjectMembers(sc2,mi,vals);
```

The *GetSerializableMembers* method returns an array of *System.Reflection.MemberInfo* instances for a specified type. If you pass a type that isn't serializable to *GetSerializableMembers*, the common language runtime will raise a *System.Runtime.Serialization.SerializationException* exception. Note that passing a type implementing the *ISerializable* interface to the *GetSerializableMembers* method doesn't result in the *GetSerializableMembers* method calling *ISerializable.GetObjectData*. This means that you might not actually get all the serialization members that the type implementer intended.

To obtain the values for each serializable member, you pass the *MemberInfo* array to the *GetObjectData* method, which returns an object array whose elements correspond to the values for the serializable members. The two arrays are populated so that the ith element of the object array is the value of the member defined by the ith element in the *MemberInfo* array.

To reverse the process we've just described, you create an uninitialized instance of the *SomeClass2* type by using *FormatterServices.GetUninitializedObject*. The critical word here is *uninitialized*—the constructor isn't called, and members that reference other objects are set to *null* or 0. To initialize the uninitialized object instance, you use the *PopulateObjectMembers* method, passing it the uninitialized object instance, the *MemberInfo* array describing each member you are initializing, and a matching object array with the values for the members. The return value of *PopulateObjectMembers* is the object being populated.

Traversing an Object Graph

The object being serialized corresponds to the root node in the object graph. All other nodes in the graph represent an object that's reachable from the object being serialized, either directly as a member or indirectly via a member of a referenced object. The basic procedure to traverse an object graph for serialization is to start at the root object and obtain its serializable members. Then you traverse each serializable member's object graph and so forth until all nodes in the graph have been traversed. For acyclic object graphs, such as the one shown in Figure 8-2, the exercise is fairly simple.

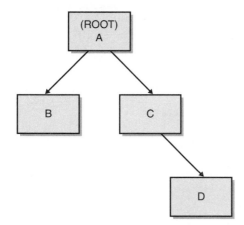

Figure 8-2   An acyclic object graph

However, some object graphs might contain cycles. A cycle occurs when one object references another object that directly or indirectly references the original object. Cycles are problematic because if you don't detect them, you'll end up traversing the cycle forever. Figure 8-3 shows an abstract view of an object graph that contains a cycle.

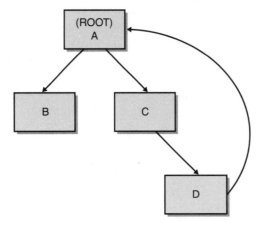

Figure 8-3 An object graph that contains a cycle

Identifying Objects by Using the *ObjectIDGenerator* Class

As the formatter traverses the object graph, it assigns each object an identifier that it can use when serializing objects that reference the object being serialized. The formatter does this by using the *ObjectIDGenerator* class, which keeps track of all objects encountered during traversal. You use the *ObjectID-Generator.GetID* method to obtain a long value that identifies the object instance passed to the *GetID* method. The *GetID* method takes two parameters. The first parameter is an object instance for which *GetID* should obtain the identifier. The second parameter is a Boolean parameter that indicates whether this is the first time the object instance has been passed to the *GetID* method. The following code snippet demonstrates how to use the *ObjectIDGenerator* class:

```
ObjectIDGenerator idgen = new ObjectIDGenerator();
SomeClass sc = new SomeClass();
bool firstTime = false;

// id_sc == 0, firstTime == true on return
long id_sc = idgen.HasId(sc, out firstTime);

// id_sc == 1, firstTime == true on return
id_sc = idgen.GetId(sc, out firstTime);

// id_sc == 1, firstTime == false on return
id_sc = idgen.HasId(sc, out firstTime);

// id_sc == 1, firstTime == false on return
id_sc = idgen.GetId(sc, out firstTime);
```

Scheduling Objects for Serialization

The .NET Framework uses a technique known as *scheduling* to help serialize an object graph. While traversing an object graph, if the formatter encounters an object instance (either the root object instance or a member of an object that references another object instance), it performs the following actions:

1. Obtains an identifier for the object instance from the *ObjectIDGenerator* class

2. Serializes a reference to the object instance by using the object identifier rather than serializing the object instance itself

3. Schedules the object instance for later serialization by placing it in a queue of objects waiting to be serialized

So far, we've discussed using the *FormatterServices* class to obtain an object instance's serializable members, traversing an object graph, and using the *ObjectIDGenerator* class. We'll use each of these tasks shortly to implement a custom formatter's *IFormatter.Serialize* method. But before we do that, let's look at how we can use the *ObjectManager* class to aid in deserialization.

Using the *ObjectManager* Class

The *ObjectManager* class allows you to construct an object graph from scratch. If you have all the object instances in a graph and know how they relate to one another, you can use the *ObjectManager* class to construct the object graph. Table 8-5 lists the useful members of the *ObjectManager* class.

Table 8-5 Significant Public Methods of *System.Runtime. Serialization.ObjectManager*

Method	Description
DoFixups	Call after all objects in the graph have been registered with the *ObjectManager*. When this function returns, all outstanding object references have been fixed up.
GetObject	Obtains a registered object instance by its identifier.
RaiseDeserializationEvent	Raises the deserialization event.
RecordArrayElementFixup	Records an array element fixup when an array element references another object instance in the graph.

(continued)

Table 8-5 **Significant Public Methods of *System.Runtime.*** ***Serialization.ObjectManager*** *(continued)*

Method	Description
RecordDelayedFixup	Records a fixup for members of a *Serialization-Info* instance associated with a registered object.
RecordFixup	Records a fixup for members of an object instance.
RegisterObject	Registers an object instance with its identifier.

In general, you use the *ObjectManager* to reconstruct an object graph by performing the following tasks:

1. Register object instances and their identifiers with the *ObjectManager* via the *RegisterObject* method.

2. Record fixups that map members of object instances to other object instances in the graph via the object identifiers by using the *RecordFixup*, *RecordArrayElementFixup*, and *RecordDelayedFixup* methods.

3. Instruct the *ObjectManager* to perform the recorded fixups via the *DoFixups* method.

4. Query the *ObjectManager* for the root object in the graph via the *GetObject* method.

The following code uses the *ObjectManager* class to reconstruct the object graph depicted in Figure 8-1:

```
// Create an ObjectManager instance.
ObjectManager om =
    new ObjectManager(new SurrogateSelector(),
    new StreamingContext(StreamingContextStates.All));

// Set up object 1, the root object.
object sc3 =
    FormatterServices.GetUninitializedObject(typeof(SomeClass3));

// Register object 1.
om.RegisterObject(sc3, 1);

// Set up to initialize the members of object 1.
System.Reflection.MemberInfo[] mi =
    FormatterServices.GetSerializableMembers(typeof(SomeClass3));
```

```
// Record a fixup for the first member of object 1 to reference
// object 2.
om.RecordFixup(1,mi[0],2);

// Initialize the second member of object 1 using FormatterServices.
FormatterServices.PopulateObjectMembers( sc3,
                                    new MemberInfo[]{ mi[1] },
                                    new Object[]{ 2112 });

// Set up object 2, the instance of SomeClass2.
SerializationInfo info =
    new SerializationInfo( typeof(SomeClass2),
                           new FormatterConverter());
info.AddValue("m1", 4000);
info.AddValue("m2", 4001);

// Record a delayed fixup for the TimeStamp member
// for object 2 referencing object 3.
om.RecordDelayedFixup(2, "TimeStamp", 3);

// Register object 2 and its associated SerializationInfo instance.
object sc2 =
    FormatterServices.GetUninitializedObject(typeof(SomeClass2));
om.RegisterObject(sc2, 2, info);

// Register object 3, the TimeStamp value--technically not
// part of the object graph, but required because SomeClass2 expects
// the TimeStamp value to be in the SerializationInfo.
om.RegisterObject(DateTime.Now,3);

// The ObjectManager now has enough information to
// construct the object graph--perform the fixups.
om.DoFixups();

// Obtain the root object.
SomeClass3 _sc3 = (SomeClass3)om.GetObject(1);
```

The code begins by creating an instance of the *ObjectManager* class. The root object in the graph is an instance of the *SomeClass3* class. We create an uninitialized instance of the *SomeClass3* class by using the *FormatterServices.GetUninitialized* method, which we then register with the *ObjectManager*, assigning it an object identifier of 1. The next step is to initialize the members of object 1. The *m_sc2* member of the *SomeClass3* class references an instance of the *SomeClass2* class. Because we don't yet have an object instance of type *SomeClass2*, we can't immediately initialize the *m_sc2* member. Therefore, we need to record a fixup for the *m_sc2* member for object 1 so that it references the object instance that has an identifier of 2. The fixup instructs the *Object-Manager* to set the *m_sc2* member equal to the object instance that has an object identifier of 2 during the fixup stage when we call the *DoFixups* method. The second member of the *SomeClass3* class is an integer value and can be initialized immediately by using the *FormatterServices.PopulateObjectMembers* method.

Next we set up the second object in the object graph, an instance of *SomeClass2*. Because *SomeClass2* implements *ISerializable*, we create a new instance of *SerializationInfo*, which we immediately populate with the two integer members, *m1* and *m2*. The *SomeClass2* implementation of *ISerializable.GetObjectData* expects a third member to be present in the *SerializationInfo*, *TimeStamp*. To demonstrate using delayed fixups, we call the *RecordDelayedFixup* method to record a delayed fixup that associates the *TimeStamp* member of object 1 with object 3, which we haven't yet registered. The *RecordDelayedFixup* method defers initialization of a *SerializationInfo* member that references an object that hasn't yet been registered until the required object is registered with the *ObjectManager*. After recording the delayed fixup, we register the uninitialized instance of *SomeClass2* and its associated *SerializationInfo* with the *ObjectManager*, assigning it an object ID of 2. At this point, the *SerializationInfo* contains two members, *m1* and *m2*, and their corresponding values. Because of the delayed fixup, when we register an instance of *DateTime* as object ID 3, the *ObjectManager* adds a member named *TimeStamp* to the *SerializationInfo* for object 2. The *TimeStamp* member references the object instance corresponding to object 3.

Next we call the *DoFixups* method on the *ObjectManager* instance. This causes the *ObjectManager* to iterate over its internal data structures, performing any outstanding fixups. For member fixups, the *ObjectManager* initializes the referring member with a reference to the actual object instance. For delayed fixups of objects that don't have a serialization surrogate, the *ObjectManager* invokes the object's *ISerializable.GetObjectData* method, passing it the *SerializationInfo* instance associated with it when the object was registered. If the object does have a serialization surrogate, the *ObjectManager* invokes the surrogate's *ISerializationSurrogate.SetObjectData* method, passing it the *SerializationInfo* instance associated with it when the object was registered. For array fixups, the *ObjectManager* initializes the array element with a reference to the actual object instance. Once the fixups are complete, we request the object instances by their identifier numbers.

Using the *Formatter* Class

The .NET Framework includes a class named *System.Runtime.Serialization.Formatter* that you can use as a base class when writing custom formatters. Table 8-6 lists the significant public members of the *Formatter* class. The *Schedule* and *GetNext* methods implement the scheduling technique for object serialization that we described earlier in the section. When you want to schedule an object instance for later serialization, you call the *Schedule* method, passing the object instance as a parameter. The *Schedule* method obtains and returns the object identifier assigned by the *ObjectIDGenerator* referenced by the *Formatter* instance's *m_idGenerator* member. Prior to returning, the *Schedule* method enqueues the object instance in the queue referenced by the *m_objectQueue* member. The *GetNext* method dequeues and returns the next object in the queue referenced by the *m_objectQueue* member.

Table 8-6   Significant Public Members of *System.Runtime.Serialization.Formatter*

Member	Member Type	Description
m_idGenerator	Protected field	A reference to the *ObjectIDGenerator* instance used to identify objects during traversal of the object graph.
m_objectQueue	Protected field	A queue of objects waiting to be serialized.
Schedule	Method	Schedules an object instance for later serialization. The return value indicates the object ID assigned to the object instance being scheduled.
GetNext	Method	Obtains the next object instance to be serialized.
WriteMember	Method	Serializes a member of an object instance. The method invokes one of the various *WriteXXXX* members based on the object's type.
WriteObjectRef	Method	Override this virtual method to write an object reference instead of the actual object instance. Most formatters simply write the object ID to the stream.

(continued)

Table 8-6   Significant Public Members of *System.Runtime. Serialization.Formatter* *(continued)*

Member	Member Type	Description
WriteValueType	Method	Override this virtual method to write a *ValueType* to the stream. For primitive types, override the *WriteXXXX* methods. *WriteMember* will call this method if the *ValueType* isn't a primitive type.
WriteXXXX	Method	Any one of the many methods named after the type they write—*WriteByte*, *WriteInt32*, *WriteDateTime*, and so on.

Implementing a Custom Serialization Formatter

Now that we've discussed the more significant classes that the .NET Framework provides to facilitate developing a custom serialization formatter, let's put what we've learned to use. In doing so, we'll follow these steps:

1.   Define a serialization format.

2.   Implement *IFormatter.Serialize*.

3.   Implement *IFormatter.Deserialize*.

Defining a Serialization Format

As mentioned at various points throughout this book, the *SoapFormatter* serializes object graphs by using a SOAP format. Likewise, the *BinaryFormatter* serializes object graphs by using an efficient binary format. Before developing our formatter, we need a format to implement. To facilitate explaining and demonstrating the principles required to implement a custom formatter, we'll use a human-readable format that consists of field tags followed by the string representation of their values. Each field tag delimits a specific type of information used to reconstruct the object graph. Table 8-7 shows the field tags we'll use in our formatter.

Table 8-7   A Custom Serialization Format

Field Tag	Value Meaning
o_id:	The object's ID as assigned by the *ObjectIDGenerator*.
o_assembly:	The object's full assembly name, including version, culture info, and public key token.
o_type:	The object's fully qualified type name.

Table 8-7 A Custom Serialization Format   *(continued)*

Field Tag	Value Meaning
m_count:	Present when serialized members are members of a *Serialization-Info*. Number of members serialized for the current object.
m_name:	Member name.
m_type:	Member fully qualified type name.
m_value:	Member value in string form.
m_value_type:	Indicates that the value for this member is actually a type. We serialize the name of the type rather than the *Type* instance.
m_value_refid:	Indicates that the value refers to another object in the graph by its object identifier.
array_rank:	Number of dimensions in the array.
array_length:	Length of a dimension in the array.
array_lowerbound:	Lower bound in a dimension in the array.

Here's an example of a serialized object graph produced by using the custom formatter we'll develop in this section:

```
o_id:1
o_assembly:Serialization, Version=1.0.912.37506, Culture=neutral, ⟶
PublicKeyToken=null
o_type:Serialization.TestClassA
m_count:2
m_name:__v1
m_type:System.DateTime
m_value:7/1/2002 9:50:24 PM
m_name:__v2
m_type:Serialization.TestClassB
m_value_refid:2
o_id:2
o_assembly:Serialization, Version=1.0.912.37506, Culture=neutral, ⟶
PublicKeyToken=null
o_type:Serialization.TestClassB
m_name:m_a
m_type:Serialization.TestClassA
m_value_refid:1
```

As you can see, each field tag and its associated value appear on a single line. This has one undesirable implication: values cannot contain carriage-return/linefeed characters. If we want to use this formatter in a production setting, we'll definitely need to address that issue, but because we're writing this formatter for demonstration purposes, we won't be concerned with this.

The first three lines begin the object serialization information by indicating the object identifier, full assembly name, and type name. The following line begins with *m_count* and indicates that two members are serialized for this object. The presence of the *m_count* field tag indicates that the following members should be placed in a *SerializationInfo* during deserialization. The name, type, and value for each member follow. Notice that the second member, named *__v2*, is a reference to an object with an identifier equal to 2. The next three lines begin a new object with identifier equal to 2. This object has only one member, and its name, type, and value indicate that the member references the object with an identifier equal to 1.

The following code defines a class named *FieldNames*, which we'll use to help implement the custom formatter:

```
class FieldNames
{
    // Object manager ID
    public static string OBJECT_ID         = "o_id:";

    // Assembly name
    public static string OBJECT_ASSEMBLY   = "o_assembly:";

    // Object type
    public static string OBJECT_TYPE       = "o_type:";

    // Number of members in this object
    public static string MEMBER_COUNT      = "m_count:";

    // Member name
    public static string MEMBER_NAME       = "m_name:";

    // Member type
    public static string MEMBER_TYPE       = "m_type:";

    // Member value
    public static string MEMBER_VALUE      = "m_value:";

    // Member value is a type
    public static string MEMBER_VALUE_TYPE = "m_value_type:";

    // Object manager ID
    public static string OBJECT_REFID      = "m_value_refid:";

    // Number of dimensions
    public static string ARRAY_RANK        = "array_rank:";

    // Length of a dimension
```

```csharp
public static string ARRAY_LENGTH        = "array_length:";

// Lower bound of a dimension
public static string ARRAY_LOWERBOUND    = "array_lowerbound:";

// Special null-value indicator
public static string MEMBER_VALUE_NULL   = "m_value_null";

public static long ParseObjectRefID(string s)
    { return Convert.ToInt64(s.Substring(OBJECT_REFID.Length)); }

public static long ParseObjectID(string s)
    { return Convert.ToInt64(s.Substring(OBJECT_ID.Length)); }

public static string ParseObjectAssembly(string s)
    { return s.Substring(OBJECT_ASSEMBLY.Length); }

public static string ParseObjectType(string s)
    { return s.Substring(OBJECT_TYPE.Length); }

public static long ParseMemberCount(string s)
    { return Convert.ToInt64(s.Substring(MEMBER_COUNT.Length)); }

public static string ParseMemberName(string s)
    { return s.Substring(MEMBER_NAME.Length); }

public static string ParseMemberType(string s)
    {  return s.Substring(MEMBER_TYPE.Length); }

public static string ParseMemberValue(string s)
    { return s.Substring(MEMBER_VALUE.Length); }

public static string ParseMemberValueType(string s)
    { return s.Substring(MEMBER_VALUE_TYPE.Length); }

public static long ParseArrayRank(string s)
    { return Convert.ToInt64(s.Substring(ARRAY_RANK.Length)); }

public static long ParseArrayLength(string s)
    { return Convert.ToInt64(s.Substring(ARRAY_LENGTH.Length)); }

public static long ParseArrayLowerBound(string s)
    { return Convert.ToInt64(s.Substring(
                        ARRAY_LOWERBOUND.Length)); }
}
```

The *FieldNames* class simply defines a static member for each of the field tags listed in Table 8-7. In addition, the *FieldNames* class defines *ParseXXXX* methods that parse each field tag. We'll use the *ParseXXXX* methods when we implement the *IFormatter.Deserialize* method.

Implementing the *IFormatter* Interface

Serialization formatters are classes that implement the *IFormatter* interface. Table 8-8 lists the members defined by the *IFormatter* interface.

Table 8-8   **Table 8-8 Members of *System.Runtime.Serialization.IFormatter***

Member	Member Type	Description
Binder	Read-write property	Allows equipping the formatter instance with a *SerializationBinder* instance to deserialize a serialized type to a different type
Context	Read-write property	Can reference a *StreamingContext* instance that contains information about the serialization or deserialization operation
SurrogateSelector	Read-write property	Can reference an instance of a surrogate selector class
Deserialize	Method	Deserializes an object graph from a stream
Serialize	Method	Serializes an object graph to a stream

The following code listing begins implementing the *MyFormatter* class, which we'll fully implement and explain in the next few sections:

```
public class MyFormatter : Formatter
{
    SerializationBinder _binder;
    StreamingContext    _streamingcontext;
    ISurrogateSelector  _surrogateselector;

    StreamWriter        _writer;
    StreamReader        _reader;
    ObjectManager       _om;

    public MyFormatter()
    {
    }

    public override SerializationBinder Binder
    {
        get
```

```
        { return _binder; }
        set
        { _binder = value; }
    }


    public override StreamingContext Context
    {
        get
        { return _streamingcontext; }
        set
        { _streamingcontext = value; }
    }


    public override ISurrogateSelector SurrogateSelector
    {
        get
        { return _surrogateselector; }
        set
        { _surrogateselector = value; }
    }
```

The *MyFormatter* class derives from the *System.Runtime.Serialization.Formatter* class to leverage the object graph traversal functionality, which we explained earlier in the section. Along with the members implementing the *IFormatter* properties, we've defined a *StreamWriter* member named *_writer* that we'll use for serialization. For deserialization, we've defined a *StreamReader* member named *_reader* and an *ObjectManager* member named *_om*.

Implementing the *IFormatter.Serialize* Method

The function of the *IFormatter.Serialize* method is to serialize an object graph to a stream by using a specific format to lay out the serialization information. Our implementation of *IFormatter.Serialize* follows:

```
public override void Serialize(Stream serializationStream,
                                    object graph)
{
    _writer = new StreamWriter(serializationStream);

    // Schedule the top object.
    Schedule(graph);

    // Get the next object to be serialized and serialize it.
    object oTop;
    long topId;
    while( (oTop = GetNext(out topId)) != null )
    {
```

(continued)

```
        // Execution of the WriteObject method will likely result
        // in the scheduling of more objects for serialization.
        WriteObject(oTop, topId);
    }


    _writer.Flush();
}
```

To start the serialization process, the *IFormatter.Serialize* method passes the root object of the object graph by calling *Formatter.Schedule*, passing the graph as the parameter. *Schedule* will obtain an identifier for the root object, which should be 1, and enqueue it for later serialization. To continue the serialization process, we call the *Formatter.GetNext* method to retrieve the next object in the serialization queue. Assuming *GetNext* returns an object instance rather than *null*, we pass that object instance and its identifier to the *MyFormatter.WriteObject* method. The process continues until *GetNext* returns *null*, indicating that no more objects to serialize exist. The implementation of the *WriteObject* method follows:

```
private void WriteObject(object obj, long objId)
{
    // Write object preamble.
    WriteField(FieldNames.OBJECT_ID, objId);
    WriteField(FieldNames.OBJECT_ASSEMBLY, obj.GetType().Assembly);
    WriteField(FieldNames.OBJECT_TYPE, obj.GetType().FullName);

    // Don't write members of array and
    // string types; handle these as special cases.
    if ( obj.GetType().IsArray )
    {
        WriteArray(obj, "", obj.GetType());
    }
    else if ( obj.GetType() == typeof(string) )
    {
        WriteField(FieldNames.MEMBER_VALUE, obj);
    }
    else
    {
        // Write object members.
        WriteObjectMembers(obj, objId);
    }
}
```

The *WriteObject* method handles arrays and strings as special cases. For arrays, we don't want to write all the *Array* class members to the stream. We need to write only the array rank, lower bounds, and length, followed by each array element—which is what the *WriteArray* method does. We'll look at the

WriteArray method later in this section. For strings, we just write the string value directly to the stream by using the *WriteField* method. For any other types, the *WriteObject* serializes the object instance to the serialization stream by writing the object ID, assembly information, and full type name to the stream by using the *WriteField* method. The *WriteObject* method then writes the object instance's serializable members to the stream by using the *WriteObjectMembers* method.

The implementation of the *WriteField* method simply writes the field name and the string representation of the value on a single line to the *Stream-Writer*:

```
//
// Write a format field to the stream.
void WriteField(string field_name, object oValue)
{
    _writer.WriteLine("{0}{1}", field_name, oValue);
}
```

The implementation of the *WriteObjectMembers* method is a bit more complex, as the following listing shows:

```
private void WriteObjectMembers(object obj, long  objId)
{
    // See if we need to use a surrogate for this object.
    ISerializationSurrogate surrogate = null;
    if ( _surrogateselector != null )
    {
        // Does the surrogate selector have a surrogate
        // registered for this type?
        ISurrogateSelector selector;
        surrogate = _surrogateselector.GetSurrogate( obj.GetType(),
                                        _streamingcontext,
                                        out selector );
    }

    if ( surrogate != null )
    {
        // Yes, a surrogate is registered; call its GetObjectData
        // method.
        SerializationInfo info =
            new SerializationInfo( obj.GetType(),
                            new FormatterConverter());

        surrogate.GetObjectData(obj, info, this._streamingcontext);

        // Write the serialization info members to the stream.
        WriteSerializationInfo(info);
```

(continued)

```
    }
    else if ( IsMarkedSerializable(obj) && ( obj is ISerializable ))
    {
        // The object type implements ISerializable.

        // Let the object serialize itself
        // via its GetObjectData method.
        SerializationInfo info =
            new SerializationInfo( obj.GetType(),
                                   new FormatterConverter());

        ((ISerializable)obj).GetObjectData(info,
                                           this._streamingcontext);

        // Write the serialization info members to the stream.
        WriteSerializationInfo(info);
    }
    else if ( IsMarkedSerializable(obj) )
    {
        // The object type does not implement
        // ISerializable and we have no surrogate for it.
        WriteSerializableMembers(obj, objId);
    }
    else
    {
        // The type cannot be serialized; throw an exception.
        throw new SerializationException();
    }
}
```

The *WriteObjectMembers* method utilizes several of the techniques for serializing an object that we discussed earlier in the chapter and follows the algorithm that all serialization formatters must follow for serializing object instances. First, the method determines whether the formatter has a surrogate selector. If so, the method asks the surrogate selector whether it has a serialization surrogate to serialize the object with. If so, the *WriteObjectMembers* method uses the serialization surrogate to serialize the object's members into a new instance of *SerializationInfo* that it then writes to the stream by calling the *WriteSerializationInfo* method. If the formatter doesn't have a surrogate selector or no surrogate exists for the object's type, we determine whether the object's type has the *SerializableAttribute* attribute and implements the *ISerializable* interface. If the object's type meets these criteria, we allow the object instance to serialize itself into a new instance of *SerializationInfo* that we then write to the stream by calling the *WriteSerializationInfo* method. If the object type has the *SerializableAttribute* attribute but doesn't implement the *ISerializable* interface, we manually serialize the object's members by using the *WriteSerializableMembers* method. If none of the other criteria are met, we can't serialize this object, so we throw a *SerializationException* exception.

The *IsMarkedSerializable* method inspects the type attributes for the object's *Type* for the presence of the *TypeAttributes.Serializable* mask, as follows:

```
// Is the type attributed with [Serializable]?
private bool IsMarkedSerializable(object o)
{
    Type t = o.GetType();

    TypeAttributes taSerializableMask =
            (t.Attributes & TypeAttributes.Serializable);

    return ( taSerializableMask == TypeAttributes.Serializable );
}
```

The *WriteSerializationInfo* method first writes the member count to the stream by using the *WriteField* method to facilitate deserialization of the *SerializationInfo* members. After writing the member count, we write each member of the *SerializationInfo* instance by calling the *Formatter.WriteMember* method, as the following listing shows:

```
// Write out all members of the serialization info.
private void WriteSerializationInfo(SerializationInfo info)
{
    // Write the member count to the stream.
    WriteField(FieldNames.MEMBER_COUNT, info.MemberCount);

    // Write each member of the serialization info to the stream.
    SerializationInfoEnumerator sie = info.GetEnumerator();
    while(sie.MoveNext())
    {
        WriteMember(sie.Name,sie.Value);
    }
}
```

The *WriteSerializableMembers* method uses *FormatterServices* class to obtain the serializable members and values for the object instance, as we did earlier in the chapter. After obtaining the *MemberInfo* array and object array containing the member values, the method writes each member to the stream by calling the *WriteMember* method, as the following listing shows.

```
private void WriteSerializableMembers(object obj, long objId)
{
    System.Reflection.MemberInfo[]  mi  =
        FormatterServices.GetSerializableMembers(obj.GetType());

    if ( mi.Length > 0 )
    {
        object[] od  = FormatterServices.GetObjectData(obj, mi);
        for( int i = 0; i < mi.Length; ++i )
        {
            WriteMember(mi[i].Name, od[i]);
        }
    }
}
```

The *Formatter.WriteMember* method is a protected virtual method. As shown in Table 8-6, the *WriteMember* method examines the type of the object passed as the data parameter and, based on the type, calls one of the many *WriteXXXX* methods that must be overridden by classes deriving from *Formatter*. The *Formatter.WriteMember* method doesn't discriminate on the *string* type. Instead, this method passes string objects to the *WriteObjectRef* method. To make for easier coding of the *WriteObjectRef* method (which we'll discuss shortly), we've chosen to override the implementation of *WriteMember* and handle strings as a special case. We're also handling *Type* instances as a special case, which we'll explain shortly. For all other types and if the object is *null*, we delegate to the base implementation of *WriteMember*:

```
protected override void WriteMember(string name, object data)
{
    if ( data == null )
    {
        base.WriteMember(name, data);
    }
    else if ( data.GetType() == typeof(string) )
    {
        WriteString(data.ToString(), name);
    }
    else if ( data.GetType().IsSubclassOf(typeof(System.Type)))
    {
        WriteType(data, name);
    }
    else
    {
        base.WriteMember(name, data);
    }
}
```

The *WriteString* method writes a *string* instance to the stream. In general, you have two options for serializing an instance of a *string* type, or any type for that matter. One option is to serialize the instance inline with the rest of the object members. Another option is to serialize an object reference for the instance and defer serializing the object instance until later. We've chosen to serialize *string* instances inline with the rest of the object members. We implement the *MyFormatter.WriteString* method as follows:

```
private void WriteString(string val, string name)
{
    // String types:
    // Because the Formatter class ignores the string type and
    // we've overridden the WriteMember method to handle strings
    // as a special case, calling WriteMember on a string type
    // ends up here.
    // We can treat it two ways:
    //   (1) Write the string directly, or
    //   (2) Write an object reference and schedule the
    //       string object for later serialization.
    //

    // For our purposes, we'll just inline the string.
    if ( name != "" )
    {
        WriteField(FieldNames.MEMBER_NAME, name);
    }

    // Write the member type.
    WriteField( FieldNames.MEMBER_TYPE,
              typeof(string).AssemblyQualifiedName);

    // Write the member value.
    WriteField(FieldNames.MEMBER_VALUE, val);
}
```

The *MyFormatter.WriteMember* implementation also handles *Type* instances as a special case. The implementation for the *WriteType* method follows:

```
private void WriteType(object data, string name)
{
    // Member name
    if ( name != "" )
    {
        WriteField(FieldNames.MEMBER_NAME, name);
    }
```

(continued)

```
Type t = (System.Type)data;
if ( t.FullName != "System.RuntimeType" )
{
    // Instead of serializing the type itself, just
    // set up to serialize full type name as a string and
    // flag it so that it's interpreted as a type rather
    // than a string.
    data = t.AssemblyQualifiedName;
}
else
{
    throw new SerializationException("Unexpected type");
}

// Member type
WriteField(FieldNames.MEMBER_TYPE,
            typeof(string).AssemblyQualifiedName);

// The value should be interpreted as a
// type during deserialization.
WriteField(FieldNames.MEMBER_VALUE_TYPE, data);
}
```

The common language runtime treats *Type* instances as instances of *System.RuntimeType*. It just so happens that the *RuntimeType* implements the *ISerializable* interface but doesn't implement the special constructor needed for deserialization. To get around this problem, we write the assembly qualified type name of the type that the *Type* instance represents and tag the value by using the *FieldNames.MEMBER_VALUE_TYPE* field name. For example, if the *Type* instance is *typeof(SomeClass)*, we write the assembly qualified name for the *SomeClass* type rather than serialize the *RuntimeType* instance. During deserialization, we'll create a *Type* instance from the assembly qualified name by using the *Type.GetType* method.

The remaining methods needed to complete the serialization implementation are virtual members of the *Formatter* class that the *WriteMember* method calls. These methods are *WriteArray*, *WriteObjectRef*, *WriteValueType*, and the type-safe *WriteXXXX* methods for primitive types. The *WriteArray* implementation follows:

```
protected override void WriteArray( object obj,
                                    string name,
                                    Type   memberType)
{
    if ( name != "" )
    {
        //
        // Member name is not "", which indicates that this object
        // is a member of another object. Instead of serializing the
```

```
                // array inline with the parent object, we'll just
                // serialize a reference to it and schedule it for later
                // serialization.
                WriteObjectRef(obj,name, memberType);
        }
        else
        {
            //
            // Go ahead and serialize the array directly.

            // To create an array, we need the array type, lengths,
            // and lower bounds of each dimension.
            System.Array a = (Array)obj;

            // For now, this formatter supports one-dimensional arrays
            // only.
            if ( a.Rank != 1 )
            {
                throw new NotSupportedException(
                    "This formatter supports only 1-dimensional arrays");
            }

            WriteField(FieldNames.ARRAY_RANK, a.Rank);

            for(int i = 0; i < a.Rank; ++i)
            {
                WriteField(FieldNames.ARRAY_LENGTH, a.GetLength(i));
                WriteField(FieldNames.ARRAY_LOWERBOUND,
                    a.GetLowerBound(i));
            }

            // Write the array elements.
            for(int i = 0; i < a.Length; ++i)
            {
                object el = a.GetValue(i);
                if ( el != null && el.GetType().IsArray )
                {
                    // The array element itself is an array.
                    // We'll just serialize a reference to it and
                    // schedule it for later serialization.
                    WriteObjectRef(el, "", memberType);
                }
                else
                {
                    WriteMember("", el);
                }
            }
        }
    }
}
```

As shown in the previous listing, the *WriteArray* method calls the *WriteObjectRef* method to serialize an object reference to the array rather than serializing the array itself if the name parameter isn't empty. Obviously, when serializing an object, you need to serialize enough information to deserialize the object. For arrays, we write the rank of the array, lower bound, and length to the stream. We then iterate over each element of the array and write it to the stream. To prevent nested arrays, if an array element is itself an array, we write an object reference. To keep the example as simple as possible, the *MyFormatter* class supports serializing only arrays of one dimension.

The *WriteObjectRef* method needs to perform two functions. First, it should write an object reference to the stream. Second, it should schedule the object for later serialization by calling the *Formatter.Schedule* method. As with other member values, we write the member name, member type, and either a special indicator for *null* values or the object identifier returned from the *Formatter.Schedule* method:

```
// Write an object reference to the stream.
protected override void WriteObjectRef( object obj,
                                        string name,
                                        Type   memberType )
{
    // Member name
    if ( name != "" )
    {
        WriteField(FieldNames.MEMBER_NAME, name);
    }

    // Member type
    WriteField(FieldNames.MEMBER_TYPE,
            memberType.AssemblyQualifiedName);

    // Member value
    if ( obj == null )
    {
        // Null:
        // We'll use a special field indicator for null values.
        WriteField(FieldNames.MEMBER_VALUE_NULL, "");
    }
    else
    {
        // Object:
        // We need to schedule this object for serialization.
        long id = Schedule(obj);
```

```
        // Write a reference to the object ID rather than
        // the complete object.
        WriteField(FieldNames.OBJECT_REFID, id);
    }
}
```

For value types other than the primitive types, the *WriteMember* method calls the *WriteValueType* method. If specified, we write the member name, followed by the member type, and then the member value. Because the *System.Void* class represents the *void* type, we need to handle it as a special case in this method. You can't create an instance of *System.Void* directly. Therefore, we use the same technique as used in the *WriteType* method and simply write the assembly qualified name of the *System.Void* type and tag it so that it's handled correctly during deserialization:

```
protected override void WriteValueType( object obj,
                                        string name,
                                        Type   memberType )
{
    // Write the member name if specified.
    if ( name != "" )
    {
        WriteField(FieldNames.MEMBER_NAME, name);
    }

    // Write the member type.
    WriteField(FieldNames.MEMBER_TYPE,
            memberType.AssemblyQualifiedName);

    // Write the member value.
    // Special case for void types
    if ( memberType.FullName == "System.Void" )
    {
        WriteField( FieldNames.MEMBER_VALUE_TYPE,
                memberType.AssemblyQualifiedName );
    }
    else
    {
        WriteField(FieldNames.MEMBER_VALUE, obj);
    }
}
```

The implementations of the remaining virtual protected *WriteXXXX* methods forward the call to the *WriteValueType* method. With the inclusion of this code, we have a fully functional *IFormatter.Serialize* method.

```csharp
protected override void WriteBoolean(bool val, string name)
{
    WriteValueType(val, name, val.GetType());
}

protected override void WriteByte(byte val, string name)
{
    WriteValueType(val, name, val.GetType());
}

protected override void WriteChar(char val, string name)
{
    WriteValueType(val, name, val.GetType());
}

protected override void WriteDateTime(System.DateTime val,
                                      string name)
{
    WriteValueType(val, name, val.GetType());
}

protected override void WriteDecimal(decimal val, string name)
{
    WriteValueType(val, name, val.GetType());
}

protected override void WriteDouble(double val, string name)
{
    WriteValueType(val, name, val.GetType());
}

protected override void WriteInt16(short val, string name)
{
    WriteValueType(val, name, val.GetType());
}

protected override void WriteInt32(int val, string name)
{
    WriteValueType(val, name, val.GetType());
}

protected override void WriteInt64(long val, string name)
{
    WriteValueType(val, name, val.GetType());
}

protected override void WriteSByte(sbyte val, string name)
{
```

```
    WriteValueType(val, name, val.GetType());
}

protected override void WriteSingle(float val, string name)
{
    WriteValueType(val, name, val.GetType());
}

protected override void WriteTimeSpan(System.TimeSpan val,
                                       string name)
{
    WriteValueType(val, name, val.GetType());
}

protected override void WriteUInt16(ushort val, string name)
{
    WriteValueType(val, name, val.GetType());
}

protected override void WriteUInt32(uint val, string name)
{
    WriteValueType(val, name, val.GetType());
}

protected override void WriteUInt64(ulong val, string name)
{
    WriteValueType(val, name, val.GetType ());
}
```

Implementing the *IFormatter.Deserialize* Method

The function of the *IFormatter.Deserialize* method is to deserialize an object graph from a stream and return the root object of the object graph. The following code implements the *IFormatter.Deserialize* method for the *MyFormatter* class:

```
public override
    object Deserialize(System.IO.Stream serializationStream)
{
    //
    // Create an object manager to help with deserialization.
    _om = new ObjectManager( _surrogateselector, _streamingcontext );

    _reader = new StreamReader(serializationStream);

    // Read objects until end of stream.
    while( _reader.Peek() != -1 )
    {
```

(continued)

```
        ReadObject();
    }

    //
    // Now we can do fixups and get the top object.
    _om.DoFixups();

    // Return topmost object.
    return _om.GetObject(1);
}
```

The *MyFormatter.Deserialize* method uses the *ObjectManager* class that
we discussed earlier in the section to reconstruct the object graph. After creating a *StreamReader* instance around the stream, the code loops through the
stream, reading the next object until the end of the stream is reached, which is
indicated by a return value of –1 from the *StreamReader.Peek* method. After
deserializing the object graph from the stream, we get the *ObjectManager* to
perform fixups of the object graph by calling the *DoFixup* method and to return
the root of the object graph. The following listing shows the implementation of
the *ReadObject* method:

```
void ReadObject()
{
    // Read object ID.
    long oid = FieldNames.ParseObjectID(_reader.ReadLine());

    // Read object assembly.
    string s_oassembly =
        FieldNames.ParseObjectAssembly(_reader.ReadLine());

    // Read object type.
    string s_otype = FieldNames.ParseObjectType(_reader.ReadLine());

    // Read object members for this type.
    Type t = System.Type.GetType( String.Format( "{0},{1}",
                                                  s_otype,
                                                  s_oassembly ) );

    if ( t.IsArray )
    {
        ReadArray(oid, t);
    }
    else if ( t == typeof(string) )
    {
        object o = FieldNames.ParseMemberValue(_reader.ReadLine());
        _om.RegisterObject(o, oid);
    }
```

```
    else
    {
        SerializationInfo info;

        object o = ReadObjectMembers(oid, t, out info);

        if ( info == null )
        {
            _om.RegisterObject(o, oid);
        }
        else
        {
            _om.RegisterObject(o,oid,info);
        }
    }
}
```

The *ReadObject* method is basically the inverse of the *WriteObject* method. *ReadObject* reads the object identifier, assembly name, and object type from the stream. Recall that *WriteObject* handles instances of the string and array types differently than other types. That means that *ReadObject* needs to handle them differently as well. If the type is an array, it reads the array by calling the *ReadArray* method, which we'll discuss later in this section. If the object type is a string, we read the string's value from the stream by using the *Field-Names.ParseMemberValue* method, which we defined earlier. At this point, the entire object has been read, so we register the object with the *ObjectManager*, *_om*. For all other types, the *ReadObject* method reads the serialized object members from the stream by calling the *ReadObjectMembers* method, shown in the following listing:

```
private void ReadObjectMembers( long oid,
                                Type t,
                                out SerializationInfo info )
{
    info = null;

    // Try and find a surrogate for this type.
    ISerializationSurrogate surrogate = null;
    if ( _surrogateselector != null )
    {
        ISurrogateSelector selector;
        surrogate =
            _surrogateselector.GetSurrogate( t,
                                             _streamingcontext,
                                             out selector );
    }
```

(continued)

```
object o = FormatterServices.GetUninitializedObject( t );

// Read object members.
if ( surrogate != null )
{
    // Yes, a surrogate is registered; this indicates that
    // the serialized members of a serialization info follow.
    ReadSerializationInfo(o, oid, out info);
}
else if ( this.IsMarkedSerializable(o) && (o is ISerializable) )
{
    // The object handles its own serialization.
    ReadSerializationInfo(o, oid, out info);
}
else if ( this.IsMarkedSerializable(o) )
{
    ReadSerializableMembers(o,oid);
}
else
{
    // The type cannot be deserialized.
    throw new SerializationException();
}

return o;
}
```

The *ReadObjectMembers* method is the deserialization counterpart of the *WriteObjectMembers* method, and the two methods' structures are similar. *ReadObjectMembers* first checks to see whether the formatter has a surrogate selector. If so, the method asks the surrogate selector whether it has a serialization surrogate for the type. If a surrogate exists or the type implements *ISerializable*, the method calls the *ReadSerializationInfo* method, which will allocate and initialize the output parameter, *info*, with the deserialized *SerializationInfo* members. If no surrogate exists and the type doesn't implement the *ISerializable* method but is attributed with the *SerializableAttribute* attribute, we call the *ReadSerializableMembers* method. If the type doesn't support serialization, it can't be deserialized, so we throw a *SerializationException* exception. The implementation of the *ReadSerializationInfo* method follows:

```
void ReadSerializationInfo( Object o,
                            long   oid,
                            out    SerializationInfo info )
{
    info = new SerializationInfo(o.GetType(),
                                 new FormatterConverter());
```

```
    // Read the member count.
    long count = FieldNames.ParseMemberCount(_reader.ReadLine());

    for( int i = 0; i < count; ++i)
    {
        ReadMember(oid, null, o, info);
    }
}
```

The *ReadSerializationInfo* method is the counterpart to the *WriteSerializationInfo*. It reads the member count from the stream and then reads each member from the stream by calling the *ReadMember* method, which we'll discuss shortly.

Similar to *ReadSerializationInfo*, the *ReadSerializableMembers* method obtains an array of the *MemberInfo* instances for a type's serializable members and then reads each member from the stream by calling the *ReadMember* method:

```
void ReadSerializableMembers( Object o, long oid)
{
    MemberInfo[] mi =
        FormatterServices.GetSerializableMembers(o.GetType());

    // Read each member.
    for( int i = 0; i < mi.Length; ++i )
    {
        ReadMember(oid, mi[i], o, null);
    }
}
```

The following code listing shows the implementation for the *ReadMember* method that reads a member from the stream:

```
void ReadMember( long oid,
                 MemberInfo mi,
                 object o,
                 SerializationInfo info )
{
    // Read member name.
    string sname = FieldNames.ParseMemberName(_reader.ReadLine());

    // Read member type.
    string stype = FieldNames.ParseMemberType(_reader.ReadLine());

    // Read member value.
    string svalue = _reader.ReadLine();
    long roid = 0;
    object ovalue = ReadMemberValue(svalue, stype, ref roid);
```

(continued)

```
if ( roid != 0 )
{
    // Have we encountered the object yet?
    if ( ovalue == null )
    {
        // If the object has a serialization info,
        // record a delayed fixup.
        if ( info != null )
        {
            _om.RecordDelayedFixup(oid, sname, roid);
        }
        else
        {
            _om.RecordFixup(oid, mi, roid);
        }

        return;
    }
}

if ( info != null )
{
    info.AddValue(sname, ovalue);
}
else
{
    FormatterServices.PopulateObjectMembers( o,
                                new MemberInfo[]{mi},
                                new object[]{ovalue});
}
}
```

The *ReadMember* method reads the member name, member type, and member value from the stream. To read the member's value from the stream, the *ReadMember* method calls the *ReadMemberValue* method, which we'll discuss momentarily. The return value of the *ReadMemberValue* method is the value for the member, and the last parameter, named *roid*, will be nonzero if the member references another object in the object graph. If the member's value references an object in the graph that hasn't yet been deserialized, we need to record a fixup for the member to the object instance by its object identifier. If the member's object has a *SerializationInfo*, we record a delayed fixup for the member name by using the *RecordDelayedFixup* method. Otherwise, we record a fixup by using the *MemberInfo* instance. If *roid* is 0, the member's value doesn't reference another object in the object graph and we can use the value to initialize the member of the object. If the object has a *SerializationInfo*, we add the member's value to the *SerializationInfo* instance. Otherwise, we use the *FormatterServices.PopulateObjectMembers* method to initialize the object's member with the deserialized value. The following listing shows the implementation for the *ReadMemberValue* method:

```
private object ReadMemberValue(string svalue,
                              string stype,
                              ref long rfoid)
{
    if ( svalue.StartsWith( FieldNames.OBJECT_REFID ) )
    {
        // This member references another object.
        rfoid = FieldNames.ParseObjectRefID(svalue);
        return _om.GetObject(rfoid);
    }
    else if ( svalue.StartsWith( FieldNames.MEMBER_VALUE_TYPE ) )
    {
        // This member should be interpreted as a type.
        string s = FieldNames.ParseMemberValueType(svalue);
        return Type.GetType(s);
    }
    else if ( svalue.StartsWith( FieldNames.MEMBER_VALUE ) )
    {
        // Value type; convert from string representation
        // to actual type.
        string s = FieldNames.ParseMemberValue(svalue);
        return Convert.ChangeType(s, Type.GetType(stype));
    }
    else if ( svalue.StartsWith( FieldNames.MEMBER_VALUE_NULL ) )
    {
        // Value is null.
        return null;
    }
    else
    {
        throw new SerializationException("Parse error.");
    }
}
```

The *ReadMemberValue* method checks to see what kind of field tag starts the *svalue* parameter. For our formatter, four possibilities exist. The member value can be a reference to another object, in which case we parse the object identifier and return the object corresponding to the object identifier if the object has already been deserialized. Another possibility is that the member value should be interpreted as a *Type*. In that case, we parse the member value and create a *Type* instance by using the *Type.GetType* method. Or, the member value might just be the string representation of a primitive type or a value type, in which case we parse the member value and use the *Convert.ChangeType* method to convert the string to an instance of the serialized type. The last possibility is that the member value is *null*, and in that case, we return *null*.

The last two methods we need to define read an array object from the stream. The following listing defines the *ReadArray* method:

```
object ReadArray(long arrayId, Type t)
{
    // Read the array rank.
    long rank = FieldNames.ParseArrayRank(_reader.ReadLine());

    // Currently, we only support rank == 1.
    if ( rank != 1 )
    {
        throw new System.NotSupportedException(
            "This formatter supports only 1-dimensional arrays");
    }

    long length = FieldNames.ParseArrayLength(_reader.ReadLine());

    long lowerbound =
        FieldNames.ParseArrayLowerBound(_reader.ReadLine());

    // Use Array.CreateInstance to create the array.
    Array oa = Array.CreateInstance(t.GetElementType(), (int)length);

    // Need to register the array in case we need to fixup elements.
    _om.RegisterObject(oa, arrayId);

    // Read array elements.
    for(int i=0; i < length; ++i)
    {
        ReadArrayElement(oa, arrayId, i, t.GetElementType());
    }

    return oa;
}
```

The *ReadArray* method reads the array rank, lower bound, and length from the stream. For the purposes of our example, we support one-dimensional arrays only. While developing this method, we tried using the *FormatterServices.GetUninitializedObject* method to create an instance of the array. This resulted in the throwing of an *ExecutionEngine* exception. We also tried simply creating a generic object array (*object []*), but that caused an exception to occur when casting the return value of the *Deserialize* method to an array of the appropriate type (for example, *int []*). The only way we could get this method to work was by calling the *Array.CreateInstance* method to create a type-safe array of the specified type and length. After creating the array instance, we registered it with the *ObjectManager*, *_om*. Following registration, we read each of the array elements by using the *ReadArrayElement* method defined in the following listing:

```
void ReadArrayElement(System.Array oa,
                      long oid,
                      int index,
                      Type el_type)
{
    // Read the type.
    string stype = FieldNames.ParseMemberType(_reader.ReadLine());
    Type t = Type.GetType(stype);

    // Read the value.
    string svalue = _reader.ReadLine();
    long roid = 0;
    object ovalue = ReadMemberValue(svalue, stype, ref roid);

    if ( roid != 0 )
    {
        // Have we encountered the object yet?
        if ( ovalue == null )
        {
            _om.RecordArrayElementFixup(oid, index, roid);
            return;
        }
    }

    oa.SetValue(ovalue,index) ;
}
```

The *ReadArrayElement* method reads the type and value from the stream. As we did for the *ReadMember* method, after calling the *ReadMemberValue* method, we check the value of the *roid* variable. A nonzero value indicates that the array element references another object instance in the graph. If the object returned by *ReadMemberValue* is *null*, we haven't yet deserialized the object that the member references. In that case, we need to record a fixup by using the *RecordArrayElementFixup* method and return. Otherwise, the array element doesn't reference another object in the graph or the array element value is *null*. Either way, we set the array element's value to the object returned by the *Read-MemberValue* method.

At this point, we have a fully functional serialization formatter. Now that we've developed a custom formatter, we can examine the procedure for plugging it into the .NET Remoting architecture.

Creating a Formatter Sink

As discussed in Chapter 2, .NET Remoting uses formatter sinks to format *IMessage* objects to a stream that's then passed to the remaining channel sinks in the channel for eventual delivery to the remote object. The .NET Remoting infrastructure separates formatter sink functionality into two types: *client formatter sinks* and *server formatter sinks*.

Client Formatter Sink

The first sink in the client-side channel sink chain is an instance of a client formatter sink that implements the *IClientFormatterSink* interface. The client formatter sink acts as a bridge between the message sink chain and the channel sink chain. As such, the client formatter sink is both a message sink and a channel sink. The *IClientFormatterSink* interface is a composite of the *IMessageSink*, *IClientChannelSink*, and *IChannelSinkBase* interfaces. The following code listing defines a class named *MyClientFormatterSink* that uses the custom formatter, *MyFormatter*, we developed in the previous section:

```
public class MyClientFormatterSink : IClientFormatterSink
{
    private IClientChannelSink  _NextChannelSink;
    private IMessageSink        _NextMessageSink;

    public MyClientFormatterSink(IClientChannelSink next)
    {
        _NextChannelSink = next;
    }

    //
    // IChannelSinkBase
    public IDictionary Properties
    {
        get{ return null; }
    }

    //
    // IClientChannelSink
    public IClientChannelSink NextChannelSink
    {
```

```
        get{return _NextChannelSink;}
}

public void AsyncProcessRequest(
    IClientChannelSinkStack sinkStack,
    IMessage msg,
    ITransportHeaders headers,
    Stream stream )
{
    // This sink must be first in the chain, so this
    // method should never be called.
    throw new NotSupportedException();
}

public void AsyncProcessResponse (
                    IClientResponseChannelSinkStack sinkStack,
                    object state,
                    ITransportHeaders headers,
                    Stream stream )
{
    // Could implement, but have not.
    throw new NotImplementedException();
}

public System.IO.Stream GetRequestStream ( IMessage msg,
                                    ITransportHeaders headers )
{
    // This sink must be first in the chain, so this
    // method should never be called.
    throw new NotSupportedException();
}

public void ProcessMessage ( IMessage msg,
                    ITransportHeaders requestHeaders,
                    Stream requestStream,
                    out ITransportHeaders responseHeaders,
                    out Stream responseStream )
{
    // This sink must be first in the chain, so this
    // method should never be called.
    throw new NotSupportedException();
}

//
// IMessageSink
public System.Runtime.Remoting.Messaging.IMessageSink NextSink
{
    get{return _NextMessageSink;}
```

(continued)

```
        }

        public IMessageCtrl AsyncProcessMessage (IMessage msg,
                                                  IMessageSink replySink)
        {
            // Could implement, but have not.
            throw new NotImplementedException();
        }

        public IMessage SyncProcessMessage ( IMessage msg )
        {
            //
            // Serialize message to a stream.
            TransportHeaders    requestHeaders = new TransportHeaders();

            Stream requestStream =
                    _NextChannelSink.GetRequestStream(msg,
                                                      requestHeaders);
            if ( requestStream == null )
            {
                requestStream = new System.IO.MemoryStream();
            }

            RemotingSurrogateSelector rem_ss =
                        new RemotingSurrogateSelector();

            MyFormatter fm = new MyFormatter();
            fm.SurrogateSelector = rem_ss;
            fm.Context = new StreamingContext(
                            StreamingContextStates.Other );

            // Serialize a MethodCall message to the stream.
            MethodCall mc = new MethodCall(msg);
            fm.Serialize(requestStream, mc);

            //
            // Let sink chain process the message.
            ITransportHeaders    responseHeaders = null;
            System.IO.Stream     responseStream =
                                    new System.IO.MemoryStream();

            this._NextChannelSink.ProcessMessage( mc,
                                                  requestHeaders,
                                                  requestStream,
                                                  out responseHeaders,
                                                  out responseStream );

            // Use our version of IMessage to deserialize.
```

```
    fm.SurrogateSelector = null;

    // The formatter handles IMessage types as a
    // special case and deserializes them as MyMessage types.
    MyMessage mr = (MyMessage)fm.Deserialize(responseStream);
    return mr.ConvertMyMessagePropertiesToMethodResponse(mc);
  }
}
```

First, we'd like to make a few remarks about the *MyClientFormatterSink* class implementation. Because the client formatter sink is the first sink in the channel sink chain, we don't expect the following *IClientChannelSink* methods to be called: *AsyncProcessRequest*, *GetRequestStream*, and *ProcessMessage*. Thus, each of these *IClientChannelSink* methods returns a *NotSupportedException* exception. We also haven't implemented the functionality to support asynchronous calls and therefore return a *NotImplementedException* exception from the *IClientChannelSink.AsyncProcessResponse* and *IMessageSink.AsyncProcessMessage* methods, the implementation of which we'll leave as an exercise for you.

The real work occurs in the *IMessage.SyncProcessMessage* method. In general, a client formatter sink's implementation of *SyncProcessMessage* should perform the following tasks:

1. Obtain a request stream for serializing the request message.

2. Serialize the message to the request stream.

3. Pass the request stream to the *ProcessMessage* method on the next channel sink in the chain.

4. Deserialize the return message from the response stream and return it.

The *MyClientFormatterSink* implementation of *SyncProcessMessage* creates a new instance of the *TransportHeaders* class, which we then use along with the *msg* parameter to obtain a request stream by calling the *GetRequestStream* method on the next sink in the channel sink chain. If *GetRequestStream* doesn't return a *Stream* instance, we create a memory stream.

Because we'll be serializing .NET Remoting infrastructure types, we configure the formatter instance with an instance of the *RemotingSurrogateSelector* class. Also notice that we serialize a new instance of a *MethodCall* message to the stream rather than the *IMessage* instance passed to *SyncProcessMessage*. The client formatter sink's *SyncProcessMessage* method receives a *System.Runtime.Remoting.Messaging.Message* instance in its *msg* parameter. The *Message* class implements *ISerializable* but doesn't implement the special constructor needed for deserialization. The *MessageSurrogate* handles serialization for the *Message* type but doesn't support deserialization of any *IMessage* types. Instead of serializing the *Message* type to the stream, we can create a new instance of the *MethodCall* class passing the *msg* instance to the constructor. Unlike the *Message* class, the *MethodCall* class implements *ISerializable* and implements the special constructor needed for deserialization. Once the new instance of *MethodCall* is in hand, we serialize it to the stream referenced by the *requestStream* variable, which we then pass to the next sink in the channel sink chain by calling the *ProcessMessage* method on the *_NextChannelSink* member. After the call to the next channel sink's *ProcessMessage* returns, we set the formatter's *SurrogateSelector* property to *null* and deserialize the response stream to the *MyMessage* type. (See the sidebar, "Why the *MyMessage* Class?") Finally, we convert the *MyMessage* type to a *MethodResponse* instance, which we then return.

Why the *MyMessage* Class?

While implementing the formatter sinks, we encountered a problem during deserialization of *MethodCall* instances. In the server formatter sink, after deserializing the *MethodCall* instance, we attempted to pass the instance to the next channel sink's *ProcessMessage* method. This resulted in the throwing of a *StackOverflowException* exception.

The only way we could get around this problem was by implementing a class named *MyMessage*, which the formatter creates in place of *IMessage* types during deserialization. We had to modify the *MyFormatter.ReadObjectMembers* method so that immediately after creating an uninitialized object instance, the method checks the object's type to determine whether it implements the *IMessage* interface. If the object's type does implement this interface, we create an instance of the *MyMessage* class in place of the uninitialized object instance created by *FormatterServices.GetUninitializedObject*.

Therefore, instead of a *MethodCall* instance occurring in the deserialized object graph, the *MyFormatter* class creates a *MyMessage* instance. The *MyMessage* class implements the *IMessage* interface and basically acts as a temporary placeholder, storing the message properties for instances of types that implement the *IMessage* interface.

The *MyMessage* class provides two methods, *ConvertMyMessagePropertiesToMethodCall* and *ConvertMyMessagePropertiesToMethodResponse*, which convert any message properties that are instances of *MyMessage* to an instance of *MethodCall* or *MethodResponse*, as appropriate.

ClientFormatterSinkProvider

Now that we have a client formatter sink, we need a channel sink provider class that we can use to install the formatter sink into the client channel sink chain. The following code listing defines the *MyFormatterClientSinkProvider* class:

```
public class MyFormatterClientSinkProvider :
            IClientFormatterSinkProvider
    {
        public MyFormatterClientSinkProvider()
        {
        }

        public MyFormatterClientSinkProvider( IDictionary properties,
            ICollection providerData)
        {
        }

        // Build the client-side channel sink chain:
        public IClientChannelSink CreateSink (
            IChannelSender channel,
            string url ,
            object remoteChannelData )
        {
            // Ask the next provider for the sink chain.
            IClientChannelSink chain =
                _Next.CreateSink(channel,url,remoteChannelData);

            // Add our formatter to the beginning of the chain.
            IClientChannelSink sinkFormatter =
                new MyClientFormatterSink(chain);

            return sinkFormatter;
        }

        private IClientChannelSinkProvider _Next=null;
        public IClientChannelSinkProvider Next
        {
            get{return _Next;}
            set{_Next = value;}
        }
    }
```

Server Formatter Sink

Unlike the client formatter sink, a server formatter sink isn't both a message sink and a channel sink; it's only a channel sink. Server formatter sinks implement the *IServerChannelSink* interface and are the last sink in the channel sink chain. The following code listing defines a class named *MyServerFormatterSink* that uses the *MyFormatter* custom formatter that we developed earlier in the chapter:

```
public class MyServerFormatterSink : IServerChannelSink
{
    private IServerChannelSink _NextChannelSink;

    public MyServerFormatterSink( IServerChannelSink snk)
    {
        _NextChannelSink = snk;
    }

    public IDictionary Properties
    {
        get
        { return null; }
    }

    public IServerChannelSink NextChannelSink
    {
        get
        { return _NextChannelSink; }
    }

    public Stream GetResponseStream(
                    IServerResponseChannelSinkStack sinkStack,
                    object state,
                    IMessage msg,
                    ITransportHeaders headers)
    {
        // We don't expect this method to be called because
        // we don't push ourselves onto the response sink stack.
        throw new NotSupportedException();
    }

    public void AsyncProcessResponse(
                    IServerResponseChannelSinkStack sinkStack,
                    object state,
                    IMessage msg,
                    ITransportHeaders headers,
                    Stream stream)
    {
        // Could implement, but have not.
        throw new NotImplementedException();
    }

    public ServerProcessing ProcessMessage(
```

```
                           IServerChannelSinkStack sinkStack,
                           IMessage requestMsg,
                           ITransportHeaders requestHeaders,
                           System.IO.Stream requestStream,
                           out IMessage responseMsg,
                           out ITransportHeaders responseHeaders,
                           out System.IO.Stream responseStream)
{
    // Initialize output parameters.
    responseMsg     = null;
    responseHeaders = null;
    responseStream  = null;

    // Set up to deserialize request stream.
    RemotingSurrogateSelector rem_ss =
        new RemotingSurrogateSelector();

    MyFormatter fm = new MyFormatter();
    fm.SurrogateSelector = null;
    fm.Context =
        new StreamingContext( StreamingContextStates.Other );

    IMessage msg = null;

    MyMessage mymsg = (MyMessage)fm.Deserialize(requestStream);

    //
    // Massage the URI property.
    string uri = (string)mymsg.Properties["__Uri"];
    int n = uri.LastIndexOf("/");
    if ( n != -1 )
    {
        uri = uri.Substring(n);
        mymsg.Properties["__Uri"] = uri;
    }

    // Convert from MyMessage to MethodCall.
    MethodCall mc =
        mymsg.ConvertMyMessagePropertiesToMethodCall();
    msg = (IMessage)mc;

    // When calling the dispatch sink (the next sink in our
    // chain), the request stream must be null.
    ServerProcessing sp =
        this._NextChannelSink.ProcessMessage( sinkStack,
                                              msg,
                                              requestHeaders,
                                              null,
```

(continued)

```
                                                    out responseMsg,
                                                    out responseHeaders,
                                                    out responseStream );

        if ( sp == ServerProcessing.Complete )
        {
            // Serialize response message to the response stream.
            if ( responseMsg != null && responseStream == null )
            {
                responseStream = sinkStack.GetResponseStream(
                                                    responseMsg,
                                                    responseHeaders);

                if ( responseStream == null )
                {
                    responseStream = new MemoryStream();
                }

                fm.SurrogateSelector = rem_ss;
                fm.Serialize(responseStream, responseMsg);
            }
        }

        return sp;
    }
}
```

The real work occurs in the *IServerChannelSink.ProcessMessage* method. In general, a server formatter sink's implementation of *ProcessMessage* should perform the following tasks:

1. Deserialize a *MethodCall* instance from the request stream.

2. Pass the *MethodCall* instance to the *ProcessMessage* method of the next sink in the chain, the *DispatchSink*.

3. Obtain a response stream for serializing the response message.

4. Serialize the response message into the response stream.

The *MyServerFormatterSink* implementation of *ProcessMessage* first initializes its output parameters, creates an instance of the *MyFormatter* class, and gets the formatter ready to deserialize the *IMessage* from the request stream. Because of the problems discussed in the "Why the *MyMessage* Class?" sidebar, we deserialize the message object as an instance of the *MyMessage* class. Next we need to convert the *__Uri* property of the message to an *objectUri*. To do so, we keep only the part of the *__Uri* property string value that follows the last "/". If we don't modify the *__Uri* property value, we'll get an exception similar to the one shown in Figure 8-4 when we try to dispatch the message.

Figure 8-4   Exception resulting from not modifying the *__Uri* property prior to passing to the *DispatchSink*

> **Important**   The .NET Remoting infrastructure requires that the message object passed to the *DispatchSink* be a .NET Framework–defined *IMessage* implementing type. Originally, we were passing the *MyMessage* type, which implements *IMessage*, but this caused the runtime to throw an exception stating, "Permission denied. Cannot call methods on *AppDomain* class remotely."

After modifying the *__Uri* property, we convert the *MyMessage* instance to a *MethodCall* instance, which we then pass to the *ProcessMessage* method on the next channel sink, the *DispatchSink*. If the return value of the *ProcessMessage* indicates that the method call is complete, we obtain a stream for serializing the response message by first calling the *GetRequestStream* method on the *IServerChannelSinkStack* object. This is the standard convention for obtaining a stream and allows sinks in the sink chain to add information to the response stream prior to the server formatter sink serializing the response message. If *GetRequestStream* doesn't return a *Stream* instance, the server formatter sink creates one. We then set the formatter's *SurrogateSelector* property to an instance of the *RemotingSurrogateSelector* class and serialize the response message to the response stream.

ServerFormatterSinkProvider

Now that we have a server formatter sink, we need a channel sink provider class that we can use to install the formatter sink into the server channel sink chain. The following code listing defines the *MyFormatterServerSinkProvider* class:

```
public class MyFormatterServerSinkProvider :
                            IServerFormatterSinkProvider
{
```

(continued)

```
public MyFormatterServerSinkProvider()
{
}

// This ctor form provides properties from configuration file.
public MyFormatterServerSinkProvider( IDictionary properties,
                                      ICollection providerData )
{
}

private IServerChannelSinkProvider _Next;

public IServerChannelSink CreateSink(IChannelReceiver channel)
{
    IServerChannelSink chain = _Next.CreateSink(channel);
    IServerChannelSink sinkFormatter =
        new MyServerFormatterSink(chain);
    return sinkFormatter;
}

public void GetChannelData(IChannelDataStore channelData)
{
    if ( _Next != null )
    {
        _Next.GetChannelData(channelData);
    }
}

public IServerChannelSinkProvider Next
{
    get
    { return _Next; }
    set
    { _Next = value; }
}
}
```

Summary

In this chapter, we discussed object serialization, looked at several classes that help serializing object graphs, and implemented a custom serialization formatter that we then used to implement a server formatter sink and client formatter sink.

Index

A

access control
  in distributed applications, 12
  in .NET Remoting applications, 85
  programming methods for, 86–87
access levels, supporting different, 85
access-time sink, 232
AccessTime custom sink
  creating, 233–40
  projects in the sample code for, 234
AccessTimeServerChannelSink class
  adding to a configuration file, 239
  implementing, 234–37
AccessTimeServerChannelSinkProvider class, 237–39
AccessTimeSinkLib project, 234
Activate request message, 121
<activated> element
  in the client configuration file, 76
  in the JobClient configuration file, 93
  in the JobServer configuration file, 94
ActivatedClientTypeEntry
  instance, 60
  objects, 142
  type, 93
ActivateResponse message, 122
activation, 28
  example for proxy objects, 138–43
  intercepting, 139
  keys, 132
  method for Web Services, 80
  mode, 59
  model, 59–60
  type, 142
_ActivationType key in a construction call message, 132
Active Server Pages. *See* ASP code
actor header attribute in SOAP, 108
acyclic object graphs, 255
Add method
  of ListView, 67
  of SurrogateSelector, 250
AddClientProviderToChain method, calling in FileClientChannel, 209
add_Delegate method, 116
add_JobEvent request message, 111–15
add_JobEvent response message, 111, 116
AddJobToListView method, 67
AddNote method of the JobNotes class, 89
AddRef and Release pairs in C++, 14
address isolation of unmanaged code, 23

AddValue method of the SerializationInfo class, 244
administration of distributed applications, 9
anonymous access, configuring, 80
application configuration files, 16
application domain identifier, 113
application domains, 24, 34
ApplicationID method of the Remoting-Configuration class, 59
ApplicationName method of the Remoting-Configuration class, 59
applications
  distributing functional areas of, 9
  extending with client-activated objects, 88–98
  reasons for choosing to distribute, 8–9
  segregating unmanaged into separate processes, 23
architectures
  .NET Remoting, 23
  distributed, 2–5
  HTTP channel, 196–203
  lifetime management, 33
  peer-to-peer, 4–5
  pluggable, 15
  server-side channel, 45–47
  server-to-server, 98
  thick-client, 9
  thin-client, 9
  three-tier, 3–4
_Args key
  in a construction call message, 132
  in a method call message, 133
array element fixup, 257
array field tags, 263
array fixups, 260
array objects, reading from the stream, 286–87
arrays, 276
ASCII text, converting binary data into, 45
ASP code, 77
ASP.NET
  applications, 16
  configuring to use Windows authentication, 84
  XML Web Services, 110
assembly
  generating with the minimum calling syntax, 82
  for SOAPSuds, 82
assembly name
  field tag for, 262
  of a stand-in class, 101

(continued)

Scott McLean

Scott McLean started programming computers on an Atari 400. After mastering Atari BASIC, he taught himself 6502 assembler. A few years later, he enlisted in the United States Navy, where he served six years as a Navy "Nuke" on a fast-attack submarine. After receiving an honorable discharge from the Navy, Scott went back to school and earned a Bachelor of Science degree in Computer Science at the University of Georgia.

Now a software engineer at XcelleNet, Inc., he focuses on enterprise server application architecture and distributed systems development. He's developed a variety of applications using multithreading, sockets, I/O completion ports, COM, ATL, and .NET. His other publications include an article on .NET Remoting for *.NET Magazine Online*, and he's a coauthor of *Visual C++.NET: A Primer for .NET Developers*, by WROX Press, Ltd. Scott is a cofounder of and contributer to *www.thinkdotnet.com*, an online resource for .NET developers.

James Naftel

James Naftel started his computing career at Allied Collection and Credit Bureau, Inc., just outside Atlanta, Georgia. When he started, he wasn't even aware of what a DOS prompt was. After being taught about computers by the owner, Rex Gallogly, he became interested in learning more and more about computers. At the time, he was a business major at Georgia State University. This newfound love for computers prompted him to change his major to Computer Science.

At the same time that he was changing majors, he convinced his then-girlfriend, April, to marry him. James and his new wife moved to Athens, Georgia, to attend the University of Georgia (UGA). While at UGA, James worked for a consulting company named PICS where he concentrated on building inventory applications in Microsoft Visual FoxPro. After moving back to the Atlanta area, James graduated from Georgia State University with a Bachelor of Science degree in Computer Science.

After graduating, James was hired by XcelleNet, Inc., where he is now a lead software engineer. He's worked in such diverse application domains as enterprise database application development and distributed systems, and he now leads a team developing database synchronization technology. He resides in the Atlanta, Georgia, area with his wife, two daughters, and two dogs. A cofounder of and contributer to *www.thinkdotnet.com*, to which he has contributed many articles, James has also written about Microsoft Visual Studio addins for *Windows Developer Journal*. His true passion is tinkering with programming languages, especially C++ and C#.

Kim Williams

Kim Williams began his professional life by earning a music degree and playing jazz piano. A few years later, he turned his computer programming hobby into a career by returning to school for a Computer Science degree. After school he landed his dream job writing antivirus software and disassembling viruses. While working with viruses, he also developed distributed enterprise security applications.

Since joining XcelleNet, Inc., Kim has worked with a variety of technologies, such as Java RMI, DCOM, ATL, and ASP, as a lead software engineer. Currently, he leads a team developing a large-scale ASP.NET Web Services solution. Kim is also a cofounder of and contributor to *www.thinkdotnet.com*. He currently resides in Atlanta, Georgia, with his wife, Patty, and son, Sean, and still manages to find time to play the piano.

Valve Spring Compressor

The *valve spring compressor* is designed to let you change your car or truck's valve springs while the cylinder head is still in the vehicle. Without it, you have to remove the complete cylinder head from the engine to swap the valve springs. Installing valve springs is a straightforward task that can be accomplished by any competent shade-tree mechanic—if you have the right tools.

At Microsoft Press, we use tools to illustrate our books for software developers and IT professionals. Tools very simply and powerfully symbolize human inventiveness. They're a metaphor for people extending their capabilities, precision, and reach. From simple calipers and pliers to digital micrometers and lasers, these stylized illustrations give each book a visual identity, and a personality to the series. With tools and knowledge, there's no limit to creativity and innovation. Our tagline says it all: *the tools you need to put technology to work*

The manuscript for this book was prepared and galleyed using Microsoft Word. Pages were composed by Microsoft Press using Adobe FrameMaker+SGML for Windows, with text in Garamond and display type in Helvetica Condensed. Composed pages were delivered to the printer as electronic prepress files.

Cover Designer:	Methodologie, Inc.
Interior Graphic Designer:	James D. Kramer
Principal Compositor:	Kerri DeVault
Interior Artist:	Rob Nance
Copy Editor:	Michelle Goodman
Indexer:	Richard Shrout

Get a **Free**
e-mail newsletter, updates,
special offers, links to related books,
and more when you

register on line!

Register your Microsoft Press® title on our Web site and you'll get a FREE subscription to our e-mail newsletter, *Microsoft Press Book Connections.* You'll find out about newly released and upcoming books and learning tools, online events, software downloads, special offers and coupons for Microsoft Press customers, and information about major Microsoft® product releases. You can also read useful additional information about all the titles we publish, such as detailed book descriptions, tables of contents and indexes, sample chapters, links to related books and book series, author biographies, and reviews by other customers.

Registration is easy. Just visit this Web page and fill in your information:

http://www.microsoft.com/mspress/register

Proof of Purchase

Use this page as proof of purchase if participating in a promotion or rebate offer on this title. Proof of purchase must be used in conjunction with other proof(s) of payment such as your dated sales receipt—see offer details.

Microsoft® .NET Remoting
0-7356-1778-3

CUSTOMER NAME

Microsoft Press, PO Box 97017, Redmond, WA 98073-9830